Bob

Jon Theemm

Patti Po___

———— 2839

925 —
3000

Food culture

D— vs NYC

2 ____ changes ____
____ ____ ____

3 ____ ____ ____

4 ____ ____
____

By Marian Burros

Keep It Simple: Thirty Minute Meals from Scratch
Pure and Simple
You've Got It Made

With Lois Levine

Come for Cocktails, Stay for Supper
Elegant but Easy Cookbook
Freeze with Ease
The Summertime Cookbook

THE BEST OF
DE GUSTIBUS

by Marian Burros

SIMON AND SCHUSTER
New York London Toronto Sydney Tokyo

Copyright © 1988 by Foxcraft, Ltd.

Published by Simon and Schuster
A Division of Simon & Schuster Inc.
Simon & Schuster Building
Rockefeller Center
1230 Avenue of the Americas
New York, NY 10020

SIMON AND SCHUSTER and colophon are registered trademarks
of Simon & Schuster Inc.

Designed by Irving Perkins Associates

Manufactured in the United States of America

1   2   3   4   5   6   7   8   9   10

Library of Congress Cataloging-in-Publication Data

Burros, Marian.

The best of de gustibus/by Marian Burros.
    p.   cm.
Includes index.
ISBN 0-671-62389-3
1. Cookery.   2. Food.   I. Title.
TX651.B87   1987
641—dc19   87–21297
                                                     CIP

The author gratefully acknowledges permission to reprint previously published
columns from *The New York Times*. © The New York Times Company, 1983,
1984, 1985, 1986, 1987.

To my mother,
who would have been both proud and amused
to learn how often she inspired me.

Acknowledgments

The readers of my column who took the time to write are responsible for this book. Without their letters—sometimes critical, sometimes admiring, often funny and always instructive—there would have been no book. This is my opportunity to say thank you.

To the style copy desk at *The New York Times,* thank you for catching most of the mistakes and improving the prose in my columns.

And to my husband, Donald, thank you for always encouraging me.

Contents

Introduction

Newspaper editors may be convinced that they are printing the most important news of the day on the front pages of their newspapers, but those of us who write about the mundane know better. And those of us who have the misfortune to print recipes with mistakes in them know that we get more mail than anyone else!

However, only a few editorial writers are willing to acknowledge that many readers find sections other than the front page of a newspaper more interesting. "The fact that a story appears on the front page holds little sway with readers," said one such editorial from a large-city daily. "They tend to respond in proportionate numbers to what interests them, what angers them, what pleases them. These are the things that do not necessarily appear on page A-1. A small item on a red-light runner can set off a storm."

And so can criticism of the American cooking bible, *Joy of Cooking,* as I found out a couple of years ago when I mentioned in a column I write each Saturday for *The New York Times* that it did not contain a recipe for a tuna fish sandwich. The column is called De Gustibus and is referred to by its newspaper shorthand name as Gusti. It has, on occasion, also been called Dis Gustibus, but only when it deals with distasteful subject matter, such as oatmeal with lumps or waiters who come up to your table and say "Hi, my name is Harold."

The column name is shorthand for the phrase *de gustibus non est disputandum* (There is no disputing about tastes).

It is sent to *New York Times* news-service subscribers all over the country under the heading "Tabletalk." No one has satisfactorily explained why the news service decided to change its name, but, in fact, when the column appears in newspapers around the country, it usually carries no name at all.

In practical terms the name De Gustibus allows me to write about anything related to food or drink that strikes my fancy. Within reason. Not necessarily my reason but my editors' reason. As any right-thinking reporter knows, editors are a capricious lot and do not know what they are doing. They have killed more than one Gusti column: on how the

11

waiter's union discriminates against women, for example, comes immediately to mind.

Just the same, I manage to range far afield, covering everything from the proper way to eat asparagus (with your fingers as long as they are not buried in hollandaise) (page 210) to the lack of sodium labeling on most packaged food (page 371); from hypnotizing a lobster (page 206) to the trouble with plastic soda bottles (page 388).

What I have not figured out after writing more than two hundred columns is what will strike the fancy of my readers. Whenever I am sure that the letters will pour in, no one seems to care. A column on lack of consideration among cigar and pipe smokers in restaurants brought only four letters: two from militant antismokers wanting to know why I didn't say that cigarettes should be banned too, and two from militant anarchists who think smoking is a God-given right to be practiced whenever the mood suits them.

On the other hand, I never imagined that a recipe for plum torte would prove so popular that it has been reprinted once a year ever since it first appeared in 1983. People keep losing the recipe, and every summer in August, as the purple plums begin to appear in the stores, letters and phone calls start, pleading for the recipe. It's easier to reprint it than to mail out copies. You will find the recipe on page 152.

Nor did I foresee the hilarious consequences a column on techniques for buttering corn would produce. Midwesterners were insulted because they felt the column cast aspersions on their manners. The column had said that two midwesterners of my acquaintance butter their corn by rolling the ear over the entire stick of butter. But the mail was only part of it. At least four midwestern newspapers held "How I Butter My Corn" contests, the results of which can be found on page 20.

What I have discovered after four years is that, as the newspaper editorial said, people respond to what interests them and to those things with which they have personal experience. Some of what they have to say is informative, much is amusing. Often the letters correct what the reader feels is an error on my part. Often they are right. Occasionally I am taken to the grammarian's woodshed for a breach of the rules of English usage. People take particular glee in exposing my mistakes. I like to share the letters about grammatical errors with the *Times'* copy desk. No newspaper in the United States has a more vigilant copy desk, but even it is not perfect.

For whatever reason readers have written, they often have something to share with other readers of the column. So this is a book of some of the more interesting columns and the most interesting responses they have elicited.

One of the most recent letters perhaps offers insight into why some people take the time to write. It is from a Manhattan resident and constant reader who was prompted to write after an end-of-the-year column of quotes from people's letters.

Often reading your column I have "thought" a letter to you, usually protestful. So far, I have succeeded in refraining from writing, each time with reluctance.... Ah well, why make the lady feel bad.

Today, I see that other readers did reach for their pens, and for the same items in the column that exasperated me, so I am finding the energy to write ... but only because I have a question that I'd like you to regard as constructive.

Do you want to entertain or inform? *Well, why not both? I can hear you think... fair enough. But I do not find it entertaining to make a comedy of eating a pomegranate, to take one example. How many people, I thought, will be discouraged from ever discovering the unique pleasures of eating that fabled fruit. I, for one, never have one without a little sense of ceremony, remembering the myths of Persephone and Pluto. So many foods bring with them certain little disciplines in their preparation.*

The informed quite respect such procedures. The uninformed may mock such cares, and thereby deprive themselves of discovery. I do not think you are uninformed, but I have thought you were a little wrongheaded at times. I feel that with so fortunate a platform as you have in De Gustibus, you have a certain duty to really enlarge the knowledge of the readers, to encourage exploration. That is entertainment enough. As the fascinating range of writers on food and its history attest, there is room for wit... but no need to reduce a food to a gag.

This is also a book dedicated to all the people who have written over the years but have never received a response. And it is a book of recipes for all the people who have written in for recipes but never received them. I have only one excuse: no secretary.

The recipes have been tested, just as they were before they appeared in a column. That way I feel confident telling anyone who writes to say the recipe didn't work that it is not my fault. With two exceptions, for which I hang my head in shame. They are corrected in this book too (see Pumpkin Cheesecake, page 251, and Salmon Hash, page 361). Two mistakes in recipes in four years isn't so bad, is it? Don't answer.

My standard responses for failed recipes follow. They are known as the ten rules for passing the buck.

1. The ingredients were not measured properly.
2. An ingredient was omitted.
3. The heat in the oven is too high.
4. The heat in the oven is too low.

5. The ingredients should have been at room temperature.
6. The ingredients should have been chilled.
7. The dish should not have been left out on the drainboard.
8. The dish should not have been frozen.
9. The dish should have been frozen.
10. The dish should have been discarded after the freezer had been defrosted for a week.

The columns have been grouped according to common interest. The largest section deals directly with food and ingredients. It follows the catchall category of fantasies and foibles. Matters pertaining to restaurants in the third category, and the last is dedicated to consumer matters—rip-offs, nutrition, cautionary tales and so on.

Among the fifty recipes included here are some that never appeared in the columns but seemed appropriate to the subject matter. Even the dessert recipe with buttercream, whipped cream and chocolate *ganache* that somewhat surprisingly appeared with a piece on spa food is appropriate once you have read the column through to the end (page 224). Délice Guy Pascal, from one of New York's foremost patissiers, Guy Pascal, is guaranteed to clog every artery, and you will love every bite.

Just as comments about the columns are appreciated, if you have comments on the comments, please write to me in care of *The New York Times,* 229 West 43rd Street, New York, New York 10036.

FANTASIES AND FOIBLES

My editor asked me to write a few introductory words for each of the four sections in this book, so I am sitting at my computer terminal on a beautiful summer afternoon wondering why I am inside.

That frame of mind is not conducive to writing engaging prose in order to draw readers into a book. I am further handicapped because I cannot figure out how to categorize this section I have called "Fantasies and Foibles."

These are the columns that expose the prejudices of people for whom food is the core of their work, the author included. They also are concerned with mothers—mine and many others—and their influence on American cooking.

Sounds to me like a little of this and that. A book with a similar title put Bette Davis on The New York Times *best-seller list.*

Buttering Corn: Variations

July 28, 1984

At an informal dinner party in Washington last month at which the hostess served the first local corn, I watched in fascination as two guests took the proffered stick of butter and rolled their ears of corn directly on it. This prompted a discussion on the proper way to butter corn. The participants included people born in the Middle West, the Far West and the Northeast, and of course, there was no agreement.

The whole-stick-of-butter school was subscribed to by the middle westerners. The far westerners melted butter in a shallow dish and rolled the corn in it. And those of us from the Northeast, more frugal, perhaps, than the others, used a butter knife to spread butter on the corn.

Accord on Corn Holders

There was accord, however, on corn holders. No one thought much of them. Even though we had silver ones at home, fashioned as ears of corn, with prongs to stick into either end of the cob, I never saw my mother use them. Some of us feel corn never tastes as good as when you have it gripped in your fingers, even if that risks a burn from a steaming cob.

As for corn cutters, the device that splits the kernels open to make creamed corn, I wasn't introduced to them until I was grown. Some people use the cutters to run over the kernels before eating them off the cob. This gives the corn a different texture, but hardly seems worth the effort unless the corn is old and tough.

I have set opinions about corn that derive from my childhood, when the only corn on the cob I ever ate at home had come from the field within two hours of picking. Not because we lived on a farm, but because my mother believed so strongly that its sweetness was in direct relationship to its freshness that she drove to the edge of town several times a week at about 4:30 or 5 P.M. to a roadside stand where it had just been picked. By 6:30 it was out of the kettle, steaming in a tea towel, awaiting its butter bath. My mother said corn older than that had already turned to starch.

In those days the most desirable variety was the white Country Gentleman. It seems to me it came later in the season. Mother peeled back a portion of the husk from every ear before she purchased it and punctured a kernel with a fingernail to test for toughness. No worms or old ears for her. Today you are lucky if they let you select the ears, much less pull away the husk.

My standards for corn haven't changed much. I've never purchased an ear in a supermarket or even an Oriental market. Country Gentleman seems to have disappeared from the commercial market. Better strains have replaced it, they say. But they don't remember Country Gentleman the way I do. Now I buy Silver Queen, and it is almost as good as the corn of my childhood.

What has changed is the way I eat and cook the corn. I stopped using butter because of the fat and calories. Then I discovered that the sweetness of a fresh young ear did not require additional embellishments. While most of the corn I am able to buy now is more than two hours old, it has always been picked the same day. The husks and silks are not removed until just before cooking because they act as a protective shield against the air. I do not put salt or sugar in the water, and instead of boiling I steam for four minutes at the most.

If, after all this loving care, the corn is not sweet or tender, I fall back on the butter, but season it with a teaspoon of ground cumin for each three tablespoons of butter.

A Cajun Dish

I am so partial to corn that I am prejudiced in favor of any dish that contains it. The revolution in American cooking finds corn in many dishes in which it never appeared before: in soups and sauces for fish, in breads and salads. I was recently introduced to a Cajun corn dish called maquechou that calls for kernels from eight ears of corn sautéed in four tablespoons of hot

butter. Two thinly sliced onions and finely chopped green pepper with freshly ground black pepper and a bit of cayenne are
added and cooked until the onions are soft. Then a mixture of
beaten egg yolk and about three-quarters of a cup of milk are
stirred in; the dish is cooked until the mixture thickens slightly.

To tell the truth, I like corn so much that, like my mother, I
relish even the leftover ears as a late-night snack, despite the
wrinkled kernels.

Another Way to Butter Corn
July 28, 1984

The local corn crop is coming to market, and this year I am more
delighted than usual to see it in the stores. I have been waiting
for eleven months to write a follow-up to last year's column on
corn. Not only because of the mail, which offered further advice
on how to butter, cook and keep corn—much of it instructive,
some of it just funny—but also because the column prompted
the *Belleville* (Ill.) *News-Democrat* to take a corn-buttering poll last
August.

It seems that a few midwestern hackles were raised when I
wrote that two guests at a dinner party, who had been raised in
the Midwest, buttered their corn by rolling the ears directly on a
stick of butter. The Belleville paper, convinced that midwesterners do not butter their corn that way, reprinted my column
next to an entry form for a "How I Butter My Corn" poll, which
listed four possible responses:

A. Melt butter in a shallow dish and roll the corn in it.

B. Use a knife to spread a pat of butter on the corn.

C. Roll corn on whole stick of butter.

D. Other.

The explanation that accompanied the poll entry blank read:

"Burros writes that folks in the Midwest butter their corn by
rolling it on a stick of butter. Sounds like a regional slur to us.

"Have you ever seen anyone butter corn by rolling it on a stick
of butter? Do you? (Would you admit it, if you did?)

"Take a moment to answer our corn poll. We'll send the results to Burros. (Unless most people vote for C—in which case we'll forget the whole thing.)"

There were more than 170 responses—the paper has a daily circulation of about 40,000, and Belleville, in southwestern Illinois about fifteen miles from St. Louis, has a population of about 42,000. A story, including a picture of one of the respondents and her method for buttering corn, appeared on the front page of the Lifestyle section on September 5, 1984. To the surprise of the editors, the poll brought a fourth method to light.

A Different Method

"Seems that in our little corner of the Midwest," wrote Mary Delach, the Lifestyle editor, "many folks use a method that's uh ... well, it's different."

More than a third of those who participated in the corn poll answered "D," for "other." Like Irene Andra of Caseyville, Illinois, who was pictured with the story, they buttered their corn by rolling it on buttered bread.

Mary Delach explained in an open letter to this columnist: "You see, you take a slice of bread, and you butter it really thick. Then you take your steaming hot ear of corn, and you roll it on the bread. Now this method may sound a little cornball to you, Marian, but folks out here swear by it."

And so did many of the people who wrote to me. I had never heard of this method before, but many readers from all over the country went to great lengths to describe how it should be done. Some rub the bread on the corn; others rub the corn on the bread. Some use a whole slice of bread; others use little pieces.

A Manhattan woman said she cut sliced bread into pieces the size of large butter pats, put salt and pepper on the butter, the butter on the bread and used it to spread the butter on each ear. "The bread is also delicious," she added.

Others used a slice of plain white bread or a dinner roll: "Butter a slice of bread or a dinner roll, and twist your ear of corn around in it," wrote one reader from Washington State. "No lost butter. No sticky fingers."

Another reader, born in Iowa, said his family used melted butter mixed with cream or half-and-half for buttering corn. "The cream makes the butter stick better, is very sweet and also extends the butter," he said.

One correspondent suggested that I was in serious jeopardy of losing my corn-eater's license for a variety of reasons, including ignorance of the proper method. "The correct procedure for buttering corn is to tear off a chunk of rude bread, plaster the torn edges with butter, then daub the kernels, using the bread as a brush," the reader said. "Vigorous chomping of the bread afterward helps rid the teeth of the clinging hulls."

The writer went on to say that a cold glass of pilsener was essential to finish the meal. And, he added: "Eating four ears of corn—the requisite minimum allowable—slathered with butter and salt, is, like Thanksgiving dinner, something we simply must overdo. The only apt description for such a joyous festival is the pop vulgarity 'pig-out.'"

Several of the poll respondents had other twists on the bread technique. One rests the corn on bread between bites so the butter doesn't run off. Another suggested adding jelly to the bread after using it for the corn.

Then, of course, there were the readers who wrote me saying they use a knife to spread butter on corn. One suggested "flattening the butter with a knife on the plate until it is the size of ravioli, adding salt and pepper and then taking some of the mixture on the knife and buttering two or three rows lengthwise— eat harmonica-fashion." He added: "This is the unmessy way; no oleaginous, dripping ear, and the stick of butter doesn't look like a new bicycle tire has run over it."

A teacher of etiquette added her 2 cents. "The proper way to eat corn, and Emily Post concurs, is to butter it across no more than *two* rows at a time, add salt (a squeeze of lime can take the place of butter) and eat it as neatly as possible."

Being an honest pollster, the *Belleville News-Democrat* admitted that some people—eleven in all—rolled their corn on sticks of butter, just like my friends at the dinner party. There was also one who didn't rub the corn on the stick of butter; she rubbed the stick of butter on the corn.

Corn

The two corn columns were not the end of the matter. In 1985 the *Milwaukee Journal* decided to have its own corn-buttering contest.

So did the *Wisconsin State Journal,* a Madison paper.

So did the *Grand Forks Herald* in Grand Forks, North Dakota.

Uncouth or not, 17 percent of those polled by the *Milwaukee Journal* used the rolling-the-corn-on-a-stick-of-butter technique. Other methods uncovered in Milwaukee included "using a push-up plastic butter spreader that holds half a stick; holding a stick or half a stick of butter in the wrapper and rubbing it on the corn; dipping the corn in a can or jar of melted butter or melted butter and water..." One claimed to use a toothbrush to apply the butter; another insisted he puts "one-quarter pound of butter in an old sweat sock and heats in microwave for forty-two seconds. The cob then is put in the hot sock."

Over in Madison at the *Wisconsin State Journal* one reader claimed to hang the boiled corn from the ceiling and apply the melted butter with a paint-can sprayer. Another takes a chunk of butter in his hand and rubs it on the ear.

Several people in Madison and in Grand Forks melt butter in a can or pot of hot water. The melted butter floats to the surface, and the corn is dipped in the water. This is recommended especially for outdoor feasts and a method also described by a New York reader.

He recalled the technique used on barrels of steaming corn served on the streets of the Bowery. "I can still savor the fragrance of the clean, early morning sea breeze blended in with the fragrance of steaming corn. My friend Mike was the 'corn chef.' There were two or three tubs of butter, huge ones on iced cakes. Mike would pick out an ear and push it into a tub and twirl it. Delish!

"Needless to say there were plenty of drippings. I always

brought along last night's *Brooklyn Eagle* and used it for a napkin!"

The *Milwaukee Journal* also surveyed the techniques for eating corn: the most popular method (59 percent) uses the typewriter or harmonica system; the round-and-round technique got less than 14 percent; 11 percent use a combination of round-and-round at the ends to get handles and the typewriter style for the middle; about 3 percent cut off the kernels and less than 1 percent start in the middle and work out or eat random fashion.

In addition to the newspaper contests, letters continued to pile up at *The New York Times*. So even after I thought I had learned everything there was to know about buttering corn, there was more.

A number of people, from all over the country, wanted to know why no one had mentioned the pastry brush method: Melted butter is served at the table, and each person spreads the butter on the corn with a pastry brush or paintbrush. In fact I have seen tiny pastry brushes designed just for use on corn.

Another corn aficionado suggested buttering the corn by placing a small piece of butter on the inside curve of a normal-size fork. "Rub butter lengthwise on the hot corn. The fork fits the shape of the corn. The butter is held between the fork tines."

A fellow *Times* reporter sent me this note: "I picked up the following habit from my father, who, I believe, learned it from his father. It was used only in family gatherings, not when company was over.

"The method is to take a hunk of butter off the pat and put it in the front of your mouth. Then simply put the corncob up to your mouth and move it back and forth against the butter, which you push forward with your tongue, like you were playing the harmonica.

"It's disgusting, but it works!"

In fact, it was mentioned by contest entrants in Wisconsin and South Dakota.

An Illinois native, now living in Connecticut, says his family always split the rows of kernels with a knife from end to end before buttering the corn. "When eaten, only the delicious insides of each kernel is released, leaving most of the 'stick between your teeth' part on the cob." The corn was buttered by placing a pat on the plate and rolling the corn in it. And then...

"After finishing eating an ear of corn, the cob is still hot. So for at least one ear per sitting we would spread some more of the butter-salt-pepper mixture on the hot, denuded cob, allow it to melt for a few seconds and suck down the eaten rows, instead of biting. It's a bit noisy but delicious, since it extracts more juices from the cob."

And finally a letter from a man in Pennsylvania who, inspired by the columns, invented a corn-buttering device but didn't have the $22,000 needed to bring it to the market. That was in January 1986. I haven't heard from him since.

Has anyone seen one of these gizmos?

Scallion? Oh, You Mean Green Onion
November 9, 1985

Just before my tenth birthday, my mother took me to a restaurant and bar in the Italian section of Waterbury, Connecticut, for a treat I had never had before. I remember this so vividly because the next day, my birthday, I came down with chicken pox. But before it was diagnosed, my mother thought perhaps I was allergic to the treat she called—and this is a phonetic stab at spelling it—"ahbeetz."

As far as I knew, that is what everyone called the thin crust covered with tomato sauce and cheese so hot it burned the roof of your mouth. Years later, when I used the word in Boston, an Italian friend laughed as she explained that what I was talking about was pizza. Subsequently, I learned that what my mother and I had heard was the Sicilian dialect, which is characterized by dropping the last vowel, as in minestron instead of ministrone.

From the Toll House Inn

I was thinking about "ahbeetz" the other night when I told an audience during a cooking demonstration that I would be making tollhouse cookies, and I could see looks of nonrecognition on several faces. When I said chocolate chip cookies, everyone understood. The original name for America's favorite cookie is not generally known to many younger people, who seem unaware of the origins of the cookie first made by Ruth Wakefield at her Toll House Inn in Whitman, Massachusetts, some fifty years ago.

Foods and ingredients have a way of changing their names as they cross the oceans, pass through the centuries or simply move from one part of the country to another.

In Louisiana they have to listen hard to figure out what you are talking about if you ask for crayfish, because they call the same little freshwater crustacean a crawfish. In Virginia, near the Blue Ridge Mountains, the elegant mushroom called a morel is a merkel. Ask for a hazelnut in California, and you could be greeted with a blank stare. They call them filberts.

In Waterbury, don't ask for a hero. Ask instead for a grinder, and then you will get a sandwich on Italian or French bread that has been sliced lengthwise and filled with meats, cheese, lettuce, etc. In Philadelphia you would order a hoagie. In New Orleans the closest relative is a poor boy, usually pronounced "po boy."

Who but born-and-bred New Englanders would know that a chowder clam and a quahog were the same thing? Or that softshell clams are usually called steamers? Most people are startled to discover that fresh coriander, cilantro and Chinese parsley are one and the same. There seems to be little rhyme or reason to what term is used for the long, slender onion sometimes called a scallion, sometimes a green onion and sometimes a spring onion. In Louisiana a scallion is a young shallot.

Over the years, citizens of the United States have done a bang-up job of confusing chili and chile. Chili is a mixture of beans, tomatoes and spices. Chili powder is a combination of spices that includes the hot pepper spelled *chile* in Spanish. But in this country we have changed the "e" to an "i" when spelling the word for hot pepper.

All this makes writing recipes difficult. And it makes following them even harder.

Scallions, "Ahbeetz" and Other Lingo

Scallions, grinders and tollhouse cookies. Someone had something to say about each of these words, but it was "ahbeetz" that brought back memories for so many.

First of all it seems that at least one publication thinks scallions and green onions are two different things, as a reader from New Hartford, New York, pointed out. Green onions, the magazine says, are pulled once a firm white bulb has developed, but before a papery skin has formed. Scallions, the magazine goes on to say, are shoots that are pulled before the bulbs have a chance to develop. They have straight sides and a fine texture. Without arguing the point, green onions and scallions taste much the same when cut into salad or cooked dishes, and most greengrocers don't, in fact, make the distinction.

In at least one state green onions have an entirely different name. Mary Cantwell, an editorial writer at *The New York Times*, came by to tell me that in Rhode Island, where she grew up, scallions were called rareripes. Not long after, I received a letter from a woman whose mother, born in Virginia in 1875, used the same word. Rareripes, according to a dictionary the woman consulted, is an adjective meaning ripening early and a noun meaning a fruit or vegetable that ripens early. Surely spring onions fit that definition.

A former Illinois resident checked in with "root beer float" for "black cow" and "Arabic" for "2 cents plain."

A professor from Trenton State College in New Jersey weighed in with stories about hoagies. "About nineteen years ago, I interviewed the man who is responsible for the term *hoggie*. This goes back to the mid-1930s in South Philadelphia and refers to the fact that you have to be a hog to eat one of the sandwiches. However, white Philadelphians have difficulty pronouncing the word in this manner. Gradually during World War II the spelling changed to meet the way the sandwich was being pronounced, hoagie. Among Black Philadelphians, the spelling and pronunciation remained hoggie." The professor said he had traced the sandwich back to 1885 in New York City and 1891 in New Orleans but did not know what it was called then.

But it was the mention of the term *ahbeetz* that brought an outpouring of mail, a sampling of which follows. Two readers may have eaten "ahbeetz" in the same restaurant where I first sampled it. "I could have written the first two paragraphs myself," said a former Naugatuck, Connecticut, resident. Naugatuck is the town on the Naugatuck River next to Waterbury. Another Waterburian, now a resident of Wilmington, Delaware, said when she was a child "going out for 'ahbeetz' was an exclusively adult treat." She also reminded me that in Delaware a hero is a submarine or a sub.

"My mouth nearly dropped when I read your column last Saturday," wrote a New Jersey reader. "Here I thought my mother was the only one who taught me 'ahbeetz' for pizza. Even years later, after I learned the truth, I could not figure out how she had arrived at 'ahbeetz.' She is not Sicilian, but apparently Neopolitans use the same dialect for this word." Which brings up another point. I think I stand corrected, but I'm not sure. I have been told by others as well that the dialect is Neopolitan, not Sicilian.

The most interesting letter of all came from a Pennsylvania Dutch reader who grew up in Reading. She recounted her visit with a friend sometime after World War II to a carnival benefiting the Holy Rosary Church in Reading. "My friend asked me if I liked 'beetz.' Never having heard of it, and with a gut feeling she wasn't referring to the pickled beets and red beet eggs I knew, I muttered something noncommittal. 'Beetz' was a specialty of Mrs. I-wish-I-could-remember-her-name of Holy Rosary. One bite and I was hooked—for me 'beetz' was not an acquired taste. As I remember, it was served tepid. Whether this was customary or dictated by the primitive cooking facilities at the Holy Rosary Carnival I do not know."

It's always nice to know a column has been genuinely helpful, so I really cherish the letter from the man who used to live in an Italian section and had "arbeetz" in the early '40s. "I'm glad, finally, to have my own memory of 'arbeetz' confirmed," he wrote. "And all these years I thought I was alone."

A former Brooklyn resident, now living in Miami, added a new "word" to my lexicon, but only after I asked several old-time New Yorkers in my office what "hamultid" was. "I am shocked that none of your correspondents reminded you about the favorite, most delectable (when affordable) and treatiest (same) item in the Brooklyn (and probably Bronx) diet, 'hamultid.'" I turned to Dick Shepard, a longtime reporter for *The New York Times,* for help. Dick knows more about New York than twenty reporters combined. He said "'hamultid' is a sort of Yiddish accent." And you would use it at the corner drugstore, if it had a soda fountain, in the following fashion: "Gimme hamultid."

Still don't get it? "Give me a malted" (as in malted milk).

To Quash Lupper, Start with Brunch
December 3, 1983

As the world's most noteworthy egg, how fitting it would have been for Humpty-Dumpty to create brunch, a portmanteau word for a meal at which eggs are invariably found. Humpty-Dumpty's creator, Lewis Carroll, however, did coin another portmanteau word—*slithy,* derived from slimy and little. And he created the phrase *portmanteau word* to describe one word that is made up of two others and suggests part of the meaning of each.

Brunch, according to most dictionaries, is a late-morning meal, but it's difficult to find a place in New York City that serves brunch before noon. Ordinarily that would be a time for lunch, and James Beard still thinks it should be. Almost twenty years ago he wrote in *James Beard's Menus for Entertaining* that he disliked the word *brunch* and would rather call it late breakfast.

By this past Friday he had not relented. "Why should we have misplaced breakfast food?" he asked. "If I'm going to have sausage and eggs, I want them in the morning. I think I'd banish brunch and ask people for late breakfast, between eleven thirty and noon, or I'd ask them for lunch at one."

Mr. Beard has taken a position without a lot of company. Ruth Baum, whose husband, Joe Baum, is a famous restaurateur in N.Y., finds the very thought of being invited to breakfast on Sunday morning "horrifying." But, she added: "You have to have some kind of fruit juice for the first meal of the day, so you can't call it lunch. A Bloody Mary has tomato juice in it, and that makes it righteous."

I must confess to confusion whenever I contemplate a brunch, because I stand somewhere between James Beard and Ruth Baum. I love the informality of the meal, but I must rack my brain to come up with food I like to eat at noon—which other people will eat as the first meal of the day. I'd like to do away with sausages, eggs, croissants and Bloody Marys. Not being a breakfaster, I can't see anything wrong with plunging right into a lunch of some lightly grilled fish or chicken and a salad of different-colored greens. But have you ever been served salad at brunch?

On the other hand, Ruth Baum's view that "brunch is the best of two worlds" is one I share. "You don't have to get up early, and you still have time to do something else," she said.

Credit for the word *brunch,* however, belongs elsewhere. The 1972 supplement to the *Oxford English Dictionary* says it first appeared in *Hunter's Weekly* in 1895. According to the August 1, 1896, issue of the magazine *Punch:* "To be fashionable nowadays we must 'brunch.' Truly an excellent portmanteau word, introduced, by the way, last year, by Mr. Guy Berlinger, in the now defunct *Hunter's Weekly,* and indicating a combined breakfast and lunch." The Oxford dictionary says the word is university slang.

Evan Jones, author of *American Food: The Gastronomic Story,* says he first became aware of brunch at the famous Pump Room in Chicago's Ambassador Hotel in 1933. In the days before jet travel made bicoastal living a matter of hours each way, movie stars with business on both coasts would stop between trains in Chicago on their way across the continent. On Sunday stopovers they brunched at the Pump Room. Mr. Jones says it was as much a scene as lunch at The Four Seasons in New York City is today.

Altered Lifestyles

But Sunday brunch, which is more popular on the East and West coasts than elsewhere in the United States, did not gain a foothold until after World War II, when lifestyles were so dramatically altered. Jones doesn't think there is anything mysterious about how brunch has replaced both lunch and Sunday midday dinner.

"We like to sleep in Sundays, read the newspapers and loll in bed," he said. "After the World War II generation went away from church altogether, Sunday became a day to enjoy doing nothing, and brunch just grew like Topsy."

Then, too, as the '50s gave way to the '60s, Americans became more casual. The formal Sunday lunch went the way of white kid gloves, girdles and fedoras. Brunch is a time for sweaters, not ties.

Joe Baum, the restaurant consultant responsible for many of the most popular dining spots in New York in the early '60s, says one of them, the Tower Suite, helped to popularize brunch. "Brunch started out as a family thing," he said. "For some it is the only day the whole family gets together for a meal. But now it has become a romantic meal as well, following the Saturday night date."

I hope, however, that William Sherk is dead wrong. In *500 Years of New Words,* a book published this year, Mr. Sherk writes that there is a new portmanteau word "struggling to be born." The word is lupper, for a midafternoon meal eaten in place of lunch and supper. I, for one, hope it dies aborning. Whatever would I serve?

. . . And Move on to Blupper and Flunch

Readers cared little about what I or anyone else should serve for brunch. They were much more interested in portmanteau words.

From New York City there was a note about a chain of restaurants in France called Flunch, for fast lunch. From Demarest, New Jersey, a reader wrote to say that I had "made a serious error. 'Blupper' is correct since it is alliteratively sound: B (Breakfast) and L (Lunch) and S (which is silent) (supper)." From Scottsdale, Arizona, a man with his mind elsewhere: "Is 'lupper' to be taken after a late nooner?" A woman in Milford, Pennsylvania, said that "dunch" would be preferable for lunch and dinner than lupper.

Brunch is beginning to sound better and better already.

For brunch, lupper or dunch I suggest:

DEBORAH'S HUEVOS RANCHEROS

> 2 *tablespoons vegetable oil*
> 2 *large onions, coarsely chopped*
> 2 *small red or green bell peppers, chopped*
> 2 *cups canned peeled tomatoes*
> 1½ *teaspoons fresh chopped basil, or* ½ *teaspoon dried*
> 1½ *teaspoons chopped fresh oregano, or* ½ *teaspoon dried*
> *Salt and freshly ground black pepper to taste*
> 8 *eggs*
> 8 *1-inch squares Muenster cheese,* ¼ *inch thick*

1. Heat the oil in a skillet large enough to hold the eggs. Sauté the onion and peppers in the hot oil about 5 minutes.
2. Drain and crush the tomatoes with your fingers before adding to the skillet with the basil, oregano, salt and pepper. Cover and cook over low heat 10 minutes.
3. Make eight wells in the tomato mixture and break one egg into each. Top each egg with cheese. Cover the skillet and cook about 10 minutes, until the eggs are done to taste.

YIELD: 4 servings

Excavating Dishes of the '60s

December 24, 1985

The invitation to the black-tie dinner read "Déjà Vu." The three hosts were professionals in the food business. So it took no great powers of deduction to figure out that the menu would look back, perhaps at some of those forgotten blockbusters such as beef Wellington and veal Orloff.

In fact, the buffet table held other equally well known if somewhat less complicated dishes. They included chicken divan, seafood Newburg, beef Stroganoff, parsleyed rice, green beans amandine and tomato aspic with avocado—retrofood, the recipes we all loved in the '60s but have long since abandoned, along with miniskirts and bouffant hairdos.

Outgrowth of Discussion

The dinner was the result of a discussion that Ellen Brown and Ann Brody, both food consultants in Washington, D.C., had about culinary archaeology. They thought it would be interesting to see how people reacted to a dinner based on recipes popular twenty years ago.

"We were very careful about the selection of the guest list," Brown said. "We did not want to offend anyone who might be serving tomato aspic today."

They chose wisely. While the fifty guests enjoyed much of the food, had seconds and thirds in some cases, the tomato aspic was an unmitigated failure. "It was universally decided," Brown said, "that our palates had progressed past the point at which we could tolerate tomato aspic." Which probably explains why it has been at least twenty years since I made my version of tomato aspic, which contained raspberry gelatin as well as horseradish.

The dinner, at which Brody's husband, Peter Finkhauser, a restaurateur, also was a host, began with cocktails and hors d'oeuvres appropriate to the period: ramaki, quiche, Swedish meatballs with dill and sweet-and-sour hot dogs. A card that provided the name of each dish and the cookbook from which it was taken accompanied each platter.

My hostesses could hardly contain their glee when they escorted me to the chafing dish of sweet-and-sour hot dogs. I didn't have to read the card to know that it had come from my first cookbook, *Elegant but Easy,* written twenty-five years ago. It is one of those recipes I would just as soon forget: slices of hot dogs cooked in a sauce of currant jelly and mustard. Ann Brody said they had tampered with the recipe, increasing the mustard in order to counteract the achingly sweet taste. But even that change did little to improve it.

Sitting next to the chafing dish were bottles of Lancer's sparkling rosé and Mateus rosé, among the first wines many Americans drank before they learned about California cabernet sauvignon and Chardonnay, both of which were provided at the dinner along with Pol Roger Champagne for the more serious enophiles.

Other than the addition of mustard to the franks, the use of fresh mushroom sauce instead of Campbell's mushroom soup with the Swedish meatballs, and the substitution of freshly made unsalted beef bouillon for the canned bouillon, the hosts stuck pretty close to the original dishes. With one important exception: They made drastic reductions in the amount of salt used in each recipe.

And, to tell the truth, they also took a few liberties with the seafood Newburg, adding crayfish, which were barely known in Washington until two years ago, and jumbo shrimp, about three times the size of the shrimp available in town twenty years ago. (I had seconds of that.)

The chocolate mousse was made the traditional French way, with egg whites instead of whipped cream. The result was so firm it was perfectly safe to turn the plate on which it rested upside-down, as one guest did, and nothing fell off.

To my taste the Nesselrode pie, made with canned Nesselrode mix, was in the same category as the tomato aspic and hot dogs in sweet-and-sour sauce, the frozen green beans not far behind. So most of us just nibbled the toasted almonds off the top and begged our hosts to serve beef Wellington and veal Orloff next time.

Retrofood

"We laughed hysterically at your column this morning," said one Washington, D.C., friend over the phone. "We were just sorry that they decided to use fresh mushrooms instead of mushroom soup. It wasn't as authentic."

"It brought back all kinds of memories about things I hadn't thought about in years. Fish on Fridays and we always had some version of tuna noodle casserole. Sometimes with nuts. Sometimes with something else," wrote one reader. "I'm always surprised when we travel to some little town in Europe and they have marvelous food. Here you can't get anything decent to eat. I suppose it's because we have no food tradition."

What the column did not say was that there are places where hot dogs in sweet-and-sour sauce are still served. At the party one guest said, "You can get food just like this at a bar mitzvah in Queens."

We all laughed a lot about the column, but I stopped laughing after I read the following letter from Westchester County, New York.

Help! *I did not realize that recipes and food are dated.* Elegant but Easy *happens to be one of my favorite cookbooks. What should I replace it with so that my cooking can be "now"?*

Your column in today's Times *was really depressing. Are there any recipes in your book that can still be used without appearing gauche? Just three or four weeks ago I made Sweet and Sour Meatballs, and all the guests thought that they were wonderful. Does this mean we are all out of touch?*

All kidding aside, is there another cookbook that tells you where to stop when preparing a recipe in advance? I have used Elegant but Easy *and* Freeze with Ease *for at least seventeen years; both books have been reliable, now I feel self-conscious when selecting a recipe."*

The letter had a P.S.: "I never made Sweet and Sour Frank-furters."

If there is one thing an author does not want to do, it is to turn people away from her books. I have tried to appease my former fan in a letter that pointed out that for this New Year's Eve I made the toasted mushroom rolls from the book, and they are just as old as the franks. The difference is that they are as good today as they were twenty-five years ago.

Worse still was a note from a former fan in New Jersey. "This takes the cake. Who wants to read about that? Hot and sour hot dogs, tomato aspic, etc.—indeed! Never will I read another arti-cle by Marian Burros. This is enough."

A Connecticut reader was equally upset: "I consider it need lessly unkind to ridicule the food preferences of other time places or people. Some of us like tomato aspic, though I nev get to serve it because my family decided it was unpalatab ("icky") in the 1940s, considerably ahead of the guests at the De Vu party."

A Cambridge, Massachusetts, correspondent who was an enough to send his comments to Letters to the Editor co barely contain his disdain. He was particularly infuriated by "treasonous onslaught on tomato aspic."

No pretenders to the status of gourmet afflicted the reading public wi
repulsive disguises and compounds of the 1960s, of which Ms. Burros'
with raspberry gelatin and horseradish is a fair example. On the othei
we had no Ellen Brown to tell us that "our palates had progressed
point at which we could tolerate tomato aspic."

No one, either in the '60s or any other decade, ever persuaded me
sume hot dogs in currant jelly or to drink sparkling rosé (or Virginia
am no devotee of anything on "divans"—at least not in the kitchen—
desecrate beef tenderloin and good cream in the unhappy concoction
beef Stroganoff. For forty years, however, my wife and I have serv
aspic, at home and abroad, to what Miss Brown might call "un
claim." We use none of Ms. Burros's ghastly adulterants, and in fa
simplified the recipe to the nub. It makes an ideal opener for almost

The correspondent's aspic is made with V-8 juice or tomato juice. The letter was accompanied by a persona dressed to me. It said: "I suppose you won't print a long as this, but I had to get it off my chest (or stom will settle for a brief public apology to partisans of asp

I can't apologize: I still don't like aspic very much, but I hope this will do.

And I hope this recipe for Toasted Mushroom Rolls will prove that some retrofood is worth preserving.

TOASTED MUSHROOM ROLLS

½   *pound mushrooms*
¼   *cup sweet butter*
3   *tablespoons flour*
    Salt to taste
1   *cup light cream*
2   *teaspoons minced fresh chives*
1   *teaspoon lemon juice*
1   *22-ounce loaf very fresh white bread*
    Additional melted butter for brushing

1. Wash, trim and finely chop the mushrooms.
2. Heat the butter and sauté the mushrooms for 5 minutes. Blend in the flour seasoned with salt, if desired.
3. Stir in the cream and cook until the mixture thickens. Add the chives and lemon juice, stir and remove from the heat and cool.
4. Remove the crusts from the bread and flatten each slice slightly with a rolling pin.
5. Spread the cooled mushroom mixture on each slice of bread and roll up. Arrange seam side down on baking sheets, brush with additional melted butter and bake at 400 degrees for about 15 minutes, until the rolls are golden. Cut each roll in half and serve warm, not hot.

If desired, the rolls may be frozen. To serve, simply defrost and follow the baking directions.

YIELD: 3½ dozen

Note: With all the wonderful wild mushrooms on the market, these rolls are even better when made with half regular white mushrooms, known as *champignons de Paris,* and half wild mushrooms, such as shiitake or Italian brown mushrooms. They add a depth of flavor not found in the ordinary mushroom.

Recipes of the '40s: Little Spice
July 13, 1985

If it is true that one person's junk is another's treasure, so it is that one person's discards are another's resources.

A recent package from a reader who was cleaning out her closet included more than a dozen recipe and menu booklets that were published between 1940 and 1943. I could hardly tear myself away from them, both transfixed and horrified at the idea of having to make three-course dinners every night with six different recipes; amused at the absence of any spices and herbs in the recipes and overwhelmed by the amount of thick cream sauces and floury gravies.

Most of the booklets were published by the now-defunct Culinary Arts Institute, a Chicago-based cooking school described on the inside cover as "one of America's foremost organizations devoted to the science of better cookery." The logo has a drawing of a woman who could be Betty Crocker's double. The recipes are a fascinating reminder of how much things have changed.

Although many more ingredient are available to cooks today, most of us would be hard pressed to take advantage of the recipe for chicken soup made from chicken feet, which is found in the booklet devoted to leftovers. In 1985 chicken feet are almost as scarce as hen's teeth. And there are those who maintain that modern-day chicken soup has lost an indescribable essence without the feet.

The cost of ingredients has also changed dramatically in forty-five years. Chickens were still a luxury in 1940 but apparently not crab and lobster. In a booklet containing 250 fish and seafood recipes, there are nineteen for crab and fourteen for lobster. Lobster in the shell probably cost a tenth then of what it costs today, crab even less. In addition there were twenty-two recipes for clams and oysters and just one for mussels.

Overcooking and Nutrition

Cooking times were vastly different too. Today we'd consider many of the dishes overcooked: A recipe for scallops suggested broiling them at 550 degrees for fifteen minutes rather than today's five to seven minutes; cubed summer squash was simmered for fifteen to twenty minutes, nearly twice the time used today.

The Culinary Arts Institute appears to have been interested in nutrition, but its nutrition advice would be laughed out of town in 1985. Adults were told to drink a pint of milk, which is not surprising, but they were also admonished to use "cream and cheese every day for good measure." Liver was to be served once a week, along with generous amounts of fresh eggs. Cholesterol levels must have been in the 700 range. Under those guidelines, the vast quantities of thick cream sauces, liberally sprinkled throughout the recipes, were considered nutritious. One recipe called for a single cup of crabmeat, two cups of grated cheese and three cups of thick white sauce. Mock terrapin stew, using three cups of leftover chicken, was made with ½ cup of melted fat and six egg yolks.

On the other hand, the variety of vegetables used in the vegetable cookbook is startling. Several of them are considered exotic or at least unusual today: kohlrabi, dasheen (taro), chayote (a squash), Jerusalem artichoke (sometimes called sunchoke), salsify, even broccoli rape, which few outside of Italian families have ever encountered.

Recipes from each of these booklets are referred to in the book of menus, which provided lunch and dinner suggestions for 365 days. Thanksgiving appears to be the one immutable meal from that day to this: roast turkey, scalloped oysters, giblet gravy, mashed potatoes, steamed squash, creamed onions, molded cranberry jelly, watercress salad and pumpkin pie and mince pie.

A typical August family dinner began with honeydew melon followed by french-fried chicken, potato soufflé, green beans, lettuce salad with chive French dressing and golden parfait. And they didn't even have air-conditioning!

My favorite suggestion is not a recipe but a garnish that is illustrated in the book of soup recipes. It calls for a stack of pretzels in a ring of sliced dill pickles that have been cored and filled with some white mixture, possibly cream cheese. According to the caption, the stuffed dills and pretzels "accompany the soup most gallantly."

'40s and '60s Food

It's hard to say which column caused more controversy, the one about '40s food or the one about food in the '60s. You be the judge.

Wrote one woman from Brooklyn: "There's no reason to be so hoity-toity about the nutritionists of that period. I daresay that forty years from now, some of the pronouncements of the current gurus will sound just as ridiculous."

Her feelings were backed up by a reader from the Bronx: "There is a smirk on the face of De Gustibus," she wrote. "So our nutrition advice would be laughed out of town in 1985? With that kind of nutrition how come there are more elderly people alive today, less infant mortality?

"Cholesterol levels? Lady, we didn't worry like you do today. We just did the best we could and lived. By the way, my husband and I are each three-quarters of a century old."

Then came a four-page letter from a lady in Amarillo setting the record straight.

I was born fifty-eight years ago last February on the Flying V Ranch in Texas. There was thick juicy steak three times a day if we so desired. Strips of meat were cut and rolled in flour, cornmeal and black pepper (that kept the flies off), then it was hung on the clothesline to dry. When dry it was put in a flour sack and hung in a convenient place. When a cowboy or someone walked by, they could get a handful of "jerky" to nibble on. Mother always cooked with pure cream and cow's butter, and there was fried chicken cooked better than Kentucky Fried. My mother was "Miss Matador" at Matador, Texas. She was not only beautiful, she was a perfectionist and everything had to be done perfectly. Anytime she wanted rabbit for supper, she went out and shot a young rabbit.

She always had vegetables and wild plums canned up for years ahead. Back then lamb's-quarter grew behind the barns and along the roads. Poison sprays have long since killed out the good lamb's-quarter. But take the dandelion. Dandelions should be our best friends.

You can make a delicious salad out of the leaves, jelly from the yellow blooms, and wine or coffee from the roots.

Back in the '40s, when a lot of things were hard to get, we cooked pinto beans, mashed them up fine, seasoned them like pumpkin pie, poured them in a pie shell and had a fine pie. And back even before that we took "squabs" (young pigeon), put them in a soup and had a feast.

And if it snowed in the winter, I took a bowl of Jell-O, put it in a snowbank and waited impatiently for it to jell. Back before "pollution," I brought in snow mixed with vanilla and sugar and milk and had instant ice cream.

And talk about biscuits that rose at least six inches high and melted in your mouth! Sourdough biscuits were made with potatoes and yeast and left to set and rise behind the wood cook stove. Everytime a batch was taken out, more sliced potatoes were added. We didn't, but some people made potato whiskey, and let it ferment behind the stove.

Don't know anyone my age or younger who can outwork me.

The mail continued on, berating me for making fun of the '40s. But I will not take the rap for the misspelling of broccoli rabe (see page 38), which came out broccoli rape and brought this note from New Jersey: "I have seen many misspelled food signs, but your 'broccolli rape' beats all." So does the correspondent's spelling of broccoli!

I'm not opposed to all '40s recipes, just bad '40s recipes. I'm equally opposed to bad '80s recipes like Watergate Cake made with a package of pistachio-flavored pudding mix.

This '40s or earlier recipe came from my friend from Arkansas, Liz Wolferman, now Haupert, who is mentioned elsewhere in this book in connection with her family recipe for fried chicken. I don't know the exact vintage of her family recipe for angel pie. But it was certainly being made in the '40s and should be now.

SOUTHERN ANGEL PIE

    3   egg whites
    ½   cup sugar
    1½ teaspoons pure vanilla extract

1 *baked 9-inch pie shell*
1 *cup heavy cream*
  Ground pecans for garnish

1. Beat the egg whites until soft peaks form. Gradually beat in the sugar and 1 teaspoon of the vanilla to form stiff, glossy peaks. Spoon into a 9-inch baked pie shell and bake at 300 degrees, until the meringue is slightly brown, about 20 minutes. Cool.
2. Two hours before serving, whip the cream with the remaining vanilla and decorate the pie with it. Sprinkle with the nuts.

YIELD: 6 servings

The Ghosts of Recipes Past

October 8, 1983

Untried recipes, many yellow with age, fill shoeboxes, folders and kitchen drawers in homes from coast to coast. Few of us ever weed them out, and as the years pass it seems that we are less and less likely to try them.

Looking at some of these recipes two, five, even fifteen years after they were clipped, it is difficult to remember what their appeal was in the first place. Fashions in cooking change just as surely as they do in clothes, though probably at a more leisurely pace. Since the advent of nouvelle cuisine and the increased interest in lighter, more healthful fare, recipes that are more than ten years old but less then fifty are not family treasures—they are simply dated.

The Impact of Revolutions

How my old recipes had been affected by the various culinary revolutions dawned on me last year when I decided to weed out mercilessly the unused bits I had been gathering for a quarter of a century. Though I had turned to them over the years in search of new concepts for each cookbook I wrote, the cookbooks have come and gone and the recipes have gathered dust.

The first one to go was for molded beet salad. Nothing was wrong with the ingredients, but I have not served a molded gelatin salad in ten years. I have three twelve-cup ring molds and one that holds twenty cups in my cupboard, not to mention at least six others that range in size from four cups to ten. These days they are used for rice, Bavarian creams and baked goods. Gelatin molds have been replaced, it seems to me, by composed salads in which the freshness of the fruit or vegetables is the primary consideration. Actually, the ingredients for that molded beet salad—shoestring beets, green onions and sour cream—would make a delicious salad with the addition of an herb or two and without the gelatin.

Yet another recipe for beef in pastry reminded me of my fruitless efforts to produce a beef Wellington without a soggy crust. It took years of trying various recipes before I came to the conclusion that a rare fillet of beef and a flaky pastry are mutually exclusive. The closest I ever came to the flaky crust was lamb chops in pastry; because the chops cooked so quickly the pastry did not have time to soak up the juices. Out went the beef-in-pastry recipe.

Similar treatment was accorded a recipe for a mock strudel that was made with a sour cream–pastry dough. The result bore absolutely no resemblance to the translucent sheets that are essential for strudel. Today even some of the commercial ones, which are easy to find, are excellent. Twenty years ago, when they were not available in the town where I lived, I clipped the recipe because I knew I was not going to spend hours, as my mother had, pulling and stretching strudel dough over the kitchen table.

Though Hello Dollys have become part of Americana, which is certainly the reason I saved the recipe, I have given the heave-ho to the achingly sweet bars named for the role Carol Channing created on Broadway in the '60s. The recipe calls for a cup of graham cracker crumbs, six ounces of chocolate chips, a cup of coconut and a can of sweetened condensed milk, along with some butter and pecans.

Gone, too, are the recipes calling for any kind of convenience food. After a few years of cooking I discovered that I could do better than any food technologist in a white coat—and usually for considerably less money.

$80 to Serve Eight Guests

It was more difficult to throw out the recipe for flamed lobster in a brandy sauce that called for four pounds of meat. It was clipped when lobster meat was $3 a pound; enough to serve eight people would cost $80 now. A recipe that called for one black truffle a person met a similar fate.

I have not discarded all my outdated recipes. Some can be refashioned, like the one calling for a single chopped onion sautéed in a quarter of a cup of butter, and the Chinese dish for four that includes two teaspoons of salt as well as two tablespoons of soy sauce. For sautéing one onion the amount of butter is cut in half; dishes with soy sauce seldom require additional salt, so the salt is eliminated and, indeed, the amount of soy sauce is reduced.

My recipe file is slimmer now. Yet when I went looking for a spectacular end to a birthday dinner party, none of the simple fruit desserts whose recipes I had filled the bill. Fortunately I had kept a recipe from 1970 for a large almond cake that is frosted with mocha buttercream. After I tasted a slightly revised version (a little less sugar, a little more almond extract and some ground almonds added to the batter), I had second thoughts about all the other old recipes I had thrown away.

Unfashionable Recipes

Irene Sax, a food writer and cookbook author, said The Ghosts of Recipes Past column reminded her of the piece she'd "always wanted to write on these files as a history of female friendships."

For example, I have in my file not only my mother's chocolate-wafer cake and my Aunt Hilda's marmalade coating for chicken (the women in my family were not celebrated cooks), but two recipes from Mrs. Kronenberg. Yet I never met

Mrs. Kronenberg: She was my mother's best friend's mother. Her pot roast is one of those truly delicious recipes with a shameful ingredient: ketchup is the principal seasoning.

Most of all, the file reminds me of how sharing recipes used to be a way of making friends when I was first married, traveling from city to city with a young physician-in-training. We'd be invited to dinner. The next day, when I made my thank-you call (!!), I'd ask the hostess how she made the shrimp casserole or the German chocolate cake, and we might arrange to push strollers to the bookmobile together that afternoon.

Or, on late-afternoon duty in the playground, rumbling stomachs would lead to the inevitable conversation: What are you making for dinner? That's why I have lots of ways to use ground beef and frozen fish fillets. Lots of macaroni casseroles, Jell-O molds and cocktail snacks. There's not a one I'd dream of making today, nor one I could discard.

After reading Irene Sax's wonderful bit of nostalgia I am really sorry I discarded all my old recipes, gathered exactly as she had gathered hers.

This is one old recipe that has not disappeared because it was published in one of the cookbooks I wrote with Lois Levine, called *Come for Cocktails, Stay for Supper.* Published in 1970 many of its recipes seem old-fashioned to me now, but for the 1985 New Year's Eve dinner—an annual event my friend Sherley Koteen and I have put on for almost twenty years now. We reached back into that book for a recipe called Nova Scotia Mousse. It was such an enormous success that, with a few updated revisions, it's worth repeating in its new form.

NOVA SCOTIA MOUSSE

1 *envelope unflavored gelatin*
¼ *cup cold water*
½ *cup hot light cream*
8 *ounces cream cheese without gum, if possible, softened*
1 *cup sour cream*
1 *teaspoon Worcestershire sauce*
¼ *teaspoon hot pepper sauce*
1 *garlic clove, mashed*
2 *tablespoons chopped fresh chives*
1 *teaspoon lemon juice*
1 *tablespoon chopped fresh parsley*

1 tablespoon white horseradish
½ pound Nova Scotia or other smoked salmon, coarsely chopped
½ cup pitted chopped black French or Greek olives, packed in brine, drained
4 ounces salmon caviar
Greens for the decoration
Thinly sliced squares of rye bread

1. Sprinkle the gelatin on the cold water. Dissolve in the hot cream. Cool.
2. Mash together the cream cheese, sour cream, Worcestershire sauce, hot pepper sauce, garlic and chives. Stir into the dissolved gelatin.
3. Add the lemon juice, parsley, horseradish, salmon and black olives. Carefully fold in the caviar.
4. Pour into a lightly greased 3-cup mold. Refrigerate until firm. Unmold to serve. Decorate with greens and serve with the thinly sliced rye bread.

YIELD: 8 to 12 servings

Collector's Items: Dusty, Useless Kitchen Gadgets
November 5, 1983

Every fall, when the postman arrives with another shipment of mail-order catalogues, I have to remind myself of the second kitchen I have been outfitting in my attic almost from the day I set up housekeeping. But the kitchen equipment so artfully displayed with mouth-watering food on the catalogues' full-color pages beckons me to fill in the order blank so that I too can have an ice cream machine, a pasta machine, an espresso machine, a utensil with which to flute mushrooms and another to make lemon zest.

My attic kitchen is filled with useless equipment that has been gathering dust for twenty years. I am not even talking about the broken electric mixer and electric frying pan and the three broken electric can openers that were carried upstairs because I was sure someone could repair them. That was before I had come to understand that in this throwaway society it is less costly to buy something new than to repair something old.

I am talking about perfectly good equipment like the meat slicer my mother-in-law gave me when I was newly married. After one or two uses it always seemed to be more trouble than it was worth to assemble it. The electric knife that is up there with the slicer is equally inefficient. And so is the onion chopper, the one with the blades at the bottom of a spring plunger that fits into a plastic cup fitted with a wooden bottom. A well-sharpened knife does slicing, chopping, cubing or mincing more quickly and effectively and does not have to be assembled. It washes more quickly too.

The cheese fondue and fondue Bourguignonne pots are casualties of the fickleness of food styles. In the '60s everyone was entertaining with fondue parties, first cheese and then beef, but fondues seem to have gone the way of California dip. Do you remember that? It was sour cream mixed with a package of dry onion soup mix served with potato chips and guaranteed to produce a salt attack. California dip is no loss, but cheese fondue, made of the best Gruyère and French bread and washed down with a light Swiss wine, is a satisfying Sunday-night supper. Perhaps the thought that I might serve it again one day is the reason I have kept the fondue forks in the kitchen drawer.

My two chocolate-roll boards are also victims of food fashion. The late Dione Lucas popularized airy, flourless but deeply rich chocolate rolls in the early '60s, and as I write I am tempted to make one again. It is just that the current creative explosion in chocolate desserts compels me to try something new all the time.

The Crockpot and the pressure cooker have also been banished. It is not really their fault, but I do not cook that way anymore. If I want to stew or braise, I do it on the weekend while I am working at other things and refrigerate or freeze the dish until I am ready to serve it.

Changes in attitude toward what constitutes healthful eating have sent the minifryer to Coventry as well. It would no longer occur to me to fry anything in deep fat just for a family meal.

Too much fat, too many calories. The few times when I do fry, it is party food; a minifryer will not do.

The electric grilled-cheese sandwich maker and peanut butter maker are also more or less victims of heightened concern with fat, but the real reason I do not use them anymore is that my children no longer live at home. The cookie press falls into the same category.

Why I ever let myself be talked into the cold-water coffee maker remains a mystery. The contraption produces coffee essence without heating the grounds. A small amount of the essence is combined with boiling water to produce a cup of coffee in as much time as it takes to boil the water. It tastes about as good as instant coffee and is a lot more work.

Someone sent me the tuna salad turner that enjoyed brief stardom a few years ago. I still do not know why anyone bought it. Since it was necessary to chop all the ingredients before putting them in the gadget, I found it just as easy to mix them in a bowl with a fork.

As for the mushroom peeler, I bought it myself, in the days when people actually peeled mushrooms. I used it only once—and that was when I learned that I was too lazy to peel mushrooms. I was delighted to find out not only that it was a waste of time but that some of the wonderful flavoring was going in the garbage with the peelings.

So, tempted as I am to buy the gadget that turns heavy cream into whipped cream and the one that cooks rice to perfection, I think I'll stick to the pots and pans I already have.

Except...

Except that I just saw a sherbet maker that costs only $89.95.

Gadgets

I'm awfully glad I didn't dispose of those chocolate-roll boards. Since I wrote the collector's items column, I have made two chocolate rolls that received the same rave notices I usually get for Double Chocolate Threat.

And a reader from Plainview, New York, gave me another reason to rescue my egg slicer from oblivion.

"You know," she wrote, "the egg-slicer gadget—a hinged lid of wires which you press down on the egg? It's marvelous for slicing mushrooms! If you don't already know about it, try it. (Even if it means a trip up to the attic.)"

Since the recipe for Dione Lucas's Chocolate Roll is already included in the column on kitchen disasters, page 64, can I interest anyone in a recipe for Jean Banchet's Chocolate Cake?

Mr. Banchet is the owner of the famous Wheeling, Illinois, restaurant, Le Français. It is about forty-five minutes outside of Chicago, and my only trip there was taken with three other food people in a broken-down taxi from downtown Chicago. The taxi was minus a window, and the trip cost $50. The cake was worth the bizarre ride.

This is a flourless cake. It gets all its height from the eggs.

JEAN BANCHET'S GATEAU AU CHOCOLAT

14 ounces bittersweet chocolate broken into small pieces
¾ cup plus 2 tablespoons unsalted butter, at room temperature
1½ cups sugar
10 eggs, separated
1 tablespoon Grand Marnier
1 teaspoon pure vanilla extract
Powdered sugar for garnish

1. Melt the chocolate and the butter in the top of a double boiler over hot, not boiling, water.
2. Stir in 1¼ cups of sugar until almost dissolved.
3. Beat the egg yolks until smooth. Beat in half of the hot chocolate mixture, a little at a time, beating constantly. Add to the remaining hot mixture and continue cooking until the mixture thickens slightly; stir constantly. Add the Grand Marnier and the vanilla.
4. Remove from the heat; cool slightly.
5. Beat the egg whites until soft peaks form; gradually beat in the remaining sugar, beating until peaks are stiff.
6. Fold the whites into the chocolate mixture.
7. Pour the batter into a greased and floured 12-inch springform pan.

8. Bake at 250 degrees for 3 hours.

9. Cool the cake in the pan to room temperature. Then cover with plastic wrap and refrigerate until chilled.

10. To serve, run a knife around the sides of the pan and remove the sides. Place the cake and the bottom of the spring-form on a serving dish. Sift powdered sugar over the top. (You can use a paper doily to make a design.)

YIELD: 12 to 14 servings

Note: The cake may be frozen wrapped in plastic wrap and overwrapped with foil or placed in a heavy-duty plastic bag.

Disliked Foods: What's Hated and Why

April 27, 1985

Richard M. Nixon did not like ice cubes with holes in the middle. So a new ice machine was installed at the President's Florida retreat in Key Biscayne in 1970.

When the rest of us don't like something, instead of changing it we usually avoid it. And the things we don't like are most often associated with the dislikes of childhood. These aversions are based either on texture—lumps in oatmeal, pulp in orange juice —taste or smell, but seldom on appearance.

Many people, asked to guess the most universally disliked foods, would probably choose liver, and liver is right up there. But so is milk. I thought I was the only one who didn't like milk, but after conversations with colleagues, I found a lot of kindred spirits.

The reasons given for disliking milk are almost exclusively associated with when it has been warmed. The taste of warm milk is unappealing to many, and the skin that forms on it is even worse. I don't like milk cold *or* warm because I was forced to drink a glass of leftover milk by the family maid when I was three or four years old. She refused to listen to my protests that it tasted funny, and it wasn't until I had consumed about three-quarters of it that she realized it was evaporated milk.

"I Hate Liver Because"

Liver came in a close second to milk because of its texture and its smell. "I think I hate liver because I was forced to eat it when I was a kid and it was mushy," said one liver hater I questioned.

"I always ate it because I heard it was good for you," said another. "But I just read it has a lot of cholesterol in it, so I don't have to eat it anymore," he said, "and now when I see it in the cafeteria, I yell at it."

Vegetables are high on the list of dislikes, although spinach surprisingly did not fare any worse than brussels sprouts, okra and stewed tomatoes. The tomato hater said he didn't like them because of the "slimy skin and mushy interior," but he conceded that his feelings were probably "irrational."

The man who eats no okra said he liked all other vegetables but has never had okra because "it's the one vegetable my mother told me never to eat. She said it was slimy."

Several people connected illness with foods they disliked. Cottage cheese in one instance, and, surprisingly, Jell-O in another. "I always associate it with the aftermath of being sick," one woman said, "because it was the first thing you could eat."

Tripe was mentioned by one person because it was "like a piece of rubber," and soft-boiled eggs by another because they were "too runny."

Caraway Seeds? No, Thanks

And then there is the woman who doesn't eat caraway seeds because as a small child a woman who lived across the street whom she disliked used to call to her: "Come here, little girl. I have some cookies for you." The cookies always had caraway seeds in them.

In general, foods that were forced upon us as children are usually those we don't want as adults. Let that be a lesson to parents who insist that their children finish every morsel on their plates.

Turning to Food for Solace
March 19, 1985

What child has not been offered a lollipop to assuage the pain after skinning a knee or enduring a shot at the doctor's office? Foods that comfort us as children are not necessarily those that make us feel better as adults when everything goes wrong, but more often than not there is a link. When it comes to comforting foods, people involved professionally with food are like everyone else.

George Lang, for example, a restaurant consultant and cookbook author, said his comfort foods "are foods I can eat any time, whether I'm full or not." Foremost is goose liver. "My whole childhood is brought back with goose liver," he said. "My mother spread golden red 'paprika-ed' goose fat from the goose she had cooked on the bread she had baked and topped it with a slab of goose liver. To me, that is the most perfect comfort."

Julie Sahni, cooking teacher and restaurant consultant, finds comfort in American foods rather than those of her native India. For her, a perfectly boiled lobster is the thing, or a medium-rare steak and baked potato with sour cream. She confesses, however, that when "I feel absolutely drained to my roots, rice pudding is an absolute must. Nothing is more comforting than rice pudding."

Some people are very selective about the food that makes them feel better, tailoring it to whatever made them feel awful to begin with. When Jonathan Waxman, a co-owner and the chef at Jams, a restaurant in Manhattan that features the new American cooking, is feeling depressed over finances, he chooses caviar with blini and Champagne. If he is "tired and crazy," he says, he wants a stew—such as chicken fricassee or *daube de boeuf* or chicken with garlic and vinegar—and chocolate cake. But if he is depressed because he misses California, where he worked before, he needs tacos, guacamole and anything with chiles in it.

Not everyone's comfort foods fit the public perception of the person. Whoever would pair Barry Wine, chef and co-owner of the four-star Quilted Giraffe in Manhattan, with Oreos? "It's terrible," Mr. Wine confessed. "I eat them out of the cookie jar at home. I essentially go through the day on coffee and Oreos." He does eat his pastry chef's chocolate chip cookies when he is nervous in the kitchen. Saturday afternoons, when the Wines are at their country house, he will have two bowls of pea soup (homemade) with garlic croutons. "It gives you a warm, full tummy," he said.

Leslie Revsin, who makes extraordinary combinations of the new American cuisine, turns to peasant food when she is miserable. She makes sourdough bread with barley, oat and rye flours and slathers it "with fifteen pounds of butter per slice. It just makes you feel, 'Oh my God, it's O.K. just for the moment,'" she said.

No matter how bad the day has been, if I can have spaghetti and meat sauce—which I was served every Wednesday night as a child and enjoyed cold for Thursday-morning breakfast—I feel better. A tuna fish sandwich and tapioca pudding have the same effect.

"We live in an age like an automobile which runs a little too fast for comfort," Mr. Lang said, "and comfort foods are the perfect tranquilizer which makes up for the speed."

Comfort Foods and Disliked Foods

Shortly after the comfort foods column appeared, *Restaurants and Institutions,* an industry trade magazine, asked the same question of a number of fast-food restaurant owners. The comfort foods most often mentioned were apple crisp, oatmeal, pudding, ice cream, soup, homemade bread, peanut butter and jelly sand-

wiches, hot chocolate, chocolate candy and grilled-cheese sandwiches.

One executive of a fast-food hamburger chain said that he had
three comfort-food categories: ordinary is a cheeseburger and
shake; superindulgent is a Snickers bar or oatmeal cookies and
special-occasion indulgent is a charbroiled veal chop or grilled
swordfish steak. Another said that when he is alone, he fixes
himself Kraft macaroni and cheese, creamed corn and fried
Spam.

In the meantime, comfort foods have become trendy. Articles
are written about them, restaurants serve them, and someone has
even compiled a cookbook of comfort recipes.

Ralph Slovenko, a professor of law and psychiatry at Wayne
State University in Detroit, sent along a copy of an article he had
written for the *Journal of Psychiatry & Law.* He writes: "It may be
said that ice cream is the best drug available for both mind and
body. It is spiritually uplifting, nutritious and wholesome. According to many nutritionists, the calcium in ice cream has a
calming effect. A number of psychiatrists, instead of prescribing
tranquilizing medication, advise their patients to have some ice
cream." Professor Slovenko thinks that ice cream's psychological
benefits may be related to the "innocence and security" of childhood.

Not everyone, of course, was comforted by ice cream in childhood. This reader from New York preferred spaghetti: "I felt
the need to share my passion with you—spaghetti with gobs of
ketchup. On Sunday evenings, as a child, while listening to 'The
Shadow,' 5:30 P.M., I consumed bowl after bowl of spaghetti with
ketchup. Even now, the yearn takes over on Sundays at 5:30 and
I often succumb, much to the chagrin of my family."

Spaghetti figures in my comfort-food department, spaghetti
and meat sauce when I feel like cooking.

Here is the recipe for the spaghetti with meat sauce that comforted me as a child. It is my mother's interpretation of what her
Italian neighbors made. No one ever claimed it was authentic,
only that it tastes good. When I don't feel like cooking, I put
together a tuna sandwich, a description of which can be found in
the tuna column, page 162.

I haven't eaten the spaghetti cold for breakfast in years. But I
used to.

MEAT SAUCE FOR SPAGHETTI

1 *pound ground beef*
1 *green bell pepper, chopped*
2 *small onions, chopped*
2 *garlic cloves, chopped*
1 *16-ounce can tomatoes*
1 *6-ounce can tomato paste*
1 *8-ounce can tomato sauce*
  Salt to taste
1 *tablespoon sugar*
1 *cup boiling water*
1 *teaspoon dried oregano*
1 *pound spaghetti*

1. Brown the beef in its own fat, breaking it up as it browns.
2. Add the green pepper, onions and garlic and sauté 5 minutes.
3. Add the tomatoes, tomato paste, tomato sauce, salt to taste, sugar, boiling water and oregano. Simmer, covered, 1½ to 2 hours.
4. When ready to serve, cook the spaghetti and serve with tomato sauce. Grated Parmesan cheese is optional.

YIELD: 4 servings

Closely related to comfort foods, but on the other side of the spectrum, are foods we dislike. After that column appeared, dozens of people came up to me in the office, eager to add their pet hates. They included cottage cheese, milk, meat and liver.

Added a Manhattan reader: "Vegetables are the quiet corner of my plate; lettuce and celery are for rabbits. Also celery makes too much noise.

"Sylvia Plath, the famous poet, said with regard to liver: 'Liver makes me quiver.'"

A Food Shopper's Love Note
June 28, 1984

People who move from the suburbs or from other cities to Manhattan often long for the 55,000-square-foot store they left behind that sells everything from shoelaces to crankcase oil in between the packages of cheese sauce mix and TV dinners. And it's true, Manhattan does not have shops or markets with the space for such an assortment of goods, many of which have absolutely nothing to do with food. But what these newcomers have either chosen to ignore or simply haven't noticed is the wealth of fabulous ingredients that they can find just around the corner from where they live.

The availability of so much wonderful food in New York City dawned on me last weekend when I was cooking in my home in Bethesda, Maryland, a suburb of the nation's capital. I went grocery shopping there for several items that I would not think twice about finding in New York. After two days and visits to four stores and two roadside stands I gave up on some of the items and made substitutions.

Having lived and shopped in the Washington, D.C., area for many years, I knew I had to be flexible, so my shopping list contained the ingredients for two salads. One included tomatoes, fresh basil and goat cheese; the other oranges, red peppers and cumin.

It's not that the Washington area has no tomatoes or peaches, red peppers, goat cheese or fresh basil, although I'm not sure about the fresh basil. It's just that someone in search of them must drive all over the city and spend hours buying what would take ten minutes to purchase in New York City.

Washington is not alone. Few big cities have the variety available to New Yorkers. During a recent trip I made to Los Angeles, several food professionals suggested that I visit a new supermarket in a Beverly Hills shopping center. They said I would be astonished at the variety of foods and especially the produce in this fancy new store. But a tour of the supermarket was disappointing. Any of the larger Oriental markets in New York has as wide a selection of produce and what they sell is just as fresh.

In Washington there is no such thing as a corner Oriental fruit and vegetable market. And because there are just two major supermarket chains, competition is not as keen as it is in a city where there are four or more. So if one chain does not go to the trouble to find ripe peaches, the other doesn't have to either. If neither sells red peppers, where is the shopper going to find them? Tomatoes you can forget about. The only decent tomatoes sold there arrive in the summer, when the roadside stands offer the local crop.

Local tomatoes are available in New York during the season, and there are alternatives during the year: hydroponically grown or imports from Israel. Not as good as New Jersey tomatoes, they still make the supermarket variety look like plastic samples.

Admittedly this is not the height of the peach season so those that are in the market are small. But small does not mean hard, and all I could find in Washington supermarkets were the green peaches that a week of ripening would not change.

I asked the produce manager in one of those stores if there were any red bell peppers, and he said they were out of season. Despite such misinformation I located three bedraggled specimens at a cooperative market. That is where the peaches and tomatoes were finally purchased as well. Along with the goat cheese. Basil continued to elude me. If I had had three or four hours in which to scour the city, I would probably have found the basil.

Even though I never drove more than four miles in any one direction, it took me two hours to gather the ingredients, including all those necessary for the orange and red pepper salad and most, but not all, for the tomato and goat cheese salad. I left the tomatoes and goat cheese with my son and hoped that he enjoyed them with or without basil.

A few days later, back in Manhattan, I went shopping again. Within one block of my apartment I purchased the goat cheese.

At an Oriental market another block down I got the tomatoes and the basil. Elapsed shopping time: ten minutes. And they deliver.

A Love Note Goes Astray

Several years after I went to work for *The New York Times*, having worked for the *Washington Post* for the previous seven years and lived full time in Washington for twenty-two years, I wrote a column about how much better grocery shopping is in New York than in Washington. The District of Columbia has never been noted for its city spirit, but you couldn't have told it from the number of passionate letters I received from D.C. and its suburbs.

One physician, a former longtime resident of Manhattan who now lives in the District, assured me that "in the matter of food marketing, I'll take Washington over New York without a moment's hesitation. For such daily necessities as really fresh eggs I had to go to a tiny Polish butter-and-egg shop on the Lower East Side in New York. Here I can obtain superb Grade AA eggs anytime at my neighborhood supermarket. For USDA Prime meat in New York City I had to devote 1½ to 2 hours once a week to travel to a butcher I could depend on. In Washington, I get excellent prime meats, cut to order or out of the case both at my local supermarket and at the equally nearby Sutton Place Gourmet." The doctor goes on to say that all she could get in Manhattan were frozen fruits and vegetables except when she went to the country on the weekends. She added that I would not have had any trouble finding fresh basil if I had known where to go.

Perhaps things were different in New York when she lived there. I stand by my column but am delighted that she likes to shop in Washington so much.

On one point, however, I take exception. The doctor writes: "You are mistaken about competition in the Washington marketplace. Not too long ago we had a lively price war, which brought food prices here well below the national average."

Having covered that aspect of Washington food for twenty years, I have a different view. This price war was an aberration. As soon as it was over, Washington prices went right back up near the top of the heap. Two supermarket chains in the Washington, D.C., area have something like 70 percent market share, and they dictate prices.

Well, how did we ever get off on that serious subject.

Back to basil.

"Come on," wrote another Washingtonian. "The District of Columbia is not that bad off. Granted your points are well taken," he said, but then he went on to mention a Sutton Place Gourmet, the shop mentioned by many of the other annoyed correspondents. "Fresh basil is almost always available there. It may cost an arm and a leg by New York standards. But a good salad is worth the extra buck. Right?

"And if for any reason, during your next trip to the land of canned tomatoes and dried herbs, Sutton Place is out of supplies, give me a call. My backyard, also ten minutes from Bethesda, is teaming with enough basil to keep any pesto maker happy. And my tomato plants were imported as seedlings from New Jersey. I do apologize for the lack of goat cheese. I had to get rid of the goats. The bells around their necks disturbed the neighbors."

Another Washingtonian of Greek extraction explained that all Greeks grow basil in their backyards in order to make a salad of tomatoes, feta, onions and basil all summer long. So she suggested that the next time I visited Washington in the summer I get out the telephone book. "Then look for some Greek last names. The tip-off is that both names, first and last, be Greek, such as Plato, Xenephon, Demetia, Despon and the like. I will bet you that they have fresh basil in their gardens and would joyfully deliver it to you." A lot of other Washingtonians said if I had any more trouble finding fresh basil, I should just come by their backyards and they'd share some of theirs. I must admit few Manhattan residents could make such an offer.

The owner of an outdoor market in the Adams-Morgan, the only colorful ethnic neighborhood in Washington, suggested I stop by his stand on weekends. Incidentally the name of his "food emporium and wine bar" is De Gustibus. He sent along a color picture, and the stuff does look mouth-watering, especially as I sit here writing this on a January evening with the temperature at fifteen degrees.

After being thoroughly thrashed by my fellow Washingtonians —we still live there on weekends—I was relieved to receive mail from others who wanted to discuss ways to preserve basil.

From Chappaqua, New York, this suggestion: Remove the stems and process the leaves in the food processor. While they are being minced, a little water is poured in, and when the whole mass is the consistency of a paste, it is then spooned into ice-cube trays and frozen. When thoroughly frozen the cubes are removed from the trays and placed in plastic bags in the freezer. "They stay nice and bright and green for six months or a year and have the original fresh flavor for whatever—pesto, spaghetti sauce, etc. Each cube is about one tablespoon."

The gentleman is more patient than I. He makes about a gross of these cubes each summer.

Jeanne Lesem, formerly food editor of United Press International (UPI), shared her secret for fresh basil year-round. She grows bush basil, which has small but very flavorful leaves, in five-inch pots on her windowsill under two small fluorescent lights. Her windowsill, she says, has very little sun. She has a gauge that tells her when to water, alternating plain tap water with water plus nutrients.

Carol Greitzer, a member of the City Council in New York City, also grows basil on her windowsill, which has a southern exposure. She stores leaves in olive oil in the refrigerator and says they stay green for quite some time.

And now, for those readers who are still speaking to me, here is the recipe for pears poached in wine with basil. Several requested it (and one from Wellfleet, Massachusetts, offered her basil soup in return—I hope she sends it). This is based on a recipe from Jeremiah Tower, owner-chef of the San Francisco restaurant Stars. Jeremiah says it was created when he was working on a Time-Life dessert cookbook. He had prepared poached pears for a photograph and was making a salad for his assistants' lunch. "I had some of the syrup from the pears on my hands and some basil leaves. I licked my hand and was astonished by the taste, so I threw some leaves in the sauce."

PEARS POACHED IN WINE WITH BASIL

    8 *firm ripe pears, with stems*
    4 *cups water*
       Juice of 1 small lemon
 2¼ *cups dry red wine*
 1¼ *cups sugar*
 25 *large basil leaves*
       Additional fresh basil leaves for garnish, optional

1. Peel the pears and slice off a bit of the bottom so the pears stand up. Place the peeled pears in a mixture of water and lemon juice as they are peeled.
2. Mix the wine with the sugar and the basil and boil for 5 minutes. Add the pears and simmer, covered, until tender. That will depend on how ripe they are. Baste often.
3. When the pears are cooked, remove and boil the syrup to reduce it slightly. Pour the hot syrup over the pears. Serve at room temperature or chilled. The pears may be decorated with fresh basil leaves, if desired.

YIELD: 8 servings

In the Kitchen: Disaster Can Haunt the Best Cooks

April 13, 1985

Lucy Ricardo tried to make bread once on *I Love Lucy.* She used thirteen cakes of yeast, and I can still see the enormous loaf that pushed open the oven door as it baked. It was so large when it was finished that Lucy could not pick it up.

Everyone has had cooking experiences that recall Lucy's disaster. Even professionals.

Marion Cunningham's problem was, in part, caused by inattention. Cunningham, the author of *The Fannie Farmer Baking Book,* decided to serve her guests a chicken potpie she had made earlier and frozen. "I didn't notice anything until I went to the oven and saw that the juices bubbling out of the pie were dark," Cunningham said. The chicken potpie turned out to be a cranberry orange pie. So for dinner Cunningham's guests had asparagus, cornmeal muffins and cheese and then went on to dessert. "I usually mark my things for the freezer," Cunningham said. "But sometimes those labels don't survive the dampness and come off."

Experimentation, the lifeblood of the creative chef, can on occasion go awry, as it did a few months ago for Paul Prudhomme, owner of K-Paul's Louisiana Kitchen in New Orleans. He and his staff were trying to create a sauce based on sweet dumpling squash to serve with several different dishes. They began with one-half gallon of the mixture. "First we added veal glaze, then spices and herbs and they didn't work," Prudhomme said. "Then we added cream and pecans and raisins and tomatoes and finally chicken glaze. But no matter what we added, it got worse. Finally at five o'clock we had four gallons of stock and my final words were, 'Throw it out.' It was a baby pink sauce that tasted awful."

Dounia Rathbone, owner of the New York City catering concern Remember Basil, had made two three-foot-high croquembouches, desserts of custard-filled cream puffs, arranged in a pyramid and held together by caramel. "It was a humid night," Rathbone, granddaughter of the late Basil Rathbone, recalled, "pretty unusual for Christmastime and we'd left the croquembouche in the kitchen. When we came in the next morning, the cream puffs were all over the floor. You could have played golf with them. In the humidity the caramel, which glued them together, had melted, and it looked as if the building had been bombed. So we picked them all up and recaramelized them," she said. "They weren't dirty or anything. We had put paper on the floor while we were caramelizing, and the cream puffs fell on the paper."

"Four Seasons" Cassoulet

For her first dinner party in New York City, Mary Beth Clark chose to make a cassoulet, complete with homemade *confit d'oie*. She followed a recipe from the first Four Seasons cookbook. To make the *confit* the directions said to cool the goose and cover the pieces with goose fat, then allow it to sit for six to eight weeks. The preserved goose, the recipe concluded, would keep for a year.

"Periodically I would check it," said Clark, who is a cooking teacher in Manhattan. "When it was time to use it, I dug down into the golden goose fat, but when I reached the goose, I had to hold my breath. It was putrid. I cut off a small piece and ran to the incinerator with the rest.

"I didn't know Paul Kovi," Clark went on, referring to the co-owner of The Four Seasons, "so I knew he wouldn't see me, and I went to the restaurant without an appointment." She took along her piece of preserved goose. "Mr. Kovi couldn't have been more gracious," she said. "We talked for forty-five minutes. And then he confessed that a line had been left out of the recipe, which said to store the goose in a cold place."

Barbara Kafka, on the other hand, followed directions for a chocolate soufflé meticulously, and she was rewarded with a perfect specimen. Fresh out of college, she said she "slaved over the dinner, as we did in those days, and the chocolate soufflé was my pièce de résistance. I took it out of the oven and stumbled over the chair," she said. "The whole thing went flat as a pancake on the kitchen table."

But instead of discarding the remains, Kafka, who is now a restaurant consultant, scooped them up, spread them with ice cream and rolled up her newly created chocolate roll. "I don't recommend it as an approach to cooking," Kafka said, "but that was when I decided cooking was not so difficult."

After Alice Waters's most memorable disaster, however, she said if it ever happened again, she would quit the business. They were firing up the new roasting spit at her restaurant, Chez Panisse, in Berkeley, California, for a trial run and had lined up twenty-five birds on three spits to cook over the wood fire.

A Roaring Fire

"The fire was roaring," Waters said. "It was so hot it set off the fire extinguisher. All the chemicals came down from the ceiling, and there was an inch of chemicals on the birds, the silver and glassware, the dishes and in the stock, and there were forty-five people waiting for dinner." They started all over with the ingredients in the walk-in refrigerator. "We thought we knew all about improvisational cooking before that," Waters said, "but we learned."

Perhaps what separates these cooks and their disasters from the rest of us is that they were able to turn theirs into triumphs. Well, perhaps not exactly triumphs, but at least their dinner guests were never the wiser.

Disasters in the Kitchen

Readers were happy to share their disasters. One from Maryland who lost all the turkey stuffing down the disposal one Thanksgiving told how she solved the emergency: "I figured the sink was clean, so I just scooped it out and put it back in the bowl."

Another from Massachusetts, who tripped going from the kitchen to the dining room with a watermelon basket, picked herself and the basket and the contents up from the floor and announced: "Don't worry. I have another in the kitchen. And then I washed everything off and put it back in the same basket and went back into the dining room. Carefully."

My favorite disaster was a Dione Lucas flourless chocolate-roll recipe. I made it the day of the party, and when I went to roll it up, it collapsed into a dozen sections, the whipped cream oozing out. I spooned it into a pretty glass bowl and served it as a chocolate whipped cream pudding.

There was also the letter from the New Jersey reader who was in high dudgeon about Dounia Rathbone's croquembouche, in part because I did not fully explain the circumstances of the flop. The letter read:

I was rather appalled by your account of Dounia Rathbone's faux pas with the croquembouches. Having myself been the unwitting victim of an unrefrigerated custard in a delicious apricot tart, with unpleasant results, to say the least, I would say that Ms. Rathbone's most serious sin was not having refrig-

*erated her custard-filled cream puffs. I feel deeply for those innocent souls who
later ingested them. Really, whatever dirt was on the floor pales in signifi-
cance to a case of food poisoning. It boggles the mind that she would not know
that any custard requires refrigeration, and certainly on a night warm enough
to melt caramel.*

*Aside from that the column was a delight, and many thanks for proving
again that the gurus of cookery are fallible also.*

What I had not written in the column was that Rathbone had
told me the night had unexpectedly turned warm, after she had
left her catering firm, something she had not expected in
December.

DIONE LUCAS CHOCOLATE ROLL

    7 eggs, separated
    1 cup sugar
    ½ pound sweet dark chocolate
    7 tablespoons brewed coffee
       Pinch of salt
       Unsweetened cocoa powder
    2 cups heavy cream
    2 tablespoons rum

1. Beat the egg yolks in a small bowl with the sugar until light
and fluffy.
2. Melt the chocolate in the coffee over very low heat. Cool
slightly.
3. Beat the egg whites with a pinch of salt until stiff.
4. Mix the egg yolks and chocolate and fold the whites into the
chocolate mixture.
5. Grease an 11- by 15-inch jelly roll pan and cover the bottom
with waxed paper. Grease the waxed paper.
6. Spoon the mixture onto the jelly roll pan and bake at 350
degrees for 15 to 20 minutes in a gas oven, 12 minutes in an
electric oven. Remove and cool for 5 minutes.
7. Cover with a slightly damp cloth like a dish towel and cool
completely to room temperature. Refrigerate for 1 hour.
8. Remove the cloth carefully and sprinkle the top generously
with cocoa. Turn out onto waxed paper. Remove the waxed
paper from the bottom of the cake.

9. Beat the heavy cream. When partially whipped, add the rum and continue to beat until soft peaks form. Spoon the whipped cream evenly over the surface of the cake.

10. Using the waxed paper on the bottom to help with rolling, quickly and carefully roll up the chocolate the long way into a jelly roll. The surface will crack as it rolls. It is supposed to resemble the bark of a tree.

11. Refrigerate, well wrapped, until serving time. This may be made a day ahead and refrigerated, if desired.

YIELD: 8 servings

A Latchkey Child Learns to Cook
November 3, 1984

I recently read a column by a young writer who had grown up as a latchkey child. He wanted the world to know he had not felt deprived because his mother was not home when he got out of school. It reminded me of my own years as a latchkey child— maybe one of the first. It was certainly long before there was such a term for children who came home from school and let themselves into empty houses.

There was no sadness to the situation in those days before television, when children went out to play after school. And there was certainly no worry about safety in the small New England town where I grew up. As a matter of fact, I didn't carry the key around my neck: It was left under the doormat in front of the apartment I shared with my mother after my father died when I was five.

Learning Self-Reliance and More

Being on my own from 3:30 until 5:45 P.M., when my mother got home from work, I learned a lot about self-reliance and became quite independent. I also learned how to cook. A limited repertoire, to be sure. I never, for example, knew how to roast chicken, but more on that fiasco another time.

I'll never forget when the pressure cooker arrived via parcel post. I was excited to be the one who opened it, learned how to use it and taught my mother how to cook in it. The first thing I cooked in ours was a Hungarian beef stew (the paprika was what made it Hungarian, even though we had no Hungarian paprika then).

I even learned to prepare dried beans in it without blowing the lid off. That didn't happen until my mother cooked something in it, using it as a regular pot. She didn't tighten the seal or put on the gauge, but the lid blew off anyway, spraying food over the walls and ceiling.

I also have a distinct recollection of learning how to pluck a chicken, a task that made me itchy. In those days chickens didn't come bald as a cue ball—they had zillions of pinfeathers, and they all had to be gone before the chicken was cooked.

Once a week we had meat sauce with spaghetti, and when I had become more adept, I was permitted to make a version my mother had learned from Italian neighbors. It may not be an authentic Bolognese sauce, but I still love it, and when I can't decide what to eat I make it.

A Sampling of Tapioca

After a few years my mother had enough faith in me to allow me to make something on my own. Something on my own was almost always tapioca pudding, to which canned pineapple chunks were added after it had cooled. For dress-up occasions, whipped cream was folded in.

Even then I had the problem I have when I cook today. I sampled. And sampled. And sampled. One afternoon I made tapioca pudding and ate it all before my mother came home from work. I never told her.

All this is not to say that children should be left alone so they can learn how to cook; after all, 1984 is not 1947. But I hope my mother did not feel guilty about her latchkey child. I didn't feel deprived—I thought I was lucky.

dict." Mr. Forgione, who owns An American Place on the Upper East Side in New York City, prefers the ones on the street, but in typical hypercritical chef fashion, he says, "They aren't as fresh and as hot as they used to be. They put them in a heating cart and they get soggy, and all the salt falls off."

As a salt addict, Mr. Forgione could be expected to like potato chips too. "Only in a sandwich with peanut butter on whole wheat bread," he said.

Fudging on Technicalities

Joe Baum, on the other hand, is far less discriminating. Right out in the open, the owner of Aurora, one of the city's most glamorous East Side restaurants, will eat "anything from any street corner that has fried onions."

Absent a street corner, Mr. Baum would be content with a box of Jujubes. "I used to be able to finish a box of those before the movie started," he said. Licorice is second choice, he says, "or any open jar of candy or Fig Newtons or raisin bars," although his favorite cookie is the one with the coconut-sprinkled pink marshmallow on top.

At first Alfred Portale, chef at the Gotham Bar and Grill in Greenwich Village, said he didn't eat junk food—since pizza is technically nutritious and does not qualify. But then he thought about it and confessed that on his way to work that day he had eaten a Snickers bar and that he liked candy, especially M&M's peanuts. Finally, he admitted that if "beer qualified as junk food," it would be high on his list because he loves it with pizza.

And what is one to make of Anne Rosenzweig's eating habits— frozen Snickers, cold leftover pizza and cold leftover Chinese food for breakfast, not to mention defective fortune cookies.

"There's a little bakery in Chinatown that sells fortune cookies in bulk, ones that don't make it," explained the owner and chef of Arcadia, the East Side restaurant known for its chocolate bread pudding. "They are big, flat round fortune cookies, curved, weird shapes, and they are very fresh," Miss Rosenzweig said.

Barry Wine's junk-food indulgence made its way onto the menu of his East Side restaurant the Quilted Giraffe, where a sumptuous meal will make you $100 poorer. Called Barry's Favorite Cookie, his version of the Oreo is a white chocolate mousse filling between two cocoa-flavored *pizelles*. Mr. Wine says he eats the real thing morning, noon and night, "three of them in the morning before the pot of coffee brews—I'm a ten-Oreo-a-day person."

Sirio Maccioni, who owns Le Cirque, succumbs only occasionally. He has hot dogs with beans and chili sauce once a month. He says he eats them when he is out with his children. Somehow, Paul Kovi's candied orange peel is not in the same league as Snickers bars or hot dogs and beans. But he seems to eat a fair amount of it at his restaurant, The Four Seasons. "Whenever I pass by the station, I pick it up," he explained. "I made them increase production of it by 50 percent."

David Bouley, chef at Montrachet in TriBeCa, says he no longer eats junk food. His decadence is confined to popcorn without butter or salt, pizza and, recently, dried cherries. "I don't want to sound like Mr. Health Food," he said. But he does.

Chefs Snacking

Almost everyone was amused by the snacking column. Almost everyone. Except this "fan" from Manhattan: "What do YOU eat when you are alone? Steamed broccoli with no salt? Poached chicken with the sauce left off? I'll bet you are some fun to go to dinner with these days."

Given a choice, I will take whatever is at hand. Cake, cookies, ice cream. Nuts, raisins, leftover spaghetti and meat sauce. Popcorn, potato chips, corn chips. Really. I'm not fussy at all. But given a choice, I'll take Anne Rosenzweig's Chocolate Bread Pudding.

ARCADIA'S CHOCOLATE BREAD PUDDING

12 *slices bread, preferably brioche, trimmed of crusts, each slice about*
   1 inch by 2½ inches by 4 inches
 1 *cup unsalted melted butter, approximately*
 3 *cups heavy cream*
 1 *cup milk*
 1 *cup sugar*
10 *to 12 egg yolks, approximately 1 cup*
 ½ *pound bittersweet chocolate*
 1 *teaspoon pure vanilla extract*
   English Custard (see recipe)

1. Brush the bread slices all over with the melted butter. Arrange the pieces on a rack and place in a 425-degree oven, turning until brown, about 8 to 10 minutes.
2. Meanwhile combine the cream and milk in a saucepan and bring just to a boil. Add the sugar and stir until dissolved.
3. Put the egg yolks into a large mixing bowl and add the hot cream mixture, a ladleful at a time, beating constantly with a wire whisk. Skim off the foam that accumulates on the surface.
4. Place the chocolate in a mixing bowl. Place the bowl in a basin of simmering water and let it stand until the chocolate melts. Add the egg yolk mixture a little at a time, stirring constantly. Stir in the vanilla.
5. In a 9½- by 13½- by 2½-inch baking dish, arrange the bread slices in two rows, slightly overlapping. Pour the chocolate mixture over the bread. Let stand until some of the mixture is absorbed. Cover the bread pudding with plastic wrap and cover this with a rectangular dish that fits inside the baking dish. Add weights so the chocolate mixture barely covers all the bread and is absorbed by it. Let stand for about an hour.
6. Meanwhile preheat the oven to 325 degrees.
7. Remove the weights, the rectangular dish and the plastic wrap. Cover the top of the bread pudding with aluminum foil, not letting it touch the chocolate filling. Punch a few holes in the foil with a knife. Seal the foil around the edges.
8. Place the dish in a larger dish and pour boiling water around it. Bring this to a boil on top of the stove. Place the dish in its water bath in the oven and bake about 1¾ hours, or until all the liquid has been absorbed, on touch the pudding springs

back and the top has a slightly glossy look. Serve warm cut into squares with English custard on the side.

YIELD: 8 or more servings

Note: Anne recommends Belgian Callebaut chocolate.

ENGLISH CUSTARD

   3 *egg yolks*
   ⅓ *cup sugar*
   ⅓ *cup milk*
   1 *cup heavy cream*
   ¼ *cup brandy*

1. Place the egg yolks in a saucepan and add the sugar. Beat with a wire whisk until the mixture is thick and lemon-colored.
2. Bring the milk almost but not quite to a boil.
3. Gradually add the milk and cream to the egg yolk mixture, beating constantly. Stir constantly with a wooden spoon, making certain the spoon touches the bottom of the saucepan all over. Cook, stirring, until the mixture has a custardlike consistency and coats the side of a spoon. Do not let the sauce boil or it may curdle.
4. Immediately remove the sauce from the stove and continue stirring. Set the saucepan in a basin of cold water. Let the sauce cool to room temperature, then add the brandy. Chill an hour or longer.

How Mother Really Cooked
October 4, 1986

Ask any number of young Americans in the food business if their mothers were good cooks, and there is a pause and then a small nervous laugh at the other end of the telephone conversation. The notion that every good cook must have learned at his or her mother's knee is a myth. But being loving sons and daughters, these food professionals are not eager to burst the bubble.

Their complaints about their mothers' culinary talents can be summed up in a word—overcooking. In fact, most of these professionals are ambivalent about their mother's cooking, to judge by the responses received from five of New York City's better known restaurateurs.

"My mother's cooking was heroic," said Robert Pritsker, chef-owner of Brive, a new restaurant on 58th Street near First Avenue. "That means she had no particular love, no particular talent, but an extraordinary desire to be a good wife and mother."

So despite the fact that Frances Pritsker of Providence, Rhode Island, cooked string beans for forty minutes until they were "Army-barracks green" and put sugar in everything, she had a positive effect on her son's attitude toward food. "I determined that eating was pretty much all there was to do in life," Mr. Pritsker said with tongue only partly in cheek, "and I haven't changed my mind."

Artistic Expression

For Karen Hubert's mother, an artist, cooking was another form of artistic expression. "I think she thought she was a very creative cook," said Hubert, host and co-owner with her husband, Len Allison, who is the chef of Hubers on East 22nd Street near Lexington Avenue.

"My mother's cooking fell into two categories," she said. "Either she cooked everything in the refrigerator in one pot, or she'd discover one ingredient, fall in love with it and put it in everything she made. There was the year of the pimiento: mashed potatoes with pimientos, meatballs with pimientos, rice with pimientos." Hubert added, as delicately as possible, "I didn't always like what my mother cooked."

Larry Forgione, on the other hand, has changed his mind about his mother's cooking as he has grown older. "At first, I used to think my mother wasn't a good cook, but the more I thought about it I realized she was," he said. "It was good honest food, but the accompaniments...like a can of mushroom soup and a can of green beans equals green beans in mushroom-cream sauce." But he remembers her pot roast, her mashed potatoes and oven-roasted potatoes with great fondness.

Despite his success as the chef-owner of An American Place at 969 Lexington Avenue, near 70th Street, Mr. Forgione has made no converts in his family. Although his mother no longer cooks vegetables for forty minutes, she doesn't cook them al dente either, and she doesn't like the fact that her son serves veal pink instead of well done.

Whether you like your food well done or rare appears to be a generational preference. Each Thanksgiving when Charles Palmer goes home to Smyrna, New York, he goes directly to the kitchen "to take out the turkey because I know it's been in there since 6 A.M."

The Best Chicken with Dumplings

Virginia Joyce Palmer cooks everything for a long time, according to her son. Charles Palmer, who is the chef at the River Cafe in Brooklyn, said his father was the real cook in the family. Yet there is one thing his mother still makes better than anyone else—chicken with dumplings.

And then there are the mothers who don't really cook: They open packages. Drew Nieporent's mother belongs in that category. Those old enough to remember the children's radio program "Let's Pretend" may recall the girl who sang "Cream of Wheat is so good to eat." That was Mr. Nieporent's mother, whose stage name was Sybil Trent.

"My mother's nickname was 'Snow Queen' because she was very good with frozen food," explained Mr. Nieporent, owner of Montrachet in TriBeCa at 239 West Broadway, at White Street. "My exposure to food came through my father, Andrew, who was an attorney for Cafe Chauveron, Le Pavillon and La Potinière in the early '60s. He took me to all those places to eat."

Expressions such as "like mother used to make" have no relevance here.

Mom Cooks

I neglected to point out a salient fact in the column: I did not call ten restaurateurs looking for five who had mothers who couldn't cook very well. I picked five Americans at random and called them. Those were the five in the column.

It's difficult to know how many people a woman who signed herself "a reader from New Jersey" represents, but she took up pen immediately upon reading this column to respond: "You're talking to the wrong children. My children have called me from all over the world for recipes, and I have cooked for them all over the world, wherever they were living at the time. We eat out very little because the food is always better at home and is less salted or has no salt at all. Even my failures are better than most restaurants. This mother just catered a party for thirty-five from soup to nuts."

This mother renews my faith in home cooking.

But not this one from Texas, who sent a copy of a letter addressed to Mr. Nieporent to me:

Cream of Wheat is so good to eat,
And we have it every day.
We sing this song, it will make us strong,
And it makes us shout hooray.
It's good for growing babies
And grown-ups too to eat.
For all the families' breakfast,
You can't beat Cream o-o-o-f Wheat!

"I sing these lyrics at least once a decade to make sure Alzheimer's isn't setting in. So far, so good.

"Sybil Trent! She must have made one heck of an impression on a then four-year-old, for I, too, am a Snow Queen of sorts. Lips that have touched fresh veg shall never touch mine, etc.

"Maybe I should do an unauthorized biography.

"Great article. As your mother's faithful fan, I remain," etc., etc., etc.

Those Old Saws About Food
July 19, 1986

Feed a cold and starve a fever.

An apple a day keeps the doctor away.

If you don't eat your okra, you won't catch any fish.

Where does fact leave off and superstition begin with the old wives' tales about food and eating that all of us were brought up on? And where do they come from?

Everyone knows an apple a day isn't going to keep you from getting sick, but is there not still a kernel of truth in the saying?

My mother always told me about starving a fever when I was sick, and I acted on the information when my first child was born. Did it make any sense? Not really. But in many old bromides there is often just enough truth to keep people following the advice. If anything, said Dr. Sidney Wolfe, the director of Health Research Group, a Washington, D.C.– based public interest group, someone with a fever should eat more. Fever causes the body to burn up more energy than normal, requiring more food. But food is often the last thing on the mind of someone running a fever.

It's important to eat, but it's more important to drink as much liquid as possible to prevent dehydration.

Apples may not keep the doctor at bay, but they are fine roughage. Other fruits, with more nutrients, as well as the fiber that apples offer, are just as good or better.

But what about the suggestion that insomniacs drink warm milk? More truth than fancy here. Milk contains tryptophan, an amino acid that is a precursor of serotonin, a chemical that induces drowsiness.

Even the consumption of chicken soup as symptomatic relief

from colds is worthwhile. The heat from the soup helps clear a stuffed nose. Well, you say, hot water will do the same thing. But who wants to drink hot water?

There *are* those who believe in drinking hot water and lemon as a digestive first thing in the morning. The hot water is key: The lemon simply makes the water more palatable. Any hot liquid will have a laxative-like effect.

The origin of the idea that oysters are an aphrodisiac is a bit difficult to pinpoint. Oysters are a good source of zinc. Zinc deficiencies are related to impaired sexual growth. But how did people hundreds of years ago know that, when they hadn't even heard of zinc?

Small children will be delighted to learn that eating spinach will not give them any more muscles than eating a hamburger. "If you eat lots of spinach and exercise," said Wolfe, "you will get muscles. And if you don't eat spinach but exercise, you will get muscles."

If spinach won't do much for muscles, will carrots do anything for eyesight? Only for those who have a vitamin A deficiency, which can cause night blindness and eventually total blindness. But for those without such a deficiency, it isn't necessary to overdose on carrots.

Nor is it necessary to eat fish to improve the brain. "Fish doesn't make you smarter," said Bonnie Liebman, a registered dietitian at the Center for Science in the Public Interest, in Washington. "If you had a protein deficiency, you might have impaired mental development," she said, but otherwise telling little children that fish is brain food was mother's way of getting them to eat the fish.

Children in my era were given flat ginger ale for an upset stomach, and Wolfe said that isn't a bad idea. "Nonirritating clear liquids are good for an upset stomach," he explained. A soft drink like ginger ale contains sugar, which provides energy, but the drink should be free of the carbonation that may be irritating.

And, said Wolfe, parents who insisted that eating a bowl of hot cereal was important before going to school on a cold winter morning were not so far off the mark. When it is very cold outside, it is better to eat hot food because the heat of the food warms the body, as do the calories that the food provides.

At the opposite extreme, the virtues of eating spicy food in steamy climates is not just an old wives' tale. It has some validity. In such climates, people may drink just enough water to quench their thirst when, in fact, they need at least half again as much as that to keep from becoming dehydrated. Eating spicy foods is certain to increase consumption of fluids.

As for okra and fishing, it is probably a variation on "If you don't eat your vegetables, you can't have dessert." Just more subtle.

Old Saws

"Alas," said Dr. Richard Wurtman, a physician and professor at the Massachusetts Institute of Technology, "it is not true that milk makes you sleepy by providing the brain with more trypto-phan. I'm not sure that milk makes one sleepy: To my knowledge this has never been demonstrated in a controlled study—a sharp contrast to dietary carbohydrates, which have repeatedly been shown to make most people sleepy." Wurtman goes on to explain why tryptophan can't make you sleepy, describing the chemistry of amino acids, which I'm sure you don't want to know about.

As for feeding a cold, this letter set me straight on that. "You gave what unfortunately has become the usual misread of the old saying, 'Feed a cold and starve a fever.' My grandmother, who was from England, used the practice, putting it 'Feed a cold to starve a fever' and therefore fed us up when we were ill. The meaning is just that, whether you say 'and' or 'to.' Maybe you can turn the tide and replenish the image of this old and true saying, which had fallen prey to grammar."

Another reader from New Jersey said the worst thing to do after eating spicy foods is to drink something. "Taking liquids to calm the spicy burn is like throwing gasoline on a fire. Rice is the best antidote." In Southeast Asia, says this reader, spicy foods are beneficial because eating them "promotes perspiration, which cools as it evaporates." And she closes with this thought. "I enjoy your column. I wish you a mouth-searing, eye-tearing, sinus-clearing and delicious Thai meal—with plenty of rice."

I love Thai food, but I have to go to Washington, D.C., to get any that comes close to authentic. New York City Thai food wouldn't burn the mouth of a baby. But I do quibble with the reader's suggestion that liquids are the worst thing for spicy food. Water does not work, I agree, but beer does a terrific job, and tea helps too.

And now on to the apples. (Was anything right in this column?)

"While one apple might not do the trick, two might be significant," wrote a New York man. Apples and other red-skinned fruits contain large quantities of a substance just below the skin surface that acts as a solvent for cholesterol, he said. This same substance is also found in grapes, according to our correspondent, and crushing them for wine does not destroy it. So the reader concludes, "Not being a particular fan of apples, I have found the alternative to be quite satisfactory over the years."

And finally an editor at a southern newspaper called up prior to running the column in his paper. He said he'd asked around the office and there was not one good ole boy who had ever heard the one about okra. I found it in a little book called *Momilies,* by Michele Slung. I wonder where she got it.

Debate on Kinship:
Ketchup, *Koe-chiap*
April 26, 1986

At the time it seemed like an appropriate tag line to a story about the authenticity of the food at the Chinese Embassy in Washington, D.C. "It was all very Chinese," I wrote, "except for one Western touch. Ketchup, hardly a Chinese invention, somehow made its way into the cold spiced shrimp."

Three weeks later the mail continues to arrive, all of it gleefully castigating. How could I not have known that the spelling of ketchup, also known as catsup and catchup, was derived from a Chinese word?

Faced with such a barrage of corrections there is nothing to do but acknowledge that the word, which to most of the world denotes a spicy tomato-based sauce, is derived from the Chinese. I am not about to take on the *Oxford Dictionary of English Etymology,* John Clardi's *Browser's Dictionary,* or the *Random House Unabridged Dictionary,* not to mention the food historian Reay Tannahill and *The Taste of America,* by John and Karen Hess.

But is ketchup as we know it—the kind used in the spiced shrimp and the only kind most Americans have ever heard of—a Chinese invention? The trouble is trying to pin down when or where ketchup was first made with tomatoes.

As many careful readers hastened to point out, ketchup comes from a word in the Chinese Xiamen-Shantou dialect, *koe-chiap* or *ke-tsiap,* or perhaps from the Malay *kechap,* which is thought to be from the Chinese. This Chinese form of ketchup, however, bears little resemblance to our ketchup. *Koe-chiap* is a mixture of fish brine, herbs and spices.

So much for that explanation. No tomatoes.

Three other letter writers offer a different story. They say the English word *kechup* comes from a word in Cantonese dialect, *keh-jup,* in which *ke* means tomato and *jap* means juice or sauce. But *Food in Chinese Culture,* edited by K.C. Chang and published in 1977, says tomatoes made their way to China only within the past one hundred years or so. And the first written reference to a kechup made with tomatoes dates to an English cookbook published in 1814.

Karen Hess does not think that tomato ketchup comes from China. "From what I know of traditional cuisine in China, they had no truck with tomato ketchup," she said. Others disagree and say tomatoes were known in China in the seventeenth century.

Chinese *koe-chiap,* the fish brine variety, made its way to the West with British, or possibly Dutch or Portuguese, seamen in the late seventeenth century. Lacking the essential Eastern ingredients, Western cooks substituted mushrooms, walnuts, cucumbers, blueberries, currants, grapes, even lobster. The only similarity between *koe-chiap* and ketchup is the use of spices. In eighteenth-century England and America these ketchups, not unlike what we call chutneys, had one ingredient in common—vinegar.

Just when tomatoes were first used is unclear, but Hess has found a reference to "a tomato sauce that keeps," which she says means tomato ketchup, in the 1814 New York edition of *A New System of Domestic Cookery,* by Maria Rundell, an Englishwoman. The earliest reference to tomato ketchup is in Mary Randolph's cookbook, printed in 1824.

What all this probably means is that the word *ketchup* is derived from the Chinese, that tomato ketchup may be a Western invention and that the Chinese happily appropriate new foods as long as they like the taste.

This, undoubtedly, is not the end of the matter. Pass the *koechiap,* please.

Ketchup

No, it certainly was not the end of the matter. I had neglected to mention that there were several letters to the editor, and one of them got printed.

Not the one from Sacramento, California, that went like this:

I fear that Marian Burros's interesting piece is making the rounds of Chinese and Asian Studies Departments this week. It is not because the article dealing with dining at the Chinese Embassy is badly written—far from it. It is because of the howler in the last paragraph.

Oh, Ms. Burros. Ketchup is a Chinese invention. It is a corruption of the Cantonese word for "mushroom sauce" and one of those cross-cultural penetrations that we owe to the Dutch merchants of the seventeenth century.

On many a tattered bulletin board and office desk in colleges and universities, the name Burros has been noted and a large ha! *added. Yes, it means the same thing in Chinese.*

Another letter suggested that I be sentenced to a month in a famous cook's test kitchen for my gaffe. "While the Chinese lay no claim to chop suey [see page 83], a California invention," wrote the Denver resident, "I am sure even Mr. Heinz would place credit for the origin of his fortunes in the land of the fortune cookie."

Evan Jones, the food writer and cookbook author, weighed in with a copy of the appropriate paragraph from his book *American Food: The Gastronomic Story.* He suggests that the method of producing ketchup was adopted by English cooks from a sauce brought back from Asia, a method borrowed and changed by Americans. All the early ketchup recipes were tart, i.e., without sugar.

> In the period immediately after the Civil War, Joshua Davenport was manufacturing and selling vinegar, pickles, and catsup in the Berkshire Hills of Massachusetts. According to the recipe handed down (the story goes) in the Davenport family, Joshua added two cups of sugar to a mixture of a gallon of tomato stock and a half-pint of vinegar flavored with cinnamon, cayenne and salt. Chances are he was not the first man to sweeten the pot, but by the time Mrs. Rorer's cookbook began to influence a wide public in 1886 the sugary tomato sauce was firmly established.
>
> ...before the nation was two hundred years old, it had gone from having a president who believed in a cuisine of high standards for the United States, as did Jefferson, to one whose taste ran to cottage cheese and sweetened red catsup for lunch, according to White House reports.

Since writing the column additional mail has suggested that tomato ketchup was "introduced to this country by the Chinese cooks who fed the construction crews on the Union Pacific Railroad"; that the Chinese did not invent ketchup in any form —it came to China from Malaysia and that ketchup is an Indonesian invention.

But still no confirmation that ketchup made with tomatoes was invented in China.

Chop Suey, at 90, Is Still a Mystery

August 30, 1986

Well, we goofed. We missed the 90th anniversary of the introduction of chop suey to New York. But considering the esteem in which this faux Chinese dish is held, perhaps no one really cares.

In fact, we didn't miss the anniversary by much, only a day. Yesterday was the official celebration, but there were no firecrackers in Chinatown or parades with paper dragons. But then, chop suey was unknown in China until some time after World War II. Grace Zia Chu, cookbook author and teacher of Chinese cooking, wrote in *The Pleasure of Chinese Cooking* that she was riding in Shanghai after the Second World War and spotted a neon sign that read GENUINE AMERICAN CHOP SUEY SERVED HERE.

The origins of chop suey, however, are in dispute. According to *Famous First Facts*, by J.N. Kane, "Chop suey was concocted in New York City on August 29, 1896, by Chinese Ambassador Li Hung-Chang's chef, who devised this dish to appeal to both American and Oriental taste." The author cites as his source a book entitled *Eng Ying Gong—Tong War.*

There is a more elaborate version of this theory in *The Cooking of China*, one of the Time-Life series on "Foods of the World." This holds that the ambassador "got indigestion from rich foreign food at banquets." As a result of an "agonizing attack of biliousness following a hard week's banqueting," his aide suggested a bland diet, and together they concocted chop suey.

Most versions of chop suey's origins, however, credit the Chinese who came to this country during the last century to work on the railroads. Whether the dish was created by Chinese cooks to feed the Chinese workers or Chinese workers who stayed in the United States after the railroad was finished is unclear. There is another story that an Irishman working as a waiter in a Chinese restaurant in San Francisco invented this atrocity, which for most Americans over forty was their first introduction to Chinese food. Different sources offer different explanations, all of them, I suspect, conjecture.

Chop suey was certainly the first Chinese food I ever ate, along with chow mein, which is another kettle of noodles entirely. Chow mein is based on an authentic Chinese dish, even if it had been adjusted for American palates in the early days. Both of them seemed pretty exotic to me as a child.

Chop suey means "miscellaneous odds and ends" in the Cantonese dialect, according to Chu. In *The Dictionary of American Food and Drink,* John Mariani says the Mandarin words for chopped up odds and ends are *tsa sui,* which is close enough to chop suey to sound reasonable.

Certainly those descriptions fit the contents of the dish, which in Chu's recipe has beef, bean sprouts, mushrooms, carrots, celery, onions, tomato, soy sauce, Sherry, sugar and cornstarch.

That's fancier than I remember: I don't recollect the tomatoes. It was something more like the recipe that calls for beef, celery, mushrooms, water chestnuts, bean sprouts and soy, heavy on the celery.

Not that you are likely to find a recipe for chop suey in any modern Chinese-American cookbook. Nor in any authentic Chinese restaurant, though, no doubt, there are Chinese-American restaurants in the hinterlands that must continue to serve chop suey to customers whose most daring foray into Chinese food has never progressed beyond an egg roll.

But chop suey has become so much a part of our language that the term has been used to describe other dishes. There is chop suey sundae, farmer's chop suey (chopped raw vegetables mixed with sour cream) and American chop suey, which, according to Mr. Mariani, is made with ground beef, noodles and tomato sauce. It might be better than the original version.

Chop Suey

Offer an explanation of the origins of a dish, and several more are sure to arrive. True to form this is what the mail brought.

A letter from Massachusetts that said, "Are you sure that it wasn't the chef of Ambassador Tsai Kwok Ching in 1886?"

From David Gold, special contributing editor to Webster's New World Dictionaries: "According to *Webster's Ninth New Collegiate Dictionary*, the earliest citation for the English word *chop suey* in Merriam-Webster's files is from 1888."

A reader from New Jersey referred me to *Food in Chinese Culture*, edited by K.C. Ching and published by Yale University Press in 1977:

> Like all Chinese cuisines, Cantonese is subject to many regional variations. A distinctive one is that of Toisan, the area south of Canton from which about half of all American Chinese trace their ancestry. Its main claim to fame is that it gave the world chop suey (Cantonese *tsap sui*, "miscellaneous things," or, at worst, "miscellaneous slops"). Typically a sort of hash of leftovers warmed up with bean sprouts, a very folklike dish, this food has a widely known origin myth: One night, after hours, a Cantonese restaurateur in San Francisco was importuned by persons he could not refuse (drunken miners in one version, Li Hung-Chang or other famed Chinese visitors in others) to serve food. However, he had no food left. So he stir-fried the day's slops and thus created the dish. Its origin in old Toisan was traced down by the indefatigable hunter (of big game and food) Li Shu-fan (1964). Toisan food has many far better dishes to offer, most of them broadly similar to other Cantonese dishes but with less ingredients mixed in the same dish.

Then Anne Mendelson, a food historian, sent me a copy of the *Chinatown History Project Newsletter,* which contains an article by Renqui Yu. Renqui says there is no way the ambassador's chef could have invented chop suey because, in fact, a Chinese-American journalist wrote about its popularity in New York City's

Chinatown in 1888, eight years before the ambassador arrived. "A staple dish for the Chinese gourmand is Chow Chop Suey, a mixture of chicken's livers and gizzards, bamboo buds, pig's tripe, fungi and bean sprouts stewed in spices. The gravy of this is poured into a bowl of rice with some [sauce that was the prototype for Worcestershire], making a delicious seasoning to the favorite grain."

To appeal to Americans the ingredients were modified. Renqui concludes: "Chinese Americans, then, not only invented these Americanized chop suey dishes, they also cooked up the legend of Li Hung-Chang chop suey to promote their business."

On a related, but slightly tangential matter, a New York City correspondent said that she had seen a sign for American chop suey on Nanking Road in Shanghai in 1932 when she lived there. Perhaps, she conjectured, it is the same sign Grace Zia Chu saw after the war.

Buffets: Eat, Drink and Be Nervous
July 20, 1986

"You balance the plate between the forefinger and three other fingers, which make a little platform, and with the forefinger and the thumb you grasp the glass, and if you think that isn't hazardous, you haven't done it lately." That is Bonnie Angelo's description of how to eat and drink while standing up at a cocktail buffet. Angelo has had many years' experience in Washington and London for *Time* magazine and now as the magazine's New York bureau chief.

I prefer to rest the plate between my third and fourth fingers, but otherwise my technique is the same. I've seen people cradling glasses in the crook of one arm, the fork in the hand of that arm and the plate in the other hand. Other veteran stand-up eaters have other techniques, but none of them are totally satisfactory. Obviously people weren't meant to eat and drink standing up.

"I Try Never to Take One"

Certainly Donna Shalala doesn't think so. The president of Hunter College says she doesn't take a plate if it's humanly possible. "For one thing I talk with my hands," she said, "and I know about not waving the glass, but it's hard when you have a plate in the other hand. Plates simply do not fit in with my ethnic background, so I try never to take one." She even remembers holding a plate between her teeth, a desperation move. "I think it was because I had to tuck my blouse down," she said. Shalala is not alone in this social conundrum, and her Lebanese background has nothing to do with it.

Most people probably do what Meredith Brokaw does. When she gets her buffet plate, she stops drinking. She's tried balancing stemware on top of a plate, holding the glass with her left hand, but finds it "a high-risk enterprise." Brokaw, who owns Pennywhistle, a small chain of toy stores, says it requires "an amazing amount of concentration at the same time you are trying to have a conversation."

So Patricia Matson concentrates on the conversation. "Who wants to worry about balancing something?" she said. "I think I've tried it for about 120 seconds and given up. The purpose of a party is to talk to interesting people. I don't care whether I eat or drink." Matson is vice president of corporate communications for Capital Cities/ABC. She confessed that stand-up buffets were especially appealing because, she said, "I'm always dieting."

Well then, would a former White House social secretary have any suggestions? Not really, said Bess Abell, whose job it was to see that everyone felt right at home in the White House during the Johnson administration. "The pros," she acknowledged immediately, "find a place to sit down. Either that or you have to find a place to set your drink down while you hold your fork. You really have to be like one of those mystical figures who had extra arms. People used to wander around at the White House with a glass in one hand and a plate in the other. They were looking out of the corner of their eye for two things: the celebrities and a table."

Tea Plates Don't Work

Manufacturers have tried various gimmicks to solve the problem, but Abell, who has her own consulting firm, Bess Abell Enterprises in Washington, D.C., doesn't think any of them have been especially successful. "Those tea plates with a place for the little tea sandwiches and an indentation for the cup all ended up in antiques shops," she said, "because they weren't any good in our grandmother's day either."

In the end, Angelo's alternative technique is probably the one most people fall back on. "I put my glass down only long enough so it won't make a circle on my hostess's table," she said, "and eat as rapidly as possible."

Judith Martin, the author of the Miss Manners etiquette columns and books, discovered years ago that when she sat down at a cocktail party, people would gravitate toward her, one by one. So she recommends sitting down. "If everyone did it," she said, "you would have a civilized party. And it would solve the problem. Give sit-down parties with lightweight furniture that can be picked up and moved around and a resolution not to take all this partying standing up."

Cocktail Buffets

The De Gustibus column appears on Saturdays. First thing Monday morning, when I got into the office, the phone was ringing with a call from a New York reader.

"You've got to have one of my things that holds a plate and a glass as long as it is stemware," he said.

"Send it over," said I.

A few days later the "thing" arrived. Made of plastic, it has a hole with an opening through which the stem of a wineglass can fit and a clip, which can be attached to a plate. You hold the plate; the thing-a-ma-bob on the plate holds the glass. Not bad.

The reader said he found them in England and now has a collection of two dozen.

If anyone wants to order them, write to: Mr. Robert Hesselberger, Hesselberger Steeden Associates Ltd., Whitmore House, 6 London Road, Ascot, Berks SL5 8DH, England.

Mr. Hesselberger will tell you how to order them. They are fairly effective, but you will have to drink your highballs, club soda, soft drinks, coffee, tea or milk in a wineglass in order to make them work.

A few months later a letter arrived from Mr. Hesselberger, who said he arrived back at his office in England to find "a small mountain of mail from America requesting details."

He enclosed the price list, and the minimum order is one hundred, which will cost $82.50. On the other hand, should you need ten thousand, the unit price drops dramatically and your bill will be merely $2,490.

Crisis Calls from a Bride's Kitchen
January 12, 1985

Occasionally my daughter will call me from Boston for some cooking advice. She may want a collection of diet recipes or a recipe for a fancy cake. But she never asks how to make egg salad or how to cook a hamburger. (In the days when my son called, it was only to find out what combinations of vegetables and grains provided complete protein for a vegetarian.)

My daughter's calls are a far cry from the ones I placed to my mother when I was a bride—a bride who had done some cooking before marriage but was no professional.

I made my first long-distance call within a week or two of setting up housekeeping. My questions involved a whole chicken. I had received an indoor rotisserie as a wedding gift, one of those so-called portable appliances that weigh so much it takes two people to lift them.

Endless Detail

My mother explained in seemingly endless detail about rinsing the chicken, salting it and arranging it on the skewer. My stepfather, who filled the traditional role of outdoor cook, had to get on the line to explain how the chicken should be placed so that it was evenly balanced. But neither could tell precisely how long to cook the chicken because they had no experience with an indoor rotisserie (the accompanying directions did not include recipes). As it turned out, they omitted another, even more significant, piece of information.

After 1½ hours the chicken looked done—the skin had golden brown patches—and I removed it. I had neglected to inquire about cutting the bird, so I ended up tearing it limb from limb. Then I tried to cut the body in half, but the knife seemed to get stuck in the middle. After much fruitless sawing I looked into the cavity, which, to my amazement, contained something.

Most cooks know what had escaped me until then: that the liver, heart, gizzard and neck were packed inside and that they were to be removed before cooking. My mother assumed I was already in possession of such rudimentary information.

That night I had eggs for dinner.

The next phone call involved canned tuna. I was having last-minute guests for lunch, and all I had in the house was two recently purchased cans. I did not need a recipe for a tuna salad. But when I opened the cans, the tuna looked funny—almost brown. The tuna at home had been white.

The natural assumption was that the tuna was spoiled, so I called my mother. But she did not know what to make of it either and suggested that I compare labels to see if they offered any clue. The cans said "dark meat tuna"; my mother's had said albacore. Being a frugal shopper, I had chosen the least expensive can on the shelf. Never having been exposed to dark meat tuna, I had no idea what it tasted like nor how it should look. I have never acquired a taste for it.

I fed my guests eggs for lunch.

The Waffle Incident

The waffle incident occurred on a Sunday. With its automatic heating and shut-off device, an electric waffle iron, another wedding gift, seemed much easier to operate than my mother's, which had to be watched like a cream sauce so the waffles would not burn.

According to the directions, which included a recipe, the red light would go off when the iron was hot enough for the batter to be poured in. When the waffles were the desired color—from light to dark golden brown—the light would go off again. This gadget was so sophisticated you could set it to give you whatever color waffles you wanted.

There was no need to call home about this appliance. I made the batter, greased and heated the iron, poured in the correct amount, sat back and waited for perfect waffles. When the light went off, I tried to open the iron, but it was stuck shut. Applying a little more effort, I managed to pry it open and came face to face not with a golden brown waffle but with its pale interior. I tried without success to pull it off the top and bottom of the iron. I called my mother.

"Did you season the waffle iron?" she asked.

"What does that mean?" I said.

She explained that the iron had to be rubbed with oil and heated very slowly and then allowed to cool before it could be used. It took considerable elbow grease and several days of effort to remove the waffle from the iron before it could be seasoned.

I had eggs for breakfast.

Some Brides Never Learn

This column was originally written in the first person. My editor at the *New York Times* looked at it and said it should not be written in the first person because, not long before, I had written a column about learning to cook as a young girl. I was unable to convince the editor that it was possible to have learned something about cooking and still need a lot of help from mother. But the editor prevailed (editors usually do), and I wrote the column as if everything happened to a friend of mine.

I have now put the column back the way it belongs. I'm the one who had all the experiences. But even as it appeared, the column brought a wonderful letter from an old friend in Philadelphia who recounted her own crises. She wrote:

> Many's the time I've called my mother to find out what "coddle an egg" means or a million other things, much more basic.
>
> Yes, for a couple of years I also cooked the turkey with the giblets inside. Guess that's why I stayed in Philadelphia—so I could call mother daily for cooking instructions without a long-distance charge.
>
> Several months ago I was trying to cook crème brûlée and cooked and cooked, but the mixture didn't seem to heat enough. Then I noticed a strange odor—the electric burner was melting; I had forgotten to put water in the double boiler. Disaster!
>
> David [her husband] had to pry the molten metal out with a saw.
>
> When I read your great piece, I was sure you'd recorded the conversations with mother years ago when we were at the News. What a marvelous piece. Unfortunately I have mislaid it and want to keep it forever, so that if you could send me a copy, I would greatly appreciate it. I'll frame it and hang it next to my two-year-old unused Cuisinart.

One other letter from New Jersey reminded me of a disaster I had forgotten to mention. "As a bride preparing chestnut stuffing for my first turkey, I remember sitting on a stool and crying because the chestnuts were so hard to peel. I didn't know about blanching them first."

The same correspondent trussed her first turkey with good heavy rubber bands and said there was "quite an odor and odd flavor."

I knew enough to blanch the chestnuts before I peeled them, but I didn't think it would take very long to do. So I invited people for dinner after work, planning to cook the chestnuts, prepare the stuffing and roast the chicken (at least it wasn't a turkey) for dinner the same evening.

We ate at ten o'clock.

When the Best Way to Help Is Not To

December 13, 1986

One of my best friends has dinner parties every week and almost never has help in the kitchen. She also has an inflexible rule about guests in her kitchen. Although she will accept your offer to clear the table, you are barred at the kitchen door. No washing, no drying. Guests can't even rinse the dishes and put them in the dishwasher. "Out, out, out," she says, and she closes the kitchen door firmly.

For years a friend and I have been giving a New Year's Eve dinner together, without any help. We preferred it that way, and we didn't want anyone jumping up from the table to clear the dishes. One very persistent guest refused to listen for three years running. We stopped inviting her. Harsh remedy, but guests who insist on helping when you don't want any help can ruin the flow of the party.

"If too many people get up," says Elizabeth Crossman, a cookbook author and food writer, "the conversation is over. It's too disruptive."

Some people offer to help because they think they should and will sit down immediately if the hostess declines. But dealing politely with the aggressively eager helper is often difficult. Hosts and hostesses who do not want the help have developed different strategies for dealing with would-be assistants short of speaking sharply to them.

Irena Chalmers tells them, "No, thank you," and adds, "I promise not to help you when I go to your house."

"If you really decide you need help with the dinner," says Clark Wolf, a food consultant, "you would have asked someone before to help you, or hired someone to come in to help. It is really rude for a guest to insist. It is tantamount to someone coming into your house and taking over your party and saying, 'No, no, no, not candlelight.' I tell them to shut up and sit down and open another bottle of wine and tell me how they like it. That distracts them wonderfully."

Firmness Is the Key

Firmness is the key, according to Donna Shor, vice president of Celebrity Service International, which keeps track of the comings and goings of world notables. "I tell them this is a one-woman kitchen, and it's better if I'm the one woman. If I have some misguided soul who thinks that she can make a contribution, I ask her to be the hostess while I'm gone."

Even worse, according to Shor, is the person who wants to chat while she is cooking. "I'm a very loquacious and gregarious person, and I'll forget what I'm doing if they talk to me," she said.

Both Chalmers, who is co-author of *The Great American Food Almanac* with Milton Glaser (Harper & Row, $25), and Paul Wolfert have developed even more foolproof methods for dealing with unwanted help: Their menus require little last-minute preparation.

"I put all the food on the table at once—it's a grazing table," said Wolfert, a cooking teacher and cookbook author. "Ninety percent of my dishes take forever to make, but they take forever the day before, so almost everything is done in advance. I gave up cooking while my guests were in the living room years ago, except at our house in Martha's Vineyard where the kitchen is an eat-in kitchen."

No Wails from the Living Room

Chalmers chooses foods that come in individual portions—chicken potpies, lobster, Cornish game hens, artichokes. "For whatever last-minute work I do, I hope that whoever is there will be able to entertain themselves without me," she said, "and in fact I find that they seem never to notice that I'm not there. I've never heard any wails from the living room saying, 'Where's Irena?'"

Some people, of course, really do want help. Clark Wolf knows a hostess who passes a bowl filled with little pieces of paper that assign a chore for each guest: clear the first course, pour the drinks, pass the bread, etc. Wolf has another friend who does not like selecting his chore from the bowl. Forewarned is forearmed. He prepared for the bowl by writing his own piece of paper, and when the bowl reached him, he palmed his piece of paper, opening it later to disclose his task for the evening. "Have a good time," it said.

Sounds like the ideal guest.

Don't Help the Hostess Unless She Asks

A month after I wrote the Best Way to Help Is Not To column, I found myself in a friend's kitchen, asking if I could help. I confess it was during the play-offs for the Super Bowl, and my team was losing badly. But midway through my conversation with my hostess I remembered my column and decided I was probably distracting her rather than assisting, so I went back and watched the football game.

"Some years ago," wrote a Manhattan reader, "when I began my annual Mother's Day brunch I tacked up this poem. I've been sorry ever since that I did not copy down the author's name along with the poem."

> Please stay away from my kitchen
> From dishwashing, cooking and such;
> You were kind to have offered to pitch in
> But thanks, no, thank you so much.
> Please don't think me ungracious
> When I ask that you leave me alone;
> For my kitchen's not any too spacious
> And my routine is strictly my own.
> Tell you what: Stay out of my kitchen
> With its sodden, hot, lackluster lures
> When you're here, stay out of my kitchen
> And I promise to stay out of yours!

Carol Cutler, a cookbook author and a friend of mine, sent me a copy of the introduction she had written for her book *Woman's Day Complete Guide to Entertaining*.

"My kitchen is well organized, and I alone know where things should go. I don't allow people to help and have been known to snap at those who follow me into the kitchen and plunk down dirty plates precisely where I planned to arrange the next platter. I even dislike having my husband get up and help, but I can't hiss at him with guests in the house."

Then she goes on to express the same sentiments I had with the following note: "Did you read Charlotte Ford's comment on the same subject? She never has help in, expects guests to help and always helps when she's at a dinner. This is her etiquette column. Is she pulling our leg?"

Most people, however, seem to agree with Carol and me. "Your article skillfully disposed of all the pests who want to help at dinner," wrote one Long Island reader. "But you should have mentioned those who don't even get out of their seats but insist on scraping and stacking the dishes. They are utterly convinced that this is the height of elegance and not murmurs, whispers, pssts, sotto voce requests to desist, or finally angry shouts stop them. They look at you amazed and ask: 'Why don't you want me to help?'"

This theme was echoed by another New Yorker who asked specifically that his name be omitted since what he had to say might embarrass his friends:"We sometimes find well-intentioned dinner guests who want to assist after the main course by collecting the plates at the table and scraping the leftovers into a pile of garbage on one plate. I find this most unappetizing. This is most often done by our European-born guests and in their homes when they are hosts.

"Is this an acceptable foreign custom? Is it a breach of American etiquette?"

Only if you can't stand to see garbage on your dining room table.

Another regular correspondent, Professor Ralph Slovenko of Wayne State University in Detroit, had this to say: "I used to think that was a woman's (or servant's) job, but that's outdated thinking. I am now glad to know that helping with the dishes ought not to be done as it can 'ruin the flow of the party.'"

Do I detect a note of residual sexism?

Ah, for the Bagel of Yesteryear
March 17, 1984

An old Yiddish recipe for a bagel directs the baker to take a hole and put some dough around it. The basic concept has not changed since the recipe first appeared—the bagel is still round, more or less, and it still has a hole in the middle—but the amount and kind of dough have undergone a drastic metamorphosis.

It has been so drastic that the small "cement doughnut" is almost a relic. Most bagels today are neither small nor cement-like. Instead they are soft and enormous, and practically devoid of the chewiness for which they were known and loved. They hardly ever give you heartburn anymore.

How the modern bagel got that way is related in large part to the growth of its popularity among non-Jews. No longer a product of the Lower East Side alone, it can be found at boardroom lunches and on airline snack trays. It is even used as a symbol for another culture on St. Patrick's Day, when green food coloring is added.

The true bagel, or water bagel, is made from white, high-gluten flour and is perfectly plain. The secret to its characteristic texture—petrified—is that it is made by hand and boiled, which reduces the starch content as well as giving it an outer sheen and hard crust. Such bagels are not easy to find.

The vast majority of today's bagels, though boiled before baking as all true bagels must be, are made by machine and contain certain dough conditioners and proofing agents that counteract the effects of boiling. These additives not only keep the bagel soft longer, but also make it spread out. Hence the increased size and soft texture, hardly the stuff for teething babies. At least that is the theory expounded by Abe Moskowitz, owner of the Bagel Oasis in Queens, New York, where the bagels are still handmade and contain no preservatives.

Hymie Perlmutter, owner of Moishe's Bakery, which produces handcrafted bagels at two Lower East Side locations, has a slightly different theory. In Manhattan, Perlmutter says today's bagels aren't the same because there are no European bakers who know how to make the old kind and because the flour used now is different. But Perlmutter must have a few old bakers around: His bagel comes closest to what I remember from my childhood.

There is one final theory on the newfangled bagel, from Joan Nathan, author of *The Jewish Holiday Kitchen*. Nathan encountered the large, soft bagels in Toronto, where there is a large Rumanian Jewish community. She was told that Rumanian bagels have always been soft and big, more like bialys. And she speculates that people in the business of mass-producing bagels discovered that the softer version had more appeal to those who had not cut their teeth on the cement-doughnut variety.

For much the same reason that the taste for certain foods, like chitterlings and pork pies, is an acquired one, the old-fashioned bagels appeal more to those who grew up on them than to those who came to them late in life.

For Johnny-come-latelies the bagels of choice come, like muffins, in assorted flavors: pumpernickel, pumpernickel raisin, onion, garlic, egg, whole wheat, wheat germ, honey, cinnamon, sesame seed, rye, bran. A non-Jew partial to the bagel in its infinite varieties describes these modern versions as "reformed bagels for gentiles." When slathered with cream cheese, called a schmeer in New York, they are enough for lunch. Turned into a pizza with tomato sauce, cheese, sausage and onions, they are enough for supper.

Bagels were not always "Jewish food." In Europe everyone ate them. Their origins are unknown, but they were mentioned in community regulations in Cracow, Poland, as early as 1610. One theory is that bagel is the Yiddish corruption of the Middle High German word *bügel*, meaning twisted or curved ring or bracelet.

Molly Goldberg, the character created by the actress Gertrude Berg, said bagels should never be eaten alone. "In order for the true taste to come out you need your family," she said. "One to cut the bagels, one to toast them, one to put on the cream cheese and lox, one to put them on the table and one to supervise."

Bagels They Have Known

A reader from Syracuse, New York, says even someone who did not grow up eating the cement version of bagels prefers them. "I never had a genuine water bagel until I was twenty-one, but I deplore the big, soft, sweetened kind that come out of the corner 'hot bagel' factories."

My correspondent went on to say that "the Molly Goldberg character, who advocates first cutting the bagel and then toasting it, has the procedure reversed. The bagel should be cut *after* toasting or, preferably, oven-warming. Otherwise, the texture of the cut surface gets crusty, and the bagel loses its chewy character."

My husband would not agree.

A reader from New Haven, Connecticut, produced the startling information that in São Paulo, Brazil, where she lived for a while, she could buy thinner, crustier and chewier bagels than what's available in the United States. "Your article now suggests to me that they are 'purer' survivors of some 'real thing' of decades past."

Then there were the bagels a Brooklyn reader had at Selfridge's, the London department store. There they were called "beigels," delightfully hard, said the correspondent, "hard-petrified, and made by an American baker."

Professor Herbert Gans from Columbia University offered another theory about what has happened to the bagel. A professor of sociology, he has some interesting thoughts.

Ethnic foods, he says,

undergo acculturation (or Americanization) processes in which, e.g., ingredients become more refined (literally and figuratively) and easier on the digestive system: softer, less spicy, etc. In short they change to fit American tastes. I would guess that this theory applies to spaghetti sauces, Polish sausages, German cold cuts, Lithuanian breads, Mexican dishes, etc.

These foods can therefore also be classified by generation, and I've studied bagels along this line for many years. What you call the "bagel of yesteryear" is the immigrant bagel; the second-generation bagel being a softer version of same that I remember encountering about twenty years ago, especially outside New York. The third-generation bagel is yet softer and much larger, the machine-made version with additives you write about. You call them the "vast majority" of today's bagels; and it may not be coincidental that a vast majority of today's Jews are also third-generation. I suppose that the fourth-generation bagel, being fully Americanized, is therefore properly pluralistic and comes in assorted flavors—and also turns green on St. Patrick's Day.

Although the current wave of ethnic nostalgia has led to a revival of the immigrant bagel, I think it is safe to predict that someday there will be fifth- and sixth-generation bagels.

When Ice Cream Wasn't Haute

June 24, 1984

Standing in line for the privilege of purchasing a single scoop of ice cream for $1.60 on one of the few warm days we've had this spring, I thought of how the ice cream business has changed since the days I cajoled my mother out of a penny to buy a lemon ice. Who knew about butterfat or cared about brand names? We bought whatever the corner drugstore sold or chased a Good Humor truck, if we were lucky enough to have one come into our neighborhood.

Now we have to make choices that aren't limited to today's vast array of flavors. The country of origin is a consideration, especially since Italian *gelati* have come into their own. Then there is the percentage of butterfat. The least caloric has just 10 percent, with the proportion ranging up to 20 percent, which some people think is too rich to be considered ice cream.

And for people who don't want butterfat at all, there are almost as many flavors among the increasingly popular sorbets, once called water sherbets. Then what kind of cone? Some consider it more important than the ice cream and go for the handmade. For others the ice cream is simply a vehicle for such ingredients as candy, cookies, raisins and nuts—all at once.

Today's choices bear little resemblance to what we dripped over ourselves as children.

My first memory of ice cream was at the age of four, when I was permitted to have a scoop of chocolate in a sugar cone. But without the chocolate jimmies. Jimmies, or chocolate shot, were the fanciest accessory for an ice cream cone. Nuts were found only on top of a sundae. The jimmies were kept in a bowl on the counter, and for a penny extra you could dip your own cone in. The object was to attach as many of the jimmies to the cone as possible. But my mother wouldn't let me do it; she said it wasn't sanitary.

The Rise of the Italian Ice

A few years later the ice cream of choice wasn't ice cream at all, it was an Italian ice, though friends who remember the neighborhood better than I say the ices weren't Italian because the store was named Goldman's. The lemon ice I remember—it was the only flavor sold—was just like the Italian lemon ice I have tasted since. In those days it came in pleated paper cups: a penny for a small one, three for a large. My cousin and I were each given a penny, and we fought regularly over who was given the larger scoop. When the ice got down below the lip of the cup, you pushed the contents up from the bottom, and if you played with it too long, the cup would spring a leak or two.

But dripping lemon ice was no match for chocolate-coated vanilla ice cream on a stick, from which I systematically ate all the chocolate coating. My mother warned me about that too. She said it would fall off the stick. Sure enough, one hot summer day the ice cream slid swiftly to the ground, pausing only to hit my dress.

The most exotic combination I ever ate was called a Creamsicle. Because I didn't like the orange coating, I discarded it, but instead of taking it all off at one time, I removed just a little and ate the insides, following this procedure to the bottom of the stick.

The Good Humor truck usually came into my neighborhood before dinner, so I seldom got to buy one. On the rare occasions when I could, my favorite was the toasted almond. Its crunchy exterior coated an ordinary vanilla ice cream, but the contrast in textures was very appealing. When my children were old enough to run after the Good Humor truck, I discovered that toasted almond had not gone out of fashion. I hesitated for weeks before trying one, uncertain if the modern version or my more sophisticated taste buds might ruin my memories. Eventually I succumbed, but I shouldn't have. It seemed soggy and excessively sweet.

The ultimate childhood ice cream experience, however, was my son's. As the Good Humor truck approached one day, Michael came running in to get money to buy one for himself and one for his sister. His visiting grandfather had no change, so he gave him a $10 bill. Michael went flying out and soon staggered in with an assortment of twenty-five cups and sticks. No one had told him to get change.

Before the Dove Bar

"Did you miss the Eskimo Pie in your youth?" asked a New York native. It was that block of vanilla ice cream encased in chocolate that was kept in a ceramic vat on subway-station stands and in candy stores.

"The ones we bought were either as hard as blocks of cement from overfreezing so slow licking was the only way to get into them, or drippingly soft because of freezer failure.

"As to the lemon ice in a fluted paper cup, which eventually dripped, that was luxury. Outside my school in East Harlem there was a man who shaved a block of ice and then dripped onto the shavings one's choice of a variety of flavors from bottles that resembled the ones containing perfumed hair tonic with which the barber would put the finishing flourish on his work."

Yes, I did miss the Eskimo Pie in my youth. Deprived childhood. But that's all right. I made up for it with the Dove Bar, the glorified Eskimo Pie.

Many people insist that they cannot finish a single Dove Bar— five hundred calories. My husband once ate two—after a dinner of barbecue. When reminded, he pleads amnesia.

For Some, Summertime's Bounty Becomes a Bane

August 21, 1985

The telephone calls usually begin in late July. The stealthy visits occur in August, when the situation is desperate. The exact date is flexible and depends on the local growing season. The calls and visits don't let up until the middle of September. The caller begs, pleads and, when desperate enough, offers bribes. The visitor just drops the package at the back door and leaves, without so much as a knock.

Both the telephone and the anonymous visitor are on the same errand—they are getting rid of the fruits of their labors in their once cherished summer gardens.

The pleasure of watching things grow has now been replaced by the problem of what to do with what has grown. The successful gardens are overrun with everything from tomatoes and zucchini to basil and peppers. Because not everyone jumps at the offer of a grocery bag full of zucchini, some gardeners just leave the bags in the dead of night, knowing that the recipient will feel as guilty about throwing out good food as the donor.

Sometimes gardeners get desperate enough to invite people to dinner, but only in order to press upon them a large shopping bag of produce as they leave. They know guests would find it impolite to reject such a generous gift.

One I know has finally acknowledged that no one will take her zucchini, but people are thrilled to be offered unusual varieties of anything else: yellow tomatoes, purple okra, white eggplant. Still, she continues to plant the zucchini because "even when nothing else come up, the zucchini always does."

Gardeners somehow fail to realize that some people don't garden, not only because they don't like to plant and water and weed, but because they have no interest whatsoever in spending the glorious days of summer's end "putting things by." To do a gardener a favor, some friends will pick a few tomatoes for immediate use, a sprig or two of basil and a couple of zucchini. But they refuse to have anything to do with an amount that requires storage beyond three days.

Despite all its nostalgic, homey attributes and all the fond memories (which seldom include the tedious aspects), canning is a chore. And don't forget the hazards. Seminal literature on canning appears in a small paperback booklet, the *Ball Blue Book*. The booklet contains pages devoted to "what went wrong." In addition, every summer there is at least one notice from the local cooperative extension service warning about poisoning your family and friends by underprocessing or improperly processing tomatoes.

The Summer of a Shortage

Of course, nothing in recent years can match the famous summer of the disappearing canning lids in 1975. It was a time of upwardly spiraling food prices, and many people planted gardens in anticipation of canning for the following winter. Suddenly, there was a shortage of canning lids, complete with a congressional hearing to get to the bottom of the problem. It didn't. And eventually—about a year later—the shortage disappeared. But not before many people were substituting mayonnaise jars and other equally inappropriate containers for canning. A lot of the canned food spoiled.

For some, the charms of home-canned food lingers on, a link with the past. But for those who have a vegetable garden, freezing the overrun has often taken the place of canning. It is a much quicker and safer way to store summer's bounty. Perhaps it isn't as romantic, but, on the other hand, you never hear about anyone being poisoned by frozen tomato sauce.

Although my family did not have a garden this summer, I found myself faced on several occasions with more tomatoes and basil than I could possibly use, thanks to gifts from gardener friends. As the tomatoes began to soften and black spots appeared on the basil, that awful fear of wasting food came over me. There was no time to make anything elaborate, so I decided to do the simplest thing possible—one that took the least amount of preparatory work on my part and the shortest amount of cooking time.

I did NOT peel or seed the tomatoes, I just coarsely chopped them in the food processor and tore the basil leaves off the stems. Tomatoes and basil leaves were dumped into a large pot, where they cooked for about fifteen minutes, until the chunks of tomatoes had softened. Then I divided the contents of the pot into several batches and put them into freezer containers.

This will make a splendid beginning for a sauce to be served over pasta or chicken or beef or veal or fish. Other vegetables, such as broccoli, zucchini or green beans, can also be cooked in such a sauce. It can be varied with other seasonings, principally garlic. It can be thickened by further cooking or combined with wine and cheeses. In other words, it's an all-purpose tomato sauce that took about fifteen minutes to prepare and another fifteen minutes to cook.

It is quite comforting to know that whenever I need the base for a tomato sauce, I have it in my freezer. But this is not to be construed as an invitation to friends who have too many tomatoes to send them over.

Why Cold Is Not So Hot
August 11, 1984

We Americans like our hot foods steaming, our cold foods icy. It is one of many cultural differences between us and most if not all of the rest of the world. We have such a fetish about these extremes in temperature that it is a point of pride to advertise frosty drinks on a muggy summer's day and a bubbling pot of beef stew on a bone-chilling winter's evening.

Because of our preoccupation with hot and cold food we are missing much of the natural flavors found in dishes served at more moderate temperatures, temperatures that do not numb our taste receptors. This is not to suggest that all dishes taste better at room temperature, but what food can you think of whose flavor is not improved if it is allowed to stand long enough to cool down or warm up a little?

Some scientific evidence backs these empirical observations. According to Dr. Gary Beauchamp, a member of the Monell Chemical Senses Center in Philadelphia, we are "most sensitive to tastes that are around body temperature." He explained that "most of the subtleties of taste have to do with smell, and when a cold food warms up, the odorous molecules come off the material at a greater rate."

That being the case, boiling-hot food should taste best of all, but other factors may be working against that theory. "There has not been much research done in this area," Beauchamp said. He added, however, that common sense would indicate that very hot food might deaden some taste receptors and that it cannot be kept in the mouth long enough to savor it.

Two considerations may account for the American interest in extremely hot and overly chilled food. Because of advanced technology in the 1920s and '30s, Americans had better refrigeration and cooking equipment than others around the world. And because of the American obsession with food safety, made possible by refrigeration and efficient stoves, we have come to believe that to prevent gastrointestinal disorders food should be kept either above 140 degrees or below 40 degrees. For prolonged periods this is true, but not for the hour or two it takes to eat a meal.

Indeed, many foods are no more or less safe to eat if they sit at room temperature, fruit being a perfect example. Cherries that have been on the kitchen counter taste much better than those that have been in the refrigerator. What is better than a peach or a tomato eaten directly from the garden? It isn't just their freshness, although that has a lot to do with it. It isn't just the romantic notion of picking your own fruit, though that has some psychic value. It is that at room temperature fruit has more aroma and, consequently, more taste.

Some of the more conscientious ice cream manufacturers advise consumers to allow their products to sit at room temperature for a few minutes before serving, not because it will be easier to scoop the ice cream but because more of the flavor will come through.

Have you ever eaten a cookie as it came from the oven? Or stolen a sliver of roast beef fresh from the roasting pan? Not until the cookie is cool enough to handle and the roast beef has been sitting for about fifteen minutes do either have any flavor. And if you are willing to wait an hour or two, the roast beef will be even more flavorful. Just like the Thanksgiving turkey about two hours after dinner.

Responding to Expectations

It is difficult to convince Americans to have open minds about eating food at more moderate temperatures because much of how we react to food has to do with what we expect from it.

So far, my idea that lamb roasted with garlic puree and served at room temperature is better than lamb just half an hour from the oven has been greeted with skepticism. And when I served *pastichio*, a Greek dish made of layers of macaroni, meat and tomato sauce, topped with a cheese-flavored cream sauce at room temperature, I met with the same resistance. In Greece *pastichio* is served that way, but here, I was told, the otherwise delicious dish would have been better if it had been hotter.

If you want to satisfy your curiosity, try a simple test. The next time you serve strawberries, compare some directly from the refrigerator with some that have reached room temperature.

Room-Temperature Food

Even in the two years since this column was written, room temperature has taken on a certain cachet among foodies in this country.

It has become not only respectable, but downright chic to serve some dishes at room temperature.

The Spanish always serve this one at room temperature.

FRITTATA OR TORTILLA

⅓ cup combination of olive and corn oils
1 large onion, diced
5 cups peeled, thinly sliced potatoes
1 small green bell pepper, diced
1 garlic clove, minced
   Salt and freshly ground black pepper to taste
¼ teaspoon or more cayenne pepper to taste
6 eggs, lightly beaten

1. Heat all but 2 tablespoons of the oil in a large skillet. Add the onion, potatoes, green pepper, garlic, salt and peppers to taste. Cover the skillet and cook over medium heat, stirring the mixture occasionally to prevent sticking. When the potatoes are tender but not brown, in about 15 to 20 minutes, remove and cool slightly. Drain off the excess oil. Clean out the skillet with paper towels.
2. Add the cooled vegetable mixture to the beaten eggs.
3. Add the remaining oil to the skillet and heat. Add the egg mixture and cook over medium heat until the bottom becomes golden brown.
4. With a spatula loosen the omelet from the pan. Place a plate on top of the pan and invert. Free the skillet of any bits of omelet that may have stuck.
5. Add a bit more oil if necessary. Slide the omelet back into the skillet and cook the second side until golden.
6. Cut into wedges and serve at room temperature to bring out the flavors.

YIELD: 4 to 6 servings

A Down-to-Earth Look at Those Airline Meals

February 25, 1984

Whenever I travel on a long flight on which dinner is served, I request a fruit plate as an alternative to the regular meal. A little fruit is a nice snack until I get to my destination and can order some real food. But on a trip from New York City to Denver last week I outfoxed myself.

The centerpiece of the fruit plate was a pile of twenty midget-to-moderate-size grapes in two colors, red and black, and with one taste—sour. Their juice would have made a superior vinegar. Next to them on a limp leaf of lettuce lay three orange slices, each some two inches in diameter. They were not sour; they were not sweet either; they were tasteless. Beside them sat the one edible piece of fruit, a tasty pineapple stick about three inches long.

That trio was set off by a small mound of large-curd cottage cheese. Bean curd has more flavor. A little plastic container labeled "honey lime dressing" appeared to be the dressing for the fruit. The container also listed the ingredients, which included xanthan gum, natural and artificial flavors, artificial color, including yellow No. 5, and sodium benzoate as a preservative (Heaven knows why anyone would want to preserve it!). This mixture had the texture of whipped lime gelatin, and like lime gelatin, it did not contain much lime. One taste made that obvious.

By the time I had made my way through the fruit plate, I was no longer interested in the food as sustenance but as specimens for critical examination, so I turned to my seat companion's lettuce and tomato salad. It was topped with two wedges of egg with the consistency of an elastic band. Two anemic-looking slices of pulpy tomato made an unappetizing decoration for iceberg lettuce that was so cold it hurt my teeth.

Why Powder, Not Juice?

For the lettuce salad something mislabeled Caesar dressing was provided, but it couldn't be poured out of the container until it had been standing for half an hour. Its overwhelming flavor was derived from three ingredients: salt, anchovy paste and monosodium glutamate. It also contained an ingredient called lemon juice powder. What's wrong with lemon juice?

There was something that looked like a roll on the tray, but it was probably just a prop. It wasn't hard enough to crumble; it was tough, so tough that breaking off a piece was almost impossible. Too bad, because despite all the artificial food on airline-meal trays, there is always a pat of real butter for the bread. A satisfactory explanation for this pleasant anomaly has never been given. Why do airlines use butter instead of margarine? If it was because of the country's enormous dairy surplus, they would use cream instead of coffee whitener, wouldn't they?

Whatever happened to the plan to offer lower fares without food? Even if the saving amounted to $1.50, that would be enough to buy a small wedge of decent cheese and a fresh baguette or a piece of fruit. And why don't the airlines consider selling such simple food in flight? The cheese tray could have such long-lasting varieties as Gruyère, Port Salut and Parmigiano-Reggiano. For fruit the lines could offer Granny Smith apples, oranges, bananas and pineapple in winter, melon wedges, seedless grapes, peaches, plums and nectarines in summer.

But hope is stronger than memory, and I'll probably order another fruit plate on my next flight.

Airline Meals

Surely, I thought, no one likes airline food.
 Surely, I was wrong.
 Instead of receiving kudos, there were a lot of brickbats.
 From New Jersey:

As a frequent air traveler, I was extremely offended by your article. I have found, in every case, the food is deliciously edible and absolutely satisfactory. It is obvious to me that you are either not really a person who travels often or have never braved the regular meal. (You may find the hot dinner more to your liking than the fruit plate. How do you expect the plate to be same-day fresh when only one out of three hundred people orders it.) Moreover, your attitude concerning the freshness of the food is unnecessary. The foods ordered by the airlines—both in first class and economy—are fresh and delivered just before the passengers are asked to board.

 I would be interested in learning just what you've determined you're paying for when you buy your ticket—your safety and well-being or gourmet food?

"No," wrote a New Yorker, "the meals are not Côte Basque or Lutèce, and I don't expect them to be. Please leave your dining and your fruit and cheese shopping on the ground and think f the airlines as a pleasant way to get to the markets and restaurants of the world."

From upstate New York: "First, let me point out that I don't board an airplane with the expectation that it is a gourmet restaurant with wings. My first interest is getting to where I am going safe, on time, and as comfortable as is practical for one hundred to three hundred people in a metal sausage (excuse the food pun).

"However, the real issue here is why is it so popular to knock airline food? Why do gourmet writers even find it a topic worthy of print?"

If it were a true attempt to analyze airline food, the writer went on to say, it should have been done systematically.

So about a year later I did a systematic examination of airline food and came up with the same results. With the exception of some first-class meals and both economy and first-class meals served on Swissair, the food was essentially as described in this piece. In fact, airlines are spending less for food then they used to, and the personnel acknowledge its shortcomings.

On a United Airlines flight in April from New York City to Denver, a flight attendant announced that there were three entrée choices and then added: "Please don't be upset if your first choice is not available. They all taste the same anyway." Or as Coleman Lollar, managing editor of *Frequent Flyer* magazine, said, "The food reaches the lowest common denominator. It is designed to offend the least amount of people."

And, as one reader who approved of my remarks said, "There's a wealth of dishes that stand up well to the sort of treatment an airline meal must be subjected to. Steak is not one of them. The employees of every airline should have to eat these meals—from the president on down to the mechanics."

While there were plenty of brickbats for the piece, there were more kudos.

"I was extremely pleased to read your description of bleak airplane fare," wrote a New Hampshire reader. "If anything it was too brief. I was beginning to think the *Times* had lost all compassion. Now, my faith is restored."

A Massachusetts reader sent me a card decorated with stars and hearts.

Brava! You said it all in your column. And if you think airline food is bad, kosher airline food is the worst.

My husband and I join you in a no-star rating for airline food. One major international carrier merits a well-earned "poor" for in-flight meals. In our experience on overseas flights leaving JFK at 9 P.M., dinner is served promptly at midnight (as you are dozing off, if you are so lucky), and barely two hours later, the wake-up call comes for what they dare to call breakfast.

Our modus operandi, to foil theirs, has brought us compliments from flight attendants and fellow passengers alike. We bring our freshly made sandwiches on board and eat them soon after the plane takes off, with drinks that are served. Having previously requested a cheese and fruit platter, we reserve it and substitute it for the greasy doughnut and coffee the next morning. Whole oranges from home add a touch of first class.

The airlines could save money and do us a favor by serving less. In this instance less is more.

Today you would be har
its food service, but once a
themselves open to criticis
matter of fact, I noticed re
are even serving the one na
Now it's some combination
ing as butter.

The solution to this stuff
that of the people who br
make something simple at h
chicken, and cut up some ve
them. Buy some fruit in s
brownie or cookie. Or if ever
are busy getting ready to gc
you like their food on the ground, you'll love it 30,000 feet up.

Most of the people a
Boston out of La G
The old Eastern
food and there
It's differ
what was
ark, a
add
s

Issue on the Shuttles: Who Noshes Best?

April 25, 1987

It was the 9 A.M. Eastern Air Lines shuttle from New York to Washington. A New Yorker accepted her little bag of food, a version of what Continental calls the Flying Nosh but comes without a name on Eastern and Pan Am.

The man seated beside my friend appeared to be a Midwesterner. He eagerly accepted his nosh. Then, she said, "he inspected his bagel and cream cheese, and, looking very pleased with himself, turned to me and said, "Oh, they're giving us a nohsh.'" That was pronounced as the word "no" followed by "shh."

My friend said it took her ten seconds to figure out what he meant. "But when I realized, I couldn't say anything," she said. "I would have started laughing. I just smiled. He seemed quite pleased with his sophisticated pronunciation and ate his 'nohsh' happily."

...board the hourly trips to Washington and
...uardia and Newark airports eat theirs, too.
...shuttle didn't bother with noshes; there was no
... were no assigned seats.
...ent now. Eastern—reacting to the competition of
...hen New York Air and is now Continental out of New-
...d Pan Am out of the Marine Terminal at La Guardia—
...ed its own version of the Flying Nosh. Snacks are one of the
...lling points of its advertisement; the commercials feature appreciative passengers commenting on the food.

Pan Am advertises its free snacks, too. "No matter when you fly our shuttle we give you either a breakfast snack or an appetizing serving of fruit, cheese and crackers along with complimentary beverages," a Pan Am spokesman said. And Pan Am's ads describe Eastern's snacks this way: "On some of their midafternoon flights, what they call snacks are really called peanuts."

But do people actually choose an airline because of its food? Asking passengers in flight if they based their travel plans on what they would get to eat brought hoots, titters and smiles. Without exception, everyone I questioned had based flight decisions on convenience or a need to accumulate more mileage for free trips. Food had nothing to do with it.

It was hardly a scientific survey—I questioned about fifteen travelers. But even though they said food had not affected their decisions, they weren't indifferent to it. They all had opinions, but nothing that added up to a consensus, except, perhaps, for a generally positive feeling about the fresh fruit aboard Pan Am and a generally negative response to Eastern's snacks.

Because I could not fly at every time of day on every flight to and from Washington, I asked the airlines to send me a sample of each food combination they offer on flights from New York and Newark to Boston and Washington.

New York Air had the most extensive selection, and Continental has chosen to maintain it. Of the three airlines, only it provides hard liquor along with soft drinks, juices and wines. There are thirteen different breakfast items, such as bagel with cream cheese and croissant and cream-cheese puff. Noshes for the rest of the day include carrot cake or banana bread; bread sticks with a piece of fruit, processed cheese spread and a mint; baked bread with cheese and a mint; and honey-roasted cashews.

do we have hourly shuttles to anywhere being as how we don't care to get anywhere that rapidly."

He asked if I could identify where in the Midwest this person came from: "I mean, to me a person from Wyoming is an 'Easterner' and when I go 'back East' I go to Colorado and from there on to the Atlantic Ocean is 'East.'" Then he apparently threw up his hands in despair and said: "I realize that to a New Yorker anything west of the Hudson River (except Moonachie) is 'West,'" a reference, I suspect, to a town in New Jersey with which the New York Giants (their home stadium is in New Jersey) are associated.

If Some of the Colors of the Rainbow Fail to Please
October 22, 1983

In the days when women went to tea instead of work, my mother told me to meet her at a League of Women Voters meeting after I got out of school. The only thing I remember about the meeting were the tea sandwiches. And then only the blue ones.

The hostess has used her deck-of-cards cookie cutters—all the best-run kitchens had a set—to make sandwiches out of white bread shaped like clubs, diamonds, hearts and spades. Instead of just flavoring the standard cream cheese topping with a little jelly or chives or pimiento, this hostess decided to go one step further, coloring her little open-faced sandwiches canary yellow, baby pink, grass green and royal blue.

While they all looked like what we would now call plastic food (in those days there was no plastic), only the blue ones seemed grossly unappetizing to me, then ten years old. Long before I understood that the appearance of food was almost as important as its taste, I knew that blue cream cheese did not look good enough to eat.

That food must appeal to the eye before we are willing to taste it is something that most of us seem to learn by osmosis. And in some ways children are more finicky than adults. If food doesn't look good, they won't even try it. But what appeals to us is almost entirely a matter of acculturation. It changes from country to country, and even from generation to generation in the same country.

Which brings me back to blue cream cheese. And to holly red Maraschino cherries, green pistachio ice cream and all the other foods that are dyed today in the belief that people won't buy them otherwise. Perhaps many of them won't. But fifty years ago they would not have known what to make of orange skins that had been dyed deep orange or strawberry ice cream that had been colored crimson.

It was not until after World War II that manufacturers began to use artificial food colorings so extensively. Before that, if ripe oranges had green spots, they were sold that way. Before that, the only red in strawberry ice cream came from the strawberries. Today strawberry ice cream can be red and yet not have a single strawberry in it.

How did we ever get to the point where we thought it essential to color food in order to sell it? Ruth Winter, author of *A Consumer's Dictionary of Food Additives,* provides one plausible answer, "We want enhanced food because all of our lives we have been subjected to beautiful pictures of foods in our magazines and on television. We have come to expect an advertiser's concept of perfection in color and texture, even though Mother Nature may not turn out all her products that way. As a result the skin of the oranges we eat are dyed bright orange to match our mental image of an ideal orange."

There are other reasons: to make artificial foods look real (Tang, Jell-O) and to make cheap substitutes look expensive (caramel coloring in bread to simulate whole-grain flour, yellow dye in cakes to simulate eggs).

But just as the last two generations instinctively learned to love the intense colors of artificial foods and even natural foods that have been dyed, some of us have played the maverick and have been learning to avoid them. We have factored in another bit of information that has colored our thinking about artificial colors. The safety factor. A cloud of suspicion has been hanging over artificial colors for more than a decade. And today there are enough of us who consciously avoid artificially colored foods so that some manufacturers have found it worth their while to promote its absence in their products.

It's nice to know that the best ice creams do not use artificial colors; California oranges are never dyed; genuine whole grain breads do not need caramel coloring, and real fruit juice will never have the intense color of its fake counterparts.

Sometimes aesthetics and safety are synonymous. And those of us who care about such things are delighted with the turn of events.

Colors

This column elicited only one letter—from the president of the League of Women Voters in Morristown, New Jersey

"Dear Editor: Please assure Marian Burros, De Gustibus, October 21, that our league never has and alas never will serve blue tea sandwiches."

Food: Mugging for the Camera
September 22, 1984

The days of food advertisements with marbles in the soup to make it boil more appealingly and shaving cream in place of whipped cream are over, thanks to truth-in-advertising regulations that prohibit food fakery in commercials.

That does not mean that the people who make food look pretty for the camera—food stylists, as they are known in the trade—have turned in their paintbrushes, tweezers, oilcans and bags of tricks. For one thing, truth in advertising does not apply to food photography for magazine and newspaper articles. And the law does not prevent some cosmetic improvement of food in advertising.

Cigarette smoke can be blown through a straw to mimic steam. Angel cakes are sometimes baked in soufflé dishes because the soufflé might fall within a minute of being taken out of the oven. Lighter fluid, rubber cement or sugar cubes dipped in lemon extract may be ignited to produce a yellow flame for flambéed dishes (but not if the advertised product is an alcoholic beverage —even though people think of flames as yellow, alcohol produces blue flames, and that is the color they must be in the shot).

"People have fantasies about food," explained Helen Feingold, a food stylist and home economist in Flushing, Queens. When we spoke, she was working on a commercial featuring Crisco as an ingredient for frosting. "Cakes have to look a certain way," she said. "For the commercial you have to bake a cake according to the recipe.

"You bake plenty of them"—in this case, she made eighteen— "so you can trim them flat. Then you cut the cake with a knife that is not so sharp, so that you get a piece that looks softer and fluffier. If, when you mix the frosting according to the recipe it isn't shiny enough, you add a little more liquid."

Feingold says that food photography is getting away from the perfect "plaster of paris look." Dora Jonassen, a food stylist in Manhattan, agrees. "Thank God there's a move to the natural look," she said. "I really like to see that food isn't perfect anymore. We're more relaxed about it." Companies have realized that "food should not be threatening anymore," she said.

Still, many artifices are available to the food stylist. Most foods, for example, are undercooked to preserve their shape. If the zucchini or green beans in minestrone are vividly colored, they were probably blanched, not cooked with the soup. Chickens are seldom roasted completely because their skin wrinkles soon after they are removed from the oven; instead, they are often painted with a glaze, using a product such as Kitchen Bouquet or Angostura bitters. Sometimes a few drops of dish detergent are used to make the glaze penetrate the meat better.

Meringues are made with dried instead of fresh egg whites because they weep less. And to make their holding power even greater, meringues are sometimes made with mixtures used by commercial bakers. "Look at the lemon meringue pie in your bakery," Feingold said. "It sits there all day."

To keep ham pink, it is sliced at the last minute, and the slices are painted with Maraschino cherry syrup. "The major problem with faking," Feingold said, "is that when you fake it, it looks fake."

She laughed about the subterfuges she spots in food photography. "When they use fake ice cubes in drinks, they sometimes forget to make some stick out the top," she said. "Fake cubes sink—real ones float. When they use smoke to look like steam, you can tell because it comes out in a thin stream," she said. "Some of the chemicals that are used look smoky rather than steamy."

Less obvious tricks, Feingold said, include using a commercial whipped topping mix for real whipped cream because the commercial product is "pretty indestructible under hot lights." Real whipped cream may be stabilized with gelatin; the bottom of a soup tureen may be filled with cornmeal mush to make the vegetables stay on the surface.

"Marvelous imperfections are what make food look good," Feingold said, "but not all advertisers are convinced of that yet."

From Chic to Cliché: The Short Life of Fad Foods
December 10, 1983

Fashions in food, like fashions in clothes, are often determined by current events. And as with clothes, last year's food chic is this year's cliché.

The nostalgia craze, which brought us *Roots* and a Ralph Lauren collection inspired by the American Southwest, also established barbecued ribs and cornbread. At black tie dinners they have replaced fillet of beef and noisettes of potatoes. No matter that it is almost impossible to get barbecue-sauce stains out of a white satin blouse or damask napkins, at least two of which are needed to really enjoy the ribs.

In addition, as the American palate has become more sophisticated, manufacturers and producers have been spurred to develop more and more foods, most of them variations on the same theme—raspberry vinegar, blueberry vinegar, huckleberry vinegar, garlic vinegar, basil vinegar—but occasionally something new and wonderful. This year foie gras from ducks raised in New York State has largely taken over the market, at least in New York City, from the partly cooked imported French foie gras. Judging by the number of restaurants serving the American product, it is the new chic food. Next year it might be American truffles.

What was current and choice at the beginning of 1983 is fading fast as 1984 approaches. Will red pepper puree be as fashionable next year as it is now, or will it suffer the same fate as other vegetable purees? Now that ginger has replaced basil as the seasoning of choice, what will next year bring?

Some of the foods that have become unfashionable should never have been fashionable in the first place. White chocolate mousse and croissants filled with spinach or ratatouille or blueberries come immediately to mind.

Some foods that have become hackneyed do not deserve their fate. Kiwis are one of the more refreshing fruits available all year long. Why did chefs have to put them on top of and into everything so that no one wants to use them anymore? Unfortunately, a similar fate has befallen vegetable purees. Not only are they delicious if used sparingly, but unlike other vegetable preparations, they can be done ahead of time and reheated without any loss of flavor—a boon to the home cook.

For those who are eager to retain their status as up-to-date in the food world, a list of "in" and "out" foods follows (in each pair, what's in precedes what's out).

Fresh American duck foie gras; *demi-cuit* (partly cooked) French foie gras.

Smoke salmon and pasta; smoked salmon and cream cheese.

Muffins; croissants.

Barbecued ribs; barbecued chicken.

Cornbread; baked potatoes.

Chilled sparkling waters; iced sparkling waters.

Fresh American shiitake or chanterelle; dried imported mushrooms of any kind.

Pizza with shrimp or ratatouille; pizza with sausage and mozzarella.

Ravioli stuffed with lobster; ravioli stuffed with cheese.

Sorbetto; ice cream and candy bars mixed together.

Flourless chocolate cake; chocolate mousse, especially white chocolate mousse.

Ginger; basil.

Rabbit; steak.

Water-processed decaffeinated coffee; flavored coffee beans.

Couli; sauce.

Ganache; frosting.

Pasta salads; lentil and bean salads.

Buttered popcorn; flavored popcorn.

Hazelnuts; pecans.

Figs; kiwis.

Food Follies of 1984

December 29, 1984

Keeping up with the latest eating trends is no easy matter, especially when some foods have a life span of no more than twenty minutes. Whatever, for example, happened to rabbit, which we were all assured was the hot new food of the '80s? Did it peak too soon?

Few years are lucky enough to offer the drama that American duck foie gras brought to 1984. How often does something that unusual and that wonderful make its debut? Like other important new ingredients, American foie gras will have more than its five minutes in the spotlight. It is here to stay. So is brewed decaffeinated coffee as a replacement for Sanka.

But how long can pasta in whatever its latest guise hold center stage? Will *gelato* shops be relegated to second place by the time summer rolls around again?

And what about the fruitwoods and grapevines that are replacing mesquite for grilling meat and fish? The prescient insist that by next year the preferred method of cooking will be to wrap food in straw.

For better or worse, here is the latest reckoning of what's fashionable and what isn't. Its shelf life may be shorter than that of a glass of Champagne.

IN	OUT
Fajitas	*Tostadas*
Crayfish	*Langoustines*
Gelato *shops*	*Cookie shops*
Lemongrass	*Ginger*
Chinese parsley	*Italian parsley*
(fresh coriander)	
Cumin	*Hot peppers*
Pansotti	*Tortellini*
Miniature vegetables	*Sculptured vegetables*
Rack of lamb and veal	*Duck breast*
Chicken potpie	*Chicken McNuggets*
Squash blossoms	*Red-pepper puree*
Rosé Champagne	*Beaujolais nouveau*
Pickled walnuts	*Pickled cucumbers*
Brewed decaffeinated coffee	*Sanka*
Apple and cherry woods and grapevines for grilling	*Mesquite*
Peach, pink, beige for restaurants	*Black, silver and neon*
Tapas	*Sushi*
Fish tartare	*Steak tartare*
Fennel	*Arugula*
Grazing	*Three square meals a day*
Smoked fish	*Smoked Turkey*
Napa Valley	*South of France*
Sicily	*Rome*

IN	**OUT**
Mexican food	*Japanese food*
Wild mushrooms	Champignons de couche *(plain white mushrooms)*
Goat's milk yogurt	*Cow's milk yogurt*
Boutique beer	*National beer brands*
Peasant breads	*Baguettes*
Botarga di tonno*	Alici**

*Dried pressed tuna eggs from Sicily.
**Marinated anchovies from Italy.

In and Out

Americans, ever in search of new culinary adventures, have become quite fickle about food styles. For years the foods we ate appeared to remain the same for at least a decade. Today they are discarded as rapidly as last year's dress.

A look back at the year that has just ended is a graphic demonstration of the haste with which we throw out both the good and the bad. In the beginning of 1985, for example, *tiramisù,* the Italian dessert made with *mascarpone* and ladyfingers, was on everyone's lips. Now no one ever mentions it. Last year cold pasta salads had gone the way of pizza with duck sausage. To some the disappearance of the salads didn't come soon enough.

Scanning the horizon for this year's fashionable food while tacking the demise of last year's there is a clear trend toward American products. That's easy to see when comparing what will be in for 1986 and what will be out.

In	**Out**
Meat loaf	*Pâtés*
Mashed potatoes	*Potatoes Dauphinois*
Corn pudding	*Corn soufflé*
Chicken potpie	*Chicken paillards*

In	Out
Bread pudding	Chocolate mousse
American goat cheese	French goat cheese
Fresh salmon caviar	Canned salmon caviar
California chefs	French chefs
Margaritas	Cajun martinis
Decorative kale	Radicchio
Fiddlehead ferns	Arugula
Fennel	Coriander
Oyster mushrooms	Enoki mushrooms
Venison sausage	Boudin blanc
Marinated salmon	Smoked salmon
Southwestern cooking	Cajun cooking
Crème brûlée	Cold Grand Marnier soufflé
Eating at home	Grazing
Cottage-industry foods	Mass-produced foods

Restaurants

Mega-loud	Loud
Live music	Muzak
Monochromatic color scheme	Peach and beige
Romanesque arches	Classical columns

Well, nobody's perfect. If I could gaze without error into the future, I would abandon this profession.

So no one ever heard of *botarga di tonno* that I said would be in in 1985. Those are dried pressed tuna eggs from Sicily, and they are just about as obscure today as they were at the end of 1984. And I could hardly have been further off base than with my prediction that hot peppers would be out and cumin would be in. Hot peppers were still hot in 1986, when the southwestern food craze was reaching its stride.

I was certainly premature in suggesting that grazing would be out by the end of 1985. It probably won't be out ever. People love to snack.

Perils of a Traveling Cook
June 30, 1984

Not much is gained by being a purist when you are cooking in unfamiliar surroundings if your primary aim is to get the food on the table.

Though that seems reasonable enough to me now, it has taken a number of make-do experiences over a long period to keep me from throwing up my hands in despair and saying, "Forget it!" when I specify Grand Marnier and end up with Drambuie because someone else is doing the shopping.

I must confess that a certain queasiness still manifests itself when I have finished preparing a dish that calls for dry red wine but contains cooking wine because the shopper did not know there is a difference. Queasiness does not compare with the downright horror I felt when my shopping list said a pound of sliced raw turkey breast and the shopper turned up with sliced cooked turkey roll that came complete with corn syrup, salt and a preservative or two. It is hard to make mock veal with capers and lemon out of *cooked* slices of turkey breast, especially in front of a live audience.

Substitutions I have known came to mind this week in Pittsburgh on a book tour, where I was scheduled to make vegetarian chili. The recipe included the following ingredients but contained none of them: fresh and ground coriander, ground cumin, pure chili powder, canned beans without preservatives, and plum tomatoes. It was easy to substitute regular tomatoes for the plum tomatoes, and though I do not like to use canned beans that contain sugar and corn syrup and something to maintain the color in the beans, at least they looked the same. However, the only substitute available for the spices was premixed chili powder that had cumin and pure chili powder but no coriander and a lot of salt.

Well, the chili was good; I must acknowledge that it was. Not the same as the original recipe, but good.

I have not always been so fortunate. Several years ago, at a cooking demonstration before an audience that expected to sample the food, I discovered that the Marsala needed for a zabaglione recipe had not been purchased. It was too late to buy a bottle, but the owner of the cooking shop that housed the demonstration suggested that I substitute some brandy she had on hand. Without thinking I added the same amount of brandy as the Marsala the recipe called for! Halfway into the beating process the light dawned, as they say, and I stuck my finger into the frothy zabaglione. Too late. The far more powerful and alcoholic brandy had overwhelmed the egg and sugar mixture, and it almost overwhelmed me. It also made the zabaglione a funny brown color. There was no dessert for the audience to sample.

Not long ago a shopping list included Grand Marnier, to be poured over sliced peaches. The shopper, wanting to be frugal, supplied Drambuie, which is a Scotch liqueur, for the orange liqueur. That was one substitution I was not willing to make.

Not all cooking experiences require substitutions of lesser quality or inappropriate substance. At another recent demonstration a recipe for meat sauce called for dry wine and that's what I got. The woman who was helping me brought a bottle of Château Cantemerie 1970. Before I opened the bottle, we had the following exchange:

"You must have brought this bottle by mistake. It is very expensive."

"Oh, no. My husband and I get a lot of wine and we don't drink it, so I just put it on the shelf. I don't know anything about it. Don't worry."

Don't worry, indeed! It was the first time I had made meat sauce with a $20 bottle of wine.

The sauce has never been better.

The Times When Enough Is Enough
August 25, 1984

In the supermarket world they call it brand proliferation. In the world of gourmet foods it's called creativity. The results are exactly the same, although chefs and cooks who do the creating would not like to be compared with food technologists who make minute changes in a product to maintain the competitive edge.

When a potato chip company wants to increase its market share, it can try several approaches. Increasing the advertising budget is one method. Adding more products to the line by creating variations on a theme is another. Take the ordinary potato chip. Sitting side by side with it on the grocer's shelf are thick potato chips, potato chips with ripples, potato chips with the skins left on, potato chips without salt, with sour-cream flavor and with cheese flavor, and even potato chips made of extruded dehydrated potatoes, packaged in a tennis-ball can.

How a Display Grew

In the case of the potato chip, the manufacturer started with a natural food. Hamburger Helper is a different matter. The entire line was developed by combining a few spices, chemical additives, a lot of salt and noodles. It was designed to be added to ground beef and thereby form a main dish. With a few little changes in the primary product, Hamburger Helper became Tuna Helper and Lasagna Helper, etc. So now, instead of a single entry on the shelf, Betty Crocker has a big display. Shoppers are more likely to notice it.

Chefs and cooks are not looking to corner the market when they make changes. They do it for variety's sake and to show off their inventiveness. Since nouvelle cuisine freed professionals from following the rigid protocols of classical French cooking, they have been experimenting like mad geniuses. Some of them are geniuses. Some of them are merely mad.

Beurre blanc was once a simple but splendid mixture of butter, vinegar, wine and shallots. It is also known as *beurre Nantais,* after Nantes, the French city where it originated. When Julia Child wrote *Mastering the Art of French Cooking* in 1961, she mentioned a "minor variation" of beurre blanc called *beurre au citron,* in which the shallots are dispensed with and the vinegar and white wine are replaced by lemon juice.

And Now There Are Many

How could she have imagined what would transpire after that tiny variation? Beurre blanc now comes in different colors. Tomato beurre blanc is pale red. Basil beurre blanc is either flecked with green or is pale green. This is an example of chefs using their imaginations to produce gastronomically sound variations on a brilliant idea. Some will argue over whether the variations are as good as the original; few would say that they violate the principle of the sauce.

But the modern-day variations on pesto have changed its fundamental character and given the superb-tasting original a bad name. Not that pesto is made the same all over Italy. Sometimes this aromatic mixture of basil, olive oil and cheese has pine nuts, sometimes walnuts. Different cheeses are used depending on the region in which the pesto is made. It may be a sheep's cheese, it may be Romano or Parmigiano. But it is always made with fresh basil.

The only thing parsley pesto and spinach pesto, two of the more frequently seen versions, have in common with the fresh basil sauce is the color. For recipes to suggest that cooks can substitute parsley or spinach when basil is not available is utter nonsense. The suggested substitution of dried basil in pesto is almost worse. The uninitiated might think that pesto should actually taste that way!

The creativity that has been applied to crème brûlée in the past several years is a perfect example of how a well-trained chef with a good palate can vary a mixture of cream, eggs and brown sugar and produce something splendid and how another, with less skill, can destroy the integrity of the dish. Adding ginger to the incredibly rich mixture introduces a refreshing element that provides the perfect contrast. But adding pineapple to crème brûlée changes its character completely. It becomes a watered-down version of the original dish whose distinctive characteristic, its unctuousness, is lost.

Variation for the sake of novelty or expediency may sell in the world of mass-produced products, but for those who care about food, a croissant stuffed with ratatouille and a Key lime pie made with Persian limes can never replace the original.

Writer's Cupboards Aren't Bare
September 7, 1985

People who write about food for a living have to contend with strange public perceptions of how they cook and eat at home. More than one acquaintance has taken a sidelong glance in my kitchen cupboard to see if I have stashed away any of the processed foods of which I speak so disparagingly: marshmallows, potato chips, canned soup, maybe even SpaghettiOs. From time to time people come up to me in the supermarket and examine the contents of my shopping cart, looking for similar items that would betray me.

For years, such incidents had kept me from serving anything in my house that I hadn't made myself. It is only recently that I have had the courage to buy a dessert instead of making one.

From the comments that have been made over the years I have the impression that a food writer is supposed to serve only food that is made from scratch: bake bread every week, grow and prepare one's own sun-dried tomatoes or even buy goat's milk to make cheese.

Readers may think I churn my own butter and ice cream and have stocks and tomato sauce simmering on the back of the stove for hours. In fact I don't. And as the quality of prepared foods has improved in the past three or four years, it has become easier and easier to let someone else do it. There are a number of excellent ready-made or convenience foods on the market that one can use to speed up cooking without destroying the integrity of the finished product. Some of them I keep in stock in my cupboard, freezer and refrigerator. They sit side by side with the staples common to everyone's cupboard, food writer or otherwise.

Some, like sun-dried tomatoes and commercially prepared frozen chicken and beef stock bases, are staples that simplify inspirational cooking for those quick meals I like to put together when I get home from work. Others, like whole wheat pita and frozen ices, are handy for snacking.

Alongside the frozen ices is an assortment of breads, none of them homemade: semolina, crusty whole wheat French and whole grain English muffins. There is a package of frozen puff pastry and another of phyllo, the translucent sheets of pastry used to make Middle Eastern sweets and savories.

Oriental sesame paste is always on hand in the refrigerator, once it has been opened—upside down. Standing it on its head is some help in blending the oil that rises to the top of the nearly impenetrable paste. Minced garlic in oil, a boon for speedy cooking, must be stored in the refrigerator if you purchase the only kind worth having, without added salt or preservatives.

The cupboard also contains at least one can of tomato puree and of tomato paste, the kind without added salt. Canned corn niblets, the best canned vegetable on the market, are often in residence, along with canned white or kidney beans for a fast chili or salad. Some wonderful jams, marmalades or preserves are always available for breakfast toast.

Occasionally I run out of some of these ingredients but never out of canned tuna, packed in water. Wonderful as fresh tuna may be grilled over an open fire, only canned tuna can satisfy my periodic craving for a sandwich, preferably made with mayonnaise. Out of the jar.

Writer's Cupboards

Since writing the writer's cupboard column I have added at least one stupefyingly modern convenience food to my cupboard: canned chicken broth.

Made by Health Valley, a natural-food company, it contains no sodium, no sugar and no monosodium glutamate. It is also less expensive than Saucier's excellent frozen bases, and for many dishes in which there are numerous other flavors, Health Valley chicken broth does just fine.

The response to this column was hardly what I would have imagined. Dozens of people phoned or wrote asking for the name of the company that manufactures the frozen stock bases. Hoping that it will not change between the time I write this book and its publication date, I am including the name and address: Saucier Inc., 688 Avenue of the Americas, New York, New York 10010.

The column also brought a letter from a former colleague who is a correspondent with CBS radio. Rob Armstrong used to write free-lance food pieces for me when I was food editor of the *Washington Post.*

His letter recounted his problems: "Even today, my past persona as a 'food person' dogs me; people are stunned to learn that in moments of weakness I have let a slice or two of pizza pass my lips, that I have sipped beer and consumed a hot dog at Yankee Stadium and that (horrors!) I have been known to put ketchup on my french fries. (A friend in Dijon makes it sound so elegant —le sauce American, he calls it, and insists it is wonderful with sautéed liver and onions.)"

Frozen Puff Pastry
Worthy of Carême
September 29, 1984

My napoleons used to list. My vol-au-vent looked like cornucopias. Literally thousands of layers of puff pastry passed through my kitchen before I became proficient enough and patient enough to make the napoleons and vol-au-vent stand up straight.

While it's nice to know how to make puff pastry, it's nicer to find that there is now a frozen product on the market that is as good as anything you can make at home.

Puff pastry, or *pâte feuilletée fine,* hundreds of leaves of pastry and butter into which a considerable amount of air has been incorporated, requires a fair amount of technical skill and a lot of time to prepare—six or seven hours. Rough puff pastry, or *demi-feuilletée,* can be done in half the time, but that is still a serious chunk of the day.

Antonin Carême, the founder of *la grande cuisine,* or classic French cooking, who lived from 1784 to 1833, is credited with reviving an interest in pastry. But just who invented the pastry is unclear. Some credit the seventeenth-century French painter Claude Gelée, know as le Lorraine; others credit a pastry cook by the name of Feuillet, whom Carême called "the great Feuillet."

No matter what inspired Carême, puff pastry in one form or another was known to the ancient Greeks and in the Middle Ages. Carême's recipe for *pâte feuilleté* is found in his classic work *Le Pâtissier Royal Parisien.* Julia Child devotes ten pages to its preparation in *Mastering the Art of French Cooking* and twenty-three additional pages to recipes that make use of it.

Though I am a great believer in cooking from scratch, I draw the line at certain things. Puff pastry has become one of them. In years gone by I have tried several alternatives. Many Pepperidge

Farms patty shells were rerolled, but not very effectively, in an effort to make one solid piece. I have driven 1½ hours round-trip to buy prepared puff pastry dough from a commercial bakery that agreed to sell me five pounds. And I have tried a couple of other frozen varieties, but they have been less than satisfactory because they are not made with butter.

I had just about given up until I tried a frozen puff pastry dough made with butter, unbleached flour, water and salt—nothing else—produced by Saucier Cuisine Inc., a company known for its fine frozen sauce bases. The company has come up with a product that will turn anyone who can read into an accomplished pastry baker. The directions on the package are foolproof.

The company has done all the rolling and folding and turning. All the baker has to do is defrost the dough, cut it according to directions, in some cases chilling the shaped dough for twenty minutes, and then bake it.

In working with two packages of the puff pastry the only variations I found were with my oven. Jon Peters, principle owner of the company, says that because of variations in ovens it is best to bake most puff pastry recipes at 375 degrees. That way it will not burn before all the leaves have baked. I tried baking some at 400 as many books recommend, and while the smaller items, like miniature and medium-size vol-au-vents were fine, when I baked an entire sheet of the puff pastry in order to make a napoleon, the interior leaves were not quite done before the pastry had turned golden brown. Baking at 375 degrees solved the problem.

The Color Purple in Vegetables
September 13, 1986

Americans constantly seek change. We are enthralled with the new, bored with the old, sometimes within a matter of months, even weeks. Now that we have discovered that tomatoes come in other colors besides red, that peppers are available in every rainbow color except blue, we are not satisfied with the traditional. And thanks to the specialty-crop farmer, we don't have to be.

What we consider traditional today was not traditional in the nineteenth century. And the more we see of these old fruits and vegetables in unusual colors the more we want.

Every year there are new surprises. Last year yellow tomatoes captivated our attention in every size and variety, along with yellow watermelon, yellow raspberries and yellow beets. Before that it was white eggplant and blue potatoes, though the potatoes never caught on the way the eggplant has.

This year it is the color purple. Purple has been edging its way into vegetable bins for the past several years. Purple cauliflower will appear from time to time along with purple broccoli and purple peppers.

But last month at the annual Tasting of Summer Produce held in Oakland, California, where small farmers exhibit their wares to restaurateurs, caterers and others, I saw an array of purple vegetables that was staggering. There were purple Peruvian potatoes, deep purple Royal Burgundy beans, purple-hulled crowder peas, purple okra—which is sort of deep red—purple baby kohlrabi, and cauliflower that was a mixture of purple and white.

Lee Grimsbo, head of the produce department at Dean & DeLuca, says commercial agriculture wiped out the variety of colored foods that were once available. "But with the resurgence of market gardening," Grimsbo said, "of the small farmers who come in and sell directly to cities, different-colored foods are coming back. The little variety we have had had to do with economics, not with what people wanted."

Many of these unusual fruits and vegetables are often part of the spectacular produce displays at Dean & DeLuca.

Jefferson Lowe, marketing director for Underwood Ranches, a large grower of specialty produce in Soanis, California, traces this interest in unusually colored specialty crops to nouvelle cuisine and its emphasis on spectacular presentations. "The French have been doing baby vegetables for some time," he said. "It trickled over to New York and then came west because of our long growing season. The thing with the color revolves around plate presentation and simply offering the consumer a greater choice. People are just into it. I think it's a statement on the part of consumers who are interested in better-tasting crops."

Most of these purple vegetables turn green once they are cooked. According to Lowe, the only vegetables that retain their purple color after cooking are kohlrabi and potatoes. "If you steam some of the other vegetables very lightly, and we're talking about ninety seconds," he said, "they will retain their color. They are for people who like their vegetables just warm and very, very crunchy."

But a plate of purple mashed potatoes is a pretty spectacular visual concept, if a bit unnerving.

Purple Vegetables

There was no room in the purple vegetable column to talk about purple carrots, which, Jefferson Lowe explained, were the color of the wild carrots from which our orange cultivated carrots are descended. Lowe also explained that when any part of a carrot above the ground is exposed to frost, it turns purple.

A letter from a Connecticut reader says that he encountered purple carrots at the weekly market in a Majorcan village where he and his wife did their weekly shopping in the 1970s.

They were quite common there.

In Connecticut, a Briton Pursues Perfect Barbecue
July 21, 1984

He may sometimes wear Texas garb and he may be slicing delicious, authentic Texas barbecue, but when he speaks, you know that Robert Pearson is from the part of London where Eliza Doolittle lived. What is a Cockney doing in Stratford, Connecticut, running a barbecue carryout in a converted roadside hamburger stand that dates from the 1950s?

Improbable as that may seem, the story is stranger still. Until Pearson opened Stick to Your Ribs in September 1983, he was a hairdresser. Three years ago, at age forty-four, he thought that it was time for a career change. His avocation was cooking, so he decided to enter the food business.

After giving up the idea of selling ready-to-bake soufflés because the market was not there and discarding a pizza carryout because the field was overpopulated, he settled on barbecue, perhaps the fastest-growing trend in the country. Other people have settled on barbecue too, but they have not taken the time or trouble to explore it that Pearson has.

A Texas Aficionado

Pearson, who was away on the day I visited his stand, said in a telephone interview that he had become a barbecue devotee during many trips to Texas. Whenever he visited, he said, "the first thing friends would do is take me out to a barbecue place." He went on: "It always tasted terrific no matter what you did with it. There were always miles of people and lots of fun, and it smelled so good, you really got a high just being there."

So Pearson gave up his salon leases at several Bloomingdale's stores and traveled not only to Texas but also to the Carolinas, Kansas and Florida, exploring the nuances of barbecue. When he learned everything he could, he searched for a place in Manhattan, but, he said, "at $110 a square foot per month for rent I was frightened." Then he ran into a man who owned a soon-to-be-vacant hamburger stand in Stratford and the price was right: $12 a foot. The location, 150 yards west of I-95, was an easy stop for travelers.

More important, after the shock of seeing a spot so remote from his city apartment, Pearson realized that "all of the best barbecue places were always off the beaten track, always funky and never on Main Street."

His low rent has given him a chance to make mistakes without going broke almost at once. First he experimented with rolls, trying three kinds before discovering the Portuguese variety he now uses. He tried several cuts of the various meats he serves before finding the right ones.

In three months Pearson thinks he will have it all "exactly right"; he hardly seems far from there now, judging from two tastings of his barbecue. Butchering the meat on the premises, grinding the peppers he buys from Casa Moneo on West 14th Street to make four strengths of hot sauce, using mesquite purchased from a man in New Jersey who brings it from Texas, Stick to Your Ribs serves barbecue even a Texan would admire. The wood-burning oven, in which one thousand pounds of meat can be cooked at a time, is also from Texas.

In this part of the country, where barbecue means slathering a piece of meat with sauce and cooking it quickly over a grill, Pearson's authentic food is a surprise because the flavor of the smoking permeates the meat. Chicken is juicy-tender with a light smoke flavor, ribs are meaty without much fat, pork shoulder moist, and brisket—called Texas beef—with its strong smoke flavor lean but not at all dry.

The chopped barbecues range in heat from mild for the chicken to warm for the chewy beef and moderately hot and flavorful for the pork. A mildly hot Texas chili is suffused with the smoky flavor of the various peppers. A chili with beans is called New England chili; Pearson explained, "Texas would crucify me if I called it chili."

The sauces range from "mild" to "mean." The mean version contains not only chili pequin but also Sichuan peppercorns, known for their bite. Of the side dishes my favorite is moist corn sticks spiked with bits of jalapeño peppers and cheese.

Barbecued Rattlesnake a Sellout

There are often such specials as barbecued rattlesnake— "which sells out every time"—venison, boar, alligator and whole pigs. I did not taste the more exotic items.

"My place," Mr. Pearson says with a great deal of pride, "smells just like all those places in Texas."

Stick to Your Ribs is just off Exit 31 of the New England Thruway and is open six days a week from 10 A.M. to 9 P.M. and Sundays from 5 P.M. The telephone number is 203-377-1752.

Robert Pearson's Barbecue

Several summers ago Stick to Your Ribs barbecue was part of a taste test with barbecue from other parts of the country, including one of the best known, Sonny Bryan's of Dallas. Stick to Your Ribs brisket won first place; its sauce second only to Sonny Bryan's. It is so good that people from Texas are ordering it!

Good news: You don't have to live in Connecticut to enjoy Stick to Your Ribs barbecued brisket. It is available by mail order. Prices are subject to change, but when this was written, an eight-pound whole brisket was available with a pint of sauce for $75, shipping included, anywhere in the continental United States. The sauce comes in four strengths: mild, medium, madness and meanness.

For more information or to place an order, write Stick to Your Ribs, 1785 Stratford Avenue, Stratford, Connecticut 06497, or call 203-377-1752.

At the Automat, Memories Are Free

July 21, 1987

"Extraordinary how potent cheap music is," says a character in Noël Coward's *Private Lives*. The macaroni and cheese at the Automat is equally potent.

Although it has been forty years since I made my first trip to this precursor of the fast-food carryout, I have never forgotten the macaroni and cheese. Or the hot dog and baked beans, the brown bread or the cut-up spaghetti with tomato sauce that our group shared.

Today there is only one Automat left, anywhere—on the corner of 42nd Street and Third Avenue in Manhattan. The Horn & Hardart operations, filled with their windowed shoe boxes, have gone the way of the soda fountains and their little glass dishes of chocolate sprinkles.

I have passed the remaining Automat hundreds of times as an adult, but I had never been tempted to go in, preferring to preserve the special memories of my one childhood encounter.

This week, curiosity got the better of me. Even before I entered, I had second thoughts: a sign outside for David's cookies was clear indication that the Automat had changed. After I went through the door I was certain I had made a mistake. Off to the right loomed a vast cafeteria. But then I spotted them straight ahead. Those little windows under the white-on-black, Art Deco signs for beverages, sandwiches, hot meals, pies, pastries. It was like a trip back to the '40s before there were salad bars, croissants or yogurt.

The cashier who used to turn dollars into nickels now turns dollars into tokens, brass ones worth 75 cents each, and silver ones, which will buy you a 40-cent cup of coffee. The coffee still streams out into heavy china mugs from the same dolphin spouts Joseph V. Horn found in Italy. And the powerful brew tastes exactly the same: hot, strong and slightly burned. No wimpy decaffeinated coffee here.

In fact, everything but the hot dog tastes the same. The macaroni and cheese, flecked golden brown, is a little like Franco-American used to be in its heyday. All of the forty-year-old goodness remains. Tuna on soggy white bread with battle-fatigued lettuce that sticks to the roof of your mouth and refuses to let go is equally comforting. The apple pie has exactly the same amount of glutinous filler, I'm quite sure.

I used to love Heinz Vegetarian Beans with hot dogs on Saturday night. The Automat's deep, dark beans are just as good as the Heinz version used to be. (The hot dog, however, has not weathered the years; it's mushy.) Crisp, crusty fish cakes have that slightly fishy taste, and someone continues to cut the spaghetti into small pieces, just the way my mother (and the Automat) used to. Waves of nostalgia swept over me.

Some of the old crowd has remained faithful to this vestige of the days before McDonald's took over: men in knitted caps, women with silver-blue hair, a paunchy gray-haired man who chain-smokes and talks to an imaginary friend. But there is a new generation of Automat diner: secretaries, young executives with briefcases, mothers and children in search of reasonable prices and variety. Most of them, however, prefer to select from the cafeteria line, with its up-to-date salad bar, its steam-table meat loaf and mashed potatoes, roast beef and creamed spinach.

The cafeteria sells the same dishes that are dispensed from the machines, but somehow they just don't taste the same.

Automat—What's Left

Readers with long memories are divided over the remaining Horn & Hardart Automat I wrote about. "It seems to me that it is false to celebrate the 'survival' of a Horn and Hardart Automat that was the only modern one built, that soon offered counterfeit quality of the H and H specialties and that has remained only because the building it occupies remains," wrote a Manhattanite more cynical than I. "If it had been free-standing I doubt if it would be extant today."

I agree, it isn't the same, but it's all we have and I guess I feel more like another New Yorker who wrote:

> When I was a kid—in the days when double-decker buses moved north and south on Fifth Avenue—my mother instilled in me a profound love for the Automat. Although a certified member of what was then called "The Smart Set," she was inexorably drawn to those locations where, she swore, the best coffee and pumpkin pie in America could be had—and for 35 cents.
>
> I measured passing decades by Automat closings and wondered—and continued to wonder over the years—where their special constituencies disappeared to: the Yorkville Daily Worker readers at the 86th Street branch; the racetrack touts and show-biz hot-shots at Broadway and 46th; the Bulgarian immigrants at 57th and 6th; the hookers, pimps and deaf-and-dumb school students at 42nd and 8th, etc.

After long years of self-denial, I found myself, a few months ago, wandering like a zombie to the last remaining H&H Automat and was deeply moved, like yourself, to find that some things remained the same. The macaroni and cheese, thank god. The baked beans aren't the fat slithery kind of yore, but they'll do. The sliced bologna on whole wheat bread and still in its little window. And, of course, the coffee.

The steam table, as you pointed out, is almost a total loss. And one remembered greatness—their now long lost formula for French dressing, gone, gone forever.

Anyway, one reader's appreciation for your effort to keep the memory of my personal carbohydrate heaven alive.

China Sky: No Soy Sauce

February 28, 1987

HONG KONG, Feb. 27—What would you expect to be served on a flight from Hong Kong to Beijing on C.A.A.C., the Chinese national airline? Shrimp-fried rice, sesame noodles, litchis in syrup? Chicken and peapods, red braised beef, steamed rice?

Not on your life. Marriott or its equivalent, has beaten me to China. To Thailand, too. When the familiar serving cart rolled down the aisle on C.A.A.C. Flight 110 and a little plastic tray appeared with roll, Danish, butter, two crackers, the ubiquitous wedge of Tiger Gruyère (pasteurized processed cheese, product of Switzerland), canned pear half with dabs of aerosol whipped cream, plastic knife, fork and spoon—not a chopstick in sight—I had visions of spaghetti and meatballs for a main course.

The Inscrutable Feast

I was not far off. Inside the covered aluminum dish were noodles, possibly Chinese, and what millions of American college students have for years been calling mystery meat. Brown and thinly sliced, in a thick, equally mysterious sauce, it could have been made in New York, Australia, England, Argentina or, as it now seems, China. No Chinese seasonings were discernible: no ginger, no soy sauce, no garlic and certainly no coriander. Sitting next to the mystery meat were a few gray-green beans.

I felt right at home. This could have been Eastern or United or American, flying from New York to Los Angeles. I should not have been surprised. Earlier the drink cart had gone by with Del Monte juices, Pepsi-Cola and 7-Up.

To be absolutely fair there was a cold salad of cellophane noodles, strips of ham, chicken and carrots, all salted. The only thing that gave it away as Chinese were the noodles. Discernible Oriental seasonings were not in evidence. The accompanying salad of pickled vegetables would have been perfectly comfortable on a table at a kosher restaurant next to the dill pickles and green tomatoes.

"Where are the chopsticks?" I asked the young Chinese man sitting next to me. "And why a roll and crackers?"

"Probably because most of the people who travel on the plane are foreigners," he said, making a sandwich of his cheese wedge and crackers. "Many come from Hong Kong, and they are used to knives and forks."

Flying to Bangkok on Thai Airways International from Seattle was similar, but I was prepared: when boarding, I caught sight of a Marriott truck loading the plane's galley.

The service on Thai was impeccable, the food was continental. One dish had some subtle tones of Thai seasoning, but they were overshadowed by the pâté en gelée, the caviar, assorted cheeses, strawberry tart and unexotic fruit—apples, bananas, pineapple and oranges. In fact, it was a struggle throughout a trip to the Orient not only to persuade hosts that I preferred to dine on the food of the country instead of bacon and eggs, but also that I wanted it cooked just as if local people were eating it.

As for Gruyère cheese in China, where are standards?

Putting Exotica to the Taste Test
March 7, 1987

Every culture has at least one food that is an acquired taste for anyone not brought up on it: lutefisk in Norway, fish maw in China, haggis in Scotland, Vegemite in Australia. As such these foods present a challenge to those who have a professional interest in food. We want to know what it is that people who have eaten them from birth find so appealing. We are curious whether this appeal bridges cultural barriers.

This brings us to durian, a fruit that is grown in Thailand as well as in the Philippines and Indonesia. According to Jennifer Brennan, author of *The Original Thai Cookbook,* it has a "strong, offensive odor, comparable to rotten onions and stale cheese." She should know; she lived in Thailand for more than ten years.

Thais are often quite certain that Westerners will not like durian; many Thais don't like it. Nat Boonthanakit, public-relations officer for the Tourism Authority of Thailand in New York, said that some members of his family "simply can't stand the thought of having a durian in their house." This was all the more reason to taste one on a visit to Thailand.

I was disappointed to find that the season would not start until a few weeks after I left. But driving along a street in Chaing Mei, a city in northern Thailand, I saw a truck at roadside selling what looked like durians, rather distinctive fruit that, once you have seen them, you are unlikely to forget. They are about the size of miniature watermelons and vary in shape from irregularly ovoid to round; they are greenish-yellow when ripe, and their very thick skin is covered with short, sharp spikes, much like a mace.

I asked the driver to stop and watched while the woman who was selling this very early crop carefully selected one for another customer by tapping it, and after weighing it, painstakingly opened it. The man turned over the equivalent of about $10, a princely sum in Thailand (those who love durians are willing to rush the season). My guide couldn't believe I wanted to spend that much on something he was sure I wouldn't like.

It took the seller at least five minutes to find one she thought was ripe, but after opening it, she realized that it was not ready to eat and had to find another. The second time she chose correctly.

I expected to be bowled over by the odor when I opened the durian I bought. What a surprise to find that it was not at all unpleasant and that the pale yellow flesh had an appealingly creamy, custard-like texture and a very sweet taste. My Thai friends, it seemed, were wrong.

It was with great pleasure, then, that I discovered frozen durian at several Thai markets in New York. Freezing certainly would not improve the texture of the fruit, but it seemed unlikely to have an effect on either the smell or the taste. After defrosting a package this week, I may have to rethink that. The odor was quite as Jennifer Brennan had described it, so strong in fact that I discarded what I had defrosted after one bite. I was reminded of the advice to hold my nose while eating it.

But Mr. Boonthanakit did not want me to give up so quickly. "It may have been overripe," he said. "And when they are overripe, they tend to smell more. The only way I eat frozen durian is with sticky rice." This is the traditional way it is served. The durian is cooked with the sticky rice in coconut milk and a bit of palm sugar. The coconut milk "neutralizes the durian," Mr. Boonthanakit explained.

He has promised me a recipe, and I will give the remaining durian in my freezer one last chance.

Durian Fans All

I could not believe that I would receive five letters on the subject of the durian. I didn't think that many people knew what it was! One of the letters was from Atlanta, from Elliott Mackle, a writer who had found durian-flavored cookies in an Oriental market there. He said the cookies closely resembled our vanilla cream—sandwich wafers.

> *Except for the aroma, of course. The fragrance and taste, if not absolutely addictive, are pleasant and unusual, reminding me of moonlit coconut groves and tropical backyards. I'm now on my second bag, and luckily the metallic-foil bags are small, because the wafers must be eaten at one sitting. If saved and rewrapped, even in an airtight plastic container, the odor permeates the storage cabinet.*

I could hardly wait to prowl through Chinatown and on my very first stop I found two brands of durian cookies. One was in a heavy-duty tin and I chose that because of the odor problem. I ate one and decided that fresh durian, eaten out doors, was the only way I liked the fruit. I fed one to my husband who ate it and then realized what it was and decided one was enough. I took the rest to the office.

You have to understand something about a newspaper office in order to appreciate what happened. Newspaper people will eat anything you leave out for them. It doesn't matter how awful it is. If it's free, they take it.

People gathered round the spot where food is usually put out for giveaways when they saw this large tin arrive. Several people helped to open it, dove in for a cookie and ate one. As they were eating, a peculiar look spread across their faces: one that said they had made a mistake. After that, everyone who came by smelled the cookies first and then left them. At the end of the day the tin was still there with half the cookies.

Unheard of at *The New York Times*. I threw the rest in the trash and have no record of what happened to them after that.

A Short Hills, New Jersey, reader wrote that she was thrilled to find out that durian was available frozen here. She said she had eaten her first one about eight years ago and had been hooked ever since.

> *I would pay any price for a fresh one—truthfully the durian eating experience is one of the things I miss most about Asia.*
>
> *None of my kids, nor my husband, cares for the taste and I used to be forced to eat it out on my terrace in Hong Kong. Unfortunately they knew when I had purchased one because my car always gave me away.*

She was off to buy frozen durian.

A Key Biscayne, Florida, resident sent a drawing of a fruit which he said is called "guanabana" in Cuba. He wondered if it was the same. From his description it seems to have several characteristics in common with the durian—"soft, pulpy whitish with a creamy tinge" is how he described the inside. "A soft, thick, cold puree drink of it is called 'Champola.' They also prepare it as ice cream called 'Helado de Guanabana.'"

Does anyone know if the two fruits are related?

FOOD

No mistaking the contents of this section. It contains some of the recipes that I have cherished ever since I learned how to cook along with some newcomers that have struck my fancy.

Plum Torte probably qualifies as the oldest, having been in my recipe box for almost thirty-five years, and Tapioca Zabaglione Custard with Fresh Berries as the newest since I acquired it only last year. My love affair with this recent acquisition can be traced back to an earlier romance, one I had as a child with my mother's instant tapioca pudding.

Purple Plums: From Tree to Torte
August 14, 1984

The first thing I think of when someone says purple plums is not just those sweet shapes with yellow flesh. Instead I see a freezer full of plum tortes and feel a twinge of pain.

One of the first recipes given me after I was married was for a thin, rich torte made with purple or, as they are sometimes known, Italian or prune plums. It was also one of the first desserts that I learned could be frozen. I became so enamored of this delicious, homey recipe that when the plums were at their cheapest, between late August and October—19 cents a pound in those days—I would make half a dozen tortes and freeze them.

They were especially appealing on a raw February day, briefly warmed in the oven to emphasize the fragrance of the cinnamon and bring out the flavor of the butter and eggs and plums. They were also marvelous gifts.

I had worked out an assembly-line arrangement to speed the process of making more. A friend who loved the tortes said that in exchange for two she would let me store as many as I wanted in her freezer. A week later she went on vacation for two weeks and her mother stayed with the children. Upon my friend's return she asked:

"How many of those tortes did you leave in my freezer?"

"Twenty-four, but two of those were for you."

There was a long pause. "Well, I guess my mother either ate twelve of them or gave them away."

Nothing on the wrappings indicated to whom the tortes belonged, and my friend forgot to tell her mother about them. Her mother must have liked her first sample. The children, too, and possibly the neighbors.

Despite this painful experience I continued to make the tortes.

Purple plums are one of the few fruits that taste better cooked than raw; their full flavor and sweetness are heightened when they soften.

PLUM TORTE

    1 *cup sugar*
  ½ *cup unsalted butter*
    1 *cup unbleached flour, sifted*
    1 *teaspoon baking powder*
      Pinch of salt
    2 *eggs*
 24 *halves pitted purple plums*
      Topping: sugar, lemon juice, cinnamon

1. Cream the sugar and butter. Add the flour, baking powder, salt and eggs and beat well.
2. Spoon the batter into a 9-inch springform pan. Place the plum halves skin side up on top of the batter. Sprinkle lightly with sugar and lemon juice, depending on the sweetness of the fruit. Sprinkle with about 1 teaspoon of cinnamon, depending on how much you like cinnamon.
3. Bake at 350 degrees for 1 hour. Remove and cool; refrigerate or freeze if desired. Or cool to lukewarm and serve plain or with vanilla ice cream or whipped cream.
4. To serve frozen tortes defrost and reheat briefly at 300 degrees.

YIELD: 8 Servings

Painful Plum Memories

The recipe for the plum torte is one of the simplest I know. I was a new bride when I began making plum tortes, but there is no accounting for how people follow directions, or the ability of their ovens to perform accurately.

No recipe I ever printed brought more requests from people who had forgotten to clip it out or had misplaced the clipping.

No recipe brought more complaints from people who had failures. One reader demanded an apology because the batter leaked out of her springform pan all over the oven. Instead of an apology I should have sent her a new springform pan. I used to have a springform pan like that. It leaked cheesecake all over the oven until I began to wrap aluminum foil around it.

I had to write another column telling all these cooks with failures what they had probably done wrong. The second column read in part:

I look forward to trying several versions of plum torte that were offered after a recent column, but not the one my friend Paul Goldman of Livingston, New Jersey, mistakenly made with rye flour. He maintains it was dark in the kitchen and he didn't notice the color of the flour. (I have known him a long time, and I maintain he doesn't know much about cooking.)

One reader suggested reducing the teaspoon of baking powder in the recipe to half a teaspoon so the batter would not rise as high and fewer of the plums would fall to the bottom, but I like the plums on the bottom. There were, however, a lot of readers who do not like plums on the bottom. "The recipe seemed simple and I followed it exactly," wrote a cook from Manhattan, "and the cake swallowed up the plums! It rose and rose and the fruit disappeared. Could there have been a typo in the amount of baking powder?

"From the ingredients I anticipated a 'cookie-like' base, but sad to say, it was a disaster. Also fruit skin side up? Other open fruit tart recipes usually have the cut side up."

I won't bore you with all the similar letters.

The baking powder is correct. The dough is not cookie-like at all. It is extremely moist and cakelike. The fruit is skin side up. And this is a torte, which is a cake, not an "open fruit tart."

The questions were endless.

Some readers said they had trouble taking the torte out of the springform pan, not realizing that cakes baked in a springform can be served directly from the bottom once the sides have been removed.

For those who want to reuse the springform immediately, it may be lined with heavy-duty aluminum foil. When the torte is baked, it can be removed, foil and all.

And for the reader who found that the torte was not done after the hour's baking time, a temperature check of the oven is in order. No more than an hour should be necessary if the directions are carefully followed.

Along with the questions and complaints, one reader said she had been inspired to get up early and head for her plum tree "to beat the crows to the plums from now on." And she made three tortes and froze them for a wedding in the fall.

The column appeared in August 1984. The following February I received a letter from a reader who said she'd been waiting for that "raw February day" for the fragrances. She put her defrosted torte in the oven and, when it was warm, took it out and cut into it. It had, she wrote—and I could hear her teeth gnashing—"a pudding-like consistency." Another new oven is in order at her home.

It is now August 1986. A request came in the mail last week for the plum torte from a lady in Birmingham, Michigan. Speaking of the plum torte she wrote, "That is the best recipe and I've lost it! At our house, my son does the cooking, and I am in charge of dessert. I've never been a good cook, but that plum dessert I can handle. Please, oh please, send me a copy of the recipe. I would try anything you recommend."

Three more requests by the middle of September. Plus this lovely note from a New Jersey reader: "Your plum torte recipe is one of my family's favorites. So imagine my delight while making one a week or so ago to hear you chatting with Joan Hamburg on WOR (a local radio talk show). I felt as if I were at the party. We've already eaten two this fall and have more in the freezer."

I can't bear all the pain out there and am forced to reprint the recipe one more time. We are thinking of making it an annual event.

Tapioca Pudding: Comfort Food Fit for a President
May 2, 1987

"Tapioca is the teddy bear of desserts, an edible security blanket," wrote Jane and Michael Stern in *Square Meals*, their compendium of all the wonderful and terrible things we ate as children. My sentiments exactly. They were shared by Lyndon B. Johnson. After his heart attack in 1955, when he was Senate majority leader, the idea of being deprived of desserts was something he would not put up with. Fortunately a member of his staff, Juanita Roberts, had been a dietician, and she devised many low-calorie recipes.

Learning to Substitute

The family cook, Zephyr Wright, learned to substitute skim milk and saccharin for whole milk and sugar in desserts, including tapioca pudding, which she topped with ersatz whipped cream and a slice of red cherry. Johnson became devoted to it—so devoted that when he was on a trip to Southeast Asia as president in 1966, reporters asserted that he went to Kuala Lumpur, the capital of Malaysia, just to see cassava plants growing. The much-loved tapioca is extracted from the root of the cassava.

Several other reporters remember visiting him in the Naval Hospital in Bethesda, Maryland, when he was recovering from an operation. He insisted on spoon-feeding them some of his favorite dessert, tapioca pudding. They clearly did not think much of it, although they didn't tell the president so. Perhaps the dietetic version wasn't to their taste.

Or perhaps tapioca haters are in the majority. With descriptions like the ones in food encyclopedias, who needs enemies? "Very easily digested," one says, "and one of the most satisfactory starchy foods for persons of weak digestion." Another puts it this way: "A favorite with the cooks in large institutions such as hospitals, army mess halls and college dormitories."

Even the Sterns acknowledge that not everyone loves "the funny little pellets of cassava plant starch, known in diner lingo as 'fisheyes,' but no nursery chef can allow personal prejudices to limit his or her repertoire." In fact tapioca pudding, like bread pudding, is coming into fashion because we have tired of the overwrought and want things simple and homey. But I loved it before it was fashionable, and whenever I am asked what my favorite comfort food is, my mother's tapioca pudding comes immediately to mind. It was one of the first things I learned to make myself, and more than once I ate it before it had even cooled.

My mother did not make tapioca pudding from the old-fashioned pearl tapioca. She made it from instant tapioca—the same recipe, I suspect, as the one on the box I used this week. Hers was thicker, though, probably because she used less milk. She knew how to doctor even the most plebeian recipes, and when she was done her tapioca pudding was the best on the block. After it was cooked she folded in drained crushed pineapple, and after the mixture had cooled a bit she folded in whipped cream.

Tapioca pudding came to mind recently when I tasted the most elegant and sophisticated version I have ever had. It is the creation of the Ark Restaurant in Nahcotta, Washington, and it is little kin to the version made with instant tapioca. It fits today's image of the perfect dessert: soothing and gluttonously rich. Instead of milk the recipe calls for half-and-half. It also has Marsala wine. As if that were not enough, it is topped with whipped cream and, perhaps to cut the cream, is served with berries.

This tapioca pudding is really tapioca zabaglione custard. I recommend it without reservation. If, however, you prefer a virtuous tapioca pudding that is really quite good, follow the directions on the package of instant tapioca, but use the Johnson formula: two tablespoons of sugar instead of five, and skim milk instead of whole. Skip the saccharin and ersatz whipped cream—and the Maraschino cherry. The following recipe is adapted from the Ark Restaurant's.

TAPIOCA ZABAGLIONE CUSTARD WITH FRESH BERRIES

1/3 cup pearl tapioca
6 ounces water
2½ cups half-and-half
1/4 cup Marsala
4 to 6 tablespoons sugar
2 eggs
1/2 pint berries
1/2 pint heavy cream, whipped

1. Soak the tapioca in the water overnight or for several hours until it has absorbed almost all the water.
2. Drain and combine with the half-and-half in a heavy-bottomed pan. Bring to a boil stirring constantly with a wire whisk. Reduce the heat and simmer 20 minutes, stirring often.
3. Add the Marsala. Simmer 25 minutes longer, stirring often. Remove from the heat.
4. Beat the sugar with the eggs and, stirring constantly, spoon one-third of the tapioca mixture into the egg mixture. Then return all to the tapioca mixture, stirring.
5. Return to low heat and cook 5 minutes. Do not boil.
6. Spoon into dessert glasses and cool. When ready to serve, decorate with berries and whipped cream.

YIELD: 4 to 6 servings.

Tapioca Loved or Loathed

No loathers among the letter writers, but not many lovers, either. In fact, I must confess it was very difficult to find pearl tapioca in order to try the recipe. I tried four supermarkets; then called around to five or six specialty markets before calling a friend who advised me of a German specialty market. And sure enough, they had pearl tapioca.

That's what I have to tell a friend from Random House who

wrote: "Has pearl tapioca become a specialty-store item? We can get jicama at the local supermarket but not real tapioca?" He said he had tried four supermarkets and could find nothing but Minute tapioca and Jell-O tapioca pudding, "not, I assumed, what you (or your mother) had in mind. Luckily, in scouring the cellar pantry, I located a half-full box of pearl tapioca, dating from prehistoric times. In short, it worked fine and was, in fact, incomparably better than I remembered the stuff."

Helen Witty, a food writer, cookbook-author friend, said she was delighted to see me defending tapioca. "Like you, I have always loved it—we had a creamy, fluffy version at home, very soothing—and I have always been amused when people say 'Yuck' at the very idea."

Panzanella, a Salad Perfect for Summer
June 21, 1986

Waverley Root speaks none too fondly of *panzanella:* "a poor man's lunch," he calls it, "salad dressing on bread, producing a sogginess which accounts for its name (little swamp)." Mr. Root and his palate notwithstanding, *panzanella* is one terrific lunch. Basically a Tuscan bread salad with oil and vinegar, what else it contains depends on who is doing the cooking.

Tuscans call *panzanella* a cold picnic dish, with the ingredients put together at the last minute, the bread soaked in water at home, the tomatoes and cucumbers simply picked from the vines as needed. But one Roman source describes it as a first course served in large families to fill everyone up before the more expensive second-course dishes are put on the table. Tony May, the owner of Sandro's, Palio and La Camelia, three Italian restaurants in Manhattan, says the dish is also called *pane molle,* which means "soft bread."

Whatever its real name and its true antecedents, I have been thinking about how sorry I am I didn't have thirds of *panzanella* last week. Sandro Fioriti, the chef at Sandro's at 420 East 59th Street, was serving it from enormous Italian pottery bowls at a party. It was especially appealing on a humid evening.

Earthy and satisfying, *panzanella* is, at the same time, cool and refreshing. In *The Food of the Western World*, Theodora FitzGibbon talks about the anchovies, chilies, basil, garlic and capers it contains but never mentions tomatoes, except as a garnish. Other recipes call for onion, cucumber and celery. One calls for spring onions rather than yellow or red onions. Fioriti uses both green and red peppers.

I associate *panzanella* with summer because I had always assumed that tomatoes were an essential ingredient, and they are not worth eating unless they are perfect. The basil, too, must be fresh and sprightly.

The proportions vary from cook to cook. Some use vast quantities of olive oil—six ounces to a half pound of bread—while others use only two ounces for a pound of bread. In fact, *panzanella* is a salad designed to be made with leftover, stale bread and whatever of the other ingredients are available.

Italian bread—purists insist it must be Tuscan bread—is also indispensable, though there have been recipes suggesting the substitution of whole wheat bread or rye bread for those who are not fortunate enough to have easy access to the compactly textured Italian, or even French, country loaves. I would just as soon not make *panzanella* with rye bread, thank you, any more than I can imagine making it with dried oregano in place of fresh basil, as one cookbook suggested.

PANZANELLA

   1 *pound whole wheat Italian (or French) bread, several days old*
   3 *pounds tomatoes*
½ *pound red onion*
   1 *large red or green bell pepper*
½ *cup red wine vinegar*
   6 *tablespoons extra-virgin olive oil*
     Salt and freshly ground black pepper to taste.
20 *fresh basil leaves*

1. Cut the bread into thick slices and trim away the crust. Soak it in ice-cold water for 15 minutes. Drain and squeeze out the

water with your hands and crumble. Spread the bread out in a single layer while making the rest of the recipe.

2. Dice the tomatoes, and thinly slice the onion. Core, seed and then dice the pepper.

3. Beat the vinegar and oil with salt and pepper to taste.

4. In a salad bowl place the bread, tomatoes, onion, pepper and basil. Spoon on the dressing and toss; adjust the seasonings and serve at once.

YIELD: 6 to 8 servings

Panzanella

So much for Waverley Root, a man I thought never made any mistakes about etymology or food history.

Unless, of course, our correspondent from Jackson Heights, New York, is wrong. He wrote: "The Italian words for swamp are *pantano* and *palude*, and in no way do they contribute to the root of *panzanella*. A *panzana* in Italian is a lie, a fib. *Panza,* on the other hand, is the vulgar word for belly. The word actually refers to the English paunch, a potbelly. One would best speculate on the idea of emptying out a half loaf of crusty Italian bread, soaking it and filling it with whatever raw vegetables are edible, seasoned with garlic, olive oil, salt and vinegar. It would be filling the paunch, so to speak."

Anyone else want to weigh in on this?

Granted that the recipe is "good and correct," a reader from Arlington, Virginia, still wanted to set the record straight. "*Never, never, never* put peppers of any kind or color into this dish. Apart from not being authentic it just doesn't taste right."

Despite the sentiment expressed, an awful lot of people lost the recipe and wanted another copy.

The Tuna Sandwich:
However You Like It
March 2, 1985

The *Joy of Cooking* has failed me. After more than twenty-five years of finding everything I ever needed in it, the cookbook came up short this week when I was searching for the quintessential tuna fish sandwich.

Perhaps that is because Irma Rombauer never wanted to become embroiled in the controversy. But how can any book that purports to cover the American cooking scene omit the mainstay of almost everyone's childhood?

Mrs. Rombauer is not alone. There is no recipe for a tuna fish sandwich in *Square Meals*, Jane and Michael Stern's otherwise commendable book about American eating habits over the past sixty years. The book has recipes for tuna casseroles, meat loaf sandwiches, peanut butter sandwiches, but none for tuna fish sandwiches.

The late James Beard turned out to be either more courageous or a better culinary historian, acknowledging the importance of the tuna sandwich in *American Cookery.* He suggests four parts tuna to one part celery, with a bit of grated raw onion and egg mixed in and enough mayonnaise to make a thick paste. But there are a lot of people who would argue with his ingredients. Passions run high when it comes to the proper way to make a tuna fish sandwich.

If you are willing to accept my survey of ten people as a valid guide, nine out of ten love them. The tenth person, however, actively dislikes them because, he says, he had too many as a child. Eating too many as a child, however, does not have the same effect on everyone.

One respondent said tuna is the only kind of fish he ate as a child, and he used to brown bag two or three sandwiches to the movies on Saturday afternoon. Like most people he will eat his tuna fish sandwich only one way, though he has been experimenting with different kinds of tuna fish. His current favorite is Italian tuna in olive oil with minced celery, sweet relish, onion, pepper and mayonnaise, on white toast with lettuce.

Another aficionado wants nothing in his sandwich but mayonnaise. "Not onion, not tomatoes, not celery, just tuna and mayo, and the bread is immaterial," he said.

In other words, tuna sandwiches are nonthreatening. "They remind you of home, of lunch in school cafeterias with your friends," said another fan. "They fill you up, and you don't have to think about them." For him the ultimate tuna sandwich is made with "tons of mayo, a slice of lettuce, white bread, preferably bad white bread, and a little relish."

Among those surveyed, only one mentioned dark meat tuna, what is euphemistically called "light tuna" by the industry. His optimum tuna sandwich has lots of mayonnaise and a chopped-up gherkin or two and is on an Italian roll.

One respondent confesses that the tuna sandwich of his childhood is not his favorite now. He's gone upscale: "Curry, raisins, Dijon mustard, onion and mayo on any kind of dark bread," he said.

"Chunky tuna, mayo, some crunchy green stuff like onions or scallions," said the only tuna lover who confessed he had never made a sandwich himself. "Don't you just take it out of the can and spread it on the bread?" he asked.

There was only one tuna sandwich lover who discussed its health aspects. "I lived on them in college," she said. "It was the only thing the cafeteria made that was good, and I lost fifteen pounds."

As for me, I have no discrimination when it comes to tuna fish sandwiches. I'll gladly eat any of the above. I've made them with chopped apples and lemon juice, with chopped black olives, with capers, with yogurt or sour cream in place of some of the mayonnaise, with a bit of vinegar added to the mayonnaise, with bacon, with chopped hard-cooked eggs and with tomato slices. I've also eaten them hot with melted cheese, but the "tuna melt" doesn't count. I have put the tuna on every kind of bread and cracker, inside a pita, on an English muffin. I've even eaten the soggy white bread tuna sandwiches sold from vending machines. And loved them.

Tuna

The column on the quintessential tuna fish sandwich brought so much mail that a few weeks later I had to write another column including a sampling of the letters. Most of the mail dealt with the opening sentence as this White Plains, New York, reader took note: "'Unbelievable,' I exclaimed. 'Irma has never let anyone down.'

"Sure enough, though. I went to my much used 1964 edition of *Joy of Cooking* and discovered that you were indeed correct. Somehow my world seemed a little less secure. Refusing to believe that Mrs. Rombauer had ignored a recipe for this staple of the American diet, I turned to my 1946 edition (originally my mother's copy), and sure enough there was included not one but three—two cold and one hot—recipes for tuna fish sandwiches. The sun shone and all was right with the world."

To avoid this problem in the future someone wrote from Littleton, Colorado, to suggest that I "buy more bookshelves and keep old editions."

Another equally indignant reader from New York City referred to earlier editions of Rombauer's books and their tuna fish sandwiches and wrote: "Mrs. Rombauer didn't purport to cover the American cooking scene. She *was* the American scene. Marion Becker later used her mother's name and copyright to create quite a different book."

That dig at Becker brought an immediate response from food writer Anne Mendelson, who is researching a biography of Irma Rombauer and her daughter. She said the reader was dead wrong.

"In the first place, Mrs. Rombauer did not hold the copyright, which was acquired by Bobbs-Merrill Company of Indianapolis and New York with the second edition (1936) and has remained with them ever since. In the second place, Mrs. Becker never 'used her mother's name' to get away with anything. She became a full co-author of the work with the 1951 edition.

"The two major revisions Mrs. Becker prepared after her mother's death (1966 and 1975) continue to carry Mrs. Rombauer's name, not because Mrs. Becker sought to capitalize on what wasn't hers but because, to this day, a tremendous amount of Mrs. Rombauer's original material remains."

Mendelson goes on to defend the newer editions as far better than the old ones because they replace tuna fish sandwiches ("anyone equipped with a tuna salad recipe, two pieces of bread and average intelligence ought to be able to devise his own") with more up-to-date information.

I couldn't have said it better. Whenever I am looking for answers to questions about American cooking, I'm sure to find them in the *Joy*—with the exception of the tuna fish sandwich.

For those of us with tuna-fish-free versions of the *Joy of Cooking* several readers contributed recipes. From Trenton, New Jersey: One can of albacore tuna, liberal quantities of mayonnaise and one heaping teaspoon horseradish. Pure heaven. From Metuchen, New Jersey: My Texas mother-in-law's recipe for tuna salad sandwich spread has been a mainstay in our family for over forty years. Miss Kate's ingredients were tuna, celery, chopped pecans, chopped pimiento, mayonnaise. I never worried about proportions and neither did she, but the combination is superior to any described in your column!

And from Covent Station, New Jersey (they must eat a lot of tuna in New Jersey): one part tuna fish, one part feta cheese, grated onion and a squeeze of fresh lemon. From New Mexico: My friend Claudia always adds chopped jalapeño peppers. From parts unknown: Lightly sautéed tuna on a toasted (no butter) bagel with a little ketchup.

No comment from here.

From Washington, D.C., a health-food tuna sandwich: We do not use mayonnaise but instead use tofu mixed in a blender with corn oil, skim milk, lemon juice, fructose and curry or garlic seasoning; a few tablespoons of low-fat plain yogurt can be added.

No comment on that one either.

To the reader from Indianapolis who wanted to know: "Why do people say 'tuna fish'? I've always considered it a sort of careless idiomatic expression, but you are an excellent writer and yet you used it several times (and so, you will note, did Irma). Why not say salmon fish or mackerel fish?"

Even though this letter never appeared in the newspaper, a reader from New York City answered the question. "To a visitor from England who was totally bewildered on first seeing the inside of a New York deli the answer seems obvious. Tuna was named in southern Europe. When it was put in a can and thence into salad, which appeared on a deli counter, the customers were puzzled. Most of them came from northern Europe and had never heard of tuna. So it was described as 'tuna fish' which, of course, seemed analogous to 'gefilte fish.' The tuna fish sat next to the gefilte fish with the chopped liver on the other side."

I don't care if the answer is historically accurate. It makes perfect sense to me.

Two years after the column appeared a letter arrived from a reader who lives in Manhattan.

Perhaps it is our mutual passion for tuna fish that explains why I feel a certain closeness to you. Whatever the reason, I am writing to thank you for making Wednesdays and Saturdays so special. I'm in law school, and no matter how heavy the reading load, I always make time to sit and savor the Living Section. A small pleasure, but it makes my day.

My newest tuna craze is probably old hat to you because it is such a natural mate with fish: dill. In addition to mayo (of course), some lemon and parsley, I now chop a few sprigs (are they sprigs?) of dill in there and sprinkle the finished product with paprika. Don't ask me how I got started on the paprika habit, but I'm addicted.

My grandmother puts a little bit of sweet relish in her tuna. I've always trusted my grandmother when it comes to food, and she certainly didn't let me down on that one.

I know a women who even puts a touch of sour cream in her tuna. Sounds disgusting, but I remember lying on the beach counting down the minutes until lunch, when my friend and I would devour those rich-tasting tuna sandwiches with potato chips, seltzer, and grapes for dessert. It's no wonder we are still friends.

One final tuna note also features the beach, this time in Ostia, a coastal town a few miles outside Rome. My girlfriend and I, both of us recently graduated from Smith, were taking the usual post-baccalaureate grand tour.

A little before noon I was famished and hungrily looking around for any sign of non-pizza life. I found it in a beautiful, tiny sandwich shop. The man behind the counter spoke no English, so I pointed to two different half sandwiches. For as long as I live I will never forget walking along the beach, gazing out into the spectacular view, the sun gently warming my body, and eating Italian tuna with a moist hard-boiled egg on thin white bread lightly spread with homemade mayonnaise. The other half was the same, with arti-choke hearts substituted for the egg. I can almost taste them now.

Muffins Are a Special Way to Enjoy Blueberries
July 27, 1985

Picking wild blueberries seems like a good idea, at least for the first half hour or so. After that, especially since blueberries grow in the hot summer sun, usually in places where there is not a breath of air stirring, it becomes a chore.

Unfortunately, the only way to savor the true taste of wild blueberries is to pick them yourself. And because they are so small, it takes a long time to fill a pail, which is what we used to put them in when I went blueberry picking as a child about once a summer. A couple of uncles and aunts, several cousins and my mother and I trekked through the woods and fields outside Boston. I don't remember that we ever had enough for more than one pie. That was probably because we ate more than we collected. One for the pail; two for the stomach.

The Cultivated Berry

The large cultivated blueberries available in the market are handsome enough, but they lack the full sweetness and tartness characteristic of wild berries. These cultivated berries are best in cooked dishes, especially in blueberry muffins, most especially if the muffins are from the Ritz-Carlton Hotel in Boston.

As an aficionado of their plump, sugar-topped version, I asked the hotel for the recipe, tried it and found it reasonably close to what I had had for breakfast at their cafe. But two days after I tried the recipe, I received a call from the hotel's pastry chef telling me I had been given the wrong recipe. At first, he said, he did not want to part with his revised version. "But when you have the best blueberry muffin," Gunther Moesinger said not at all immodestly, "why not give it out?" Moesinger, pastry chef at the hotel since 1982, had made considerable changes. The shortening had been cast aside in favor of butter, the eggs and blueberries increased and the baking powder reduced.

So I tried the new version, and the new blueberry muffin tasted just about the same as the old except for the generous quantity of blueberries.

Thom Egan, public relations director for the Ritz-Carlton and a student of the hotel's blueberry muffins for thirteen years, agrees. He is particularly fond of the crusty, sugared topping. "I wonder," he said, "how many people are like me and cut off the top and don't bother with the bottom."

The Ritz-Carlton blueberry muffin recipe has been in flux for thirty-five years, ever since Charles Bonino, the executive chef who retired in 1971, decided he wanted to make a better muffin. The hotel has been serving some version or other since it opened in 1927.

One of Boston's best-known department stores, Gilchrist's—long since departed—was renowned for its blueberry muffins. The recipe was a closely guarded secret. According to Egan, Bonino bought dozens and dozens of the muffins over the years. He would take them back to the hotel kitchen, try to analyze what made them so special and try to copy them. Egan says the chef was never satisfied, so he kept fiddling.

But hundreds of patrons were satisfied, and they probably haven't noticed the difference since Moesinger made his changes. After one morning muffin, many guests ask to buy a box to take home. If the inventory that day is sufficient, the hotel obliges. The hotel does not like to mail them because they should be eaten the day they are made.

At the height of the blueberry season it is easy to make muffins at home, and they are at their best warm from the oven. In winter they can be made with frozen blueberries.

THE RITZ-CARLTON'S BLUEBERRY MUFFINS

3½ cups sifted all-purpose flour
2 tablespoons baking powder
¾ cup sugar
 Pinch of salt, optional
5 eggs, lightly beaten
½ cup milk
5 ounces unsalted butter, melted and cooled
4 to 5 cups blueberries, fresh or frozen
 Additional sugar for topping

1. Preheat the oven to 425 degrees.
2. Mix all the dry ingredients together. Stir in the eggs, milk and butter; do not overmix. Carefully stir in the berries.
3. Grease the top of large muffin tins. Insert paper cups and spoon the batter to the top of the paper cups. Sprinkle generously with sugar.
4. Reduce the heat to 400 degrees and place the muffin tins on the middle shelf of the oven. Bake about 25 minutes, until the muffins are golden brown. Remove from the muffin tins and cool.

YIELD: 15 to 16 large muffins

Blueberry Muffins

Just to prove once again that there is no accounting for tastes, one of the first responses to the blueberry column was a copy of the column with the following message written across the bottom from a Tacoma, Washington, reader: "This is a terrible recipe. What a way to waste blueberries. Did you forget some of the ingredients?"

Maybe the blueberries in Washington State are different from the ones we have on the East Coast, because a few days later I got a phone call from a resident of a Boston suburb saying she and her husband stayed at the Ritz after their wedding but "were ignorant and failed to order" the muffins for breakfast. They remedied the error by making the muffins and declared them "damn good."

So did some New Yorkers who cruise along the Maine coast in their yacht each year. Along with a thank-you note they enclosed a picture of their fourth batch of muffins. "We anticipate many happy cruises enjoying this wonderful treat," they said.

Another reader suggested I try the muffin recipe from Jordan Marsh, a Boston department store. The recipe calls for mashing half a cup of the berries in with the batter. The reader says she has wild berries growing all around the pond on her property in New Hampshire, and she solves the problem of the August heat by standing in the pond and picking berries while ankle-deep in water.

Sounds blissful.

Shortly after the column appeared I received a phone call from Cypress, Texas, from a woman who wanted me to know that the blueberry muffins she and her husband had been experimenting with for five years every Sunday morning were the very best. Could she, she wondered, deliver some to me.

One day a package arrived, fresh from a flight from Texas. The package was accompanied by a note: "We are at a disadvantage, I know, since I took the muffins from the freezer at five this morning. But perhaps you'll give 'em a try." I did but they were not, I am ungrateful enough to confess, my style. Too cakey.

From time to time over the past year I have received a few phone calls from hotels asking me for the blueberry muffin recipe, and I ask why. Someone on the other end always has the same answer: The boss of the hotel wants to try them. For their breakfast menu, I hope. If this brief column has improved hotel breakfasts in at least three locations around the country, it will have done a noble job.

I have also promised Guy Pascal, one of New York City's best pastry chefs, a copy of the recipe because he says customers at his three locations want muffins in the morning now. They appear to have overtaken croissants in popularity.

The chef at the Ritz-Carlton in Boston has just published a cookbook that includes the muffin recipe. It has a few changes for anyone who likes to experiment. The recipe calls for an additonal teaspoon of baking powder, one ounce less butter and a total of 1½ cups sugar, the additional three-quarters of a cup for sprinkling on top of the muffins. In addition, the batter is allowed to rest in the refrigerator, covered with plastic, for two hours before the muffins are baked. The batter is divided among twelve muffin cups, each mounded about one-quarter inch to the top of the cup.

Let me know what you think of the changes.

The Chocolate Chip Cookie That Money Can't Buy
October 5, 1985

Anyone under the age of ten might find it difficult to believe, but chocolate chip cookies were not always available on every street corner. It was usually necessary to bake them. At home.

Washington, D.C., was an exception. From 1946 until a few years ago, when the Y.W.C.A. moved from K Street Northwest, it sold freshly baked chocolate chip cookies every day. The lines used to snake down the corridor and out the door as cookie lovers lined up for the Y's large, warm, soft, chewy version. But the Y, now on G Street Northwest, is no longer so centrally located, and it has no baking ovens. The cookie making has been farmed out to someone who guards the recipe as closely as the Y once did. The cookies are still available at the Y and at Neiman-Marcus, but a lot of the ritual's charm has been lost.

The Y cookie also has a lot of competition these days. Lovers of chocolate chip cookies now have choices, not only in Washington but all over the country. Devotees of the crisp cookie can buy Famous Amos; aficionados of the soft kind have everything from the supermarket variety in sacks with an old-fashioned look (to suggest goodness) to Mrs. Fields.

In fact the chocolate chip cookie has come full circle in the half century it has existed. When Ruth Wakefield created it in 1930 and christened it the Toll House chocolate crunch cookie, after a restaurant in Whitman, Massachusetts, that she and her husband owned, she used broken pieces of chocolate.

Wakefield, according to one story, was using the chocolate pieces as a substitute for pecans. Others say that she was trying to make a chocolate shortbread based on a popular cookie called the Drop-Do. Whatever the truth, the chocolate pieces did not melt, and fifty-five years later there are a lot of grateful people.

Eventually a chocolate manufacturer was persuaded to produce a chocolate bar scored in tiny sections that could be snipped apart with a special tool. Then the company created already-snipped-apart pieces and called them semisweet chocolate morsels. It put a recipe for Wakefield's tollhouse cookies on the back of the package, and the "Original Toll House Cookie," as we know it, was born.

The Decline of a Cookie

Today some of the best chocolate chip cookies are also made with broken chocolate. And some cookies that bear the name chocolate chip would be unrecognizable to Wakefield. She would surely be surprised at such ingredients as coconut, cracker crumbs, candied cherries and chocolate pudding mix.

Of all the variations, none have ever really improved on Ruth Wakefield's original recipe.

Several years ago I experimented with a chocolate chip cookie mix based on the original recipe. I created a homemade mix that can sit on the shelf for six months and can be turned into cookies simply by adding eggs and vanilla, and baking—yielding warm-from-the-oven homemade chocolate chip cookies in a quarter of an hour.

CHOCOLATE CHIP COOKIES

> 7 *cups chocolate chip cookie mix (see recipe)*
> 1 *teaspoon pure vanilla extract*
> 2 *eggs, lightly beaten*

1. Stir the mix to distribute the chips and nuts evenly. Combine with the vanilla and the eggs; this creates a heavy batter.
2. Drop the batter by the heaping tablespoon on buttered baking sheets.
3. Bake at 375 degrees for 10 to 12 minutes.
4. Cool slightly on baking sheets

YIELD: About 2 dozen

Note: For flatter cookies, pat the batter down with the back of a spoon.

CHOCOLATE CHIP COOKIE MIX

    9 *cups unbleached flour*
    4 *teaspoons baking soda*
    2 *teaspoons salt*
    3 *cups firmly packed dark brown sugar*
    3 *cups granulated sugar*
    4 *cups vegetable shortening*
    4 *cups chopped pecans*
    4 *12-ounce packages semisweet real chocolate chips*

1. Combine the flour, baking soda, salt and both sugars in a very large bowl.
2. Mix in the shortening with your fingers.
3. Stir in the pecans and chocolate chips. Store in an airtight container in a cool, dry place for up to 6 months. For longer storage, refrigerate or freeze.

YIELD: 28 cups mix, approximately

Chocolate Chip Cookie

This cookie mix is so popular that I received 2,500 requests for it when I mentioned it on one television broadcast and 1,900 when I mentioned it on another. I assumed that there were at least 4,400 satisfied customers since no complaints were ever received.

But then I printed the recipe in the newspaper. First there was the letter complaining that there was too much mix. "Get it right," wrote someone who didn't read it right from Iowa.

Another, from Cleveland, wrote: "Dear Marian: I feel that I can use your first name because I look upon you as a friend." But then she got to the point: "But, Marian, with your article and recipe of last week for chocolate chip cookies I feel that you blew it. Fortunately I made only half the recipe, but even so I am left with mounds of ingredients. I do not feel that two eggs can handle seven cups of cookie mixture and come up with anything but a blob of doughy cookie. Except for the flavor of the chips there is not a hint of all that brown sugar and shortening in the taste of the cookies, etc., etc." She concluded: "This is not an end to a friendship via the food pages, and I will try to make good with the ingredients I have left. If you have any suggestions, I will be most grateful."

Yes. I have a suggestion. Please give the recipe one try before you knock it. Two eggs is all you need for the seven cups of mix. Honest.

Someone else suggested that I substitute whole wheat flour for half the white flour. She said it made a chewier, more nutritious cookie. And it probably does, but I confess that when I eat chocolate chip cookies I am not eating them for my health, at least not my physical health.

But the most disgruntled reader of all, one from St. Louis, wanted to know why I didn't devote more columns to helping people with cooking problems instead of writing about such inconsequential things as chocolate chip cookies.

Nothing, however, prepared me for the note I received from Debra Fields, owner and creator of Mrs. Fields cookies, of which I spoke so highly in the column. Along with the thank-you note was a little card with a form printed on it which someone in Fields's office fills in: "Because you are special (fill in number) free (fill in variety) at any Mrs. Fields Cookies." Mrs. Fields had sent me a certificate good for four free cookies! I suspect it costs more to write the letter, fill out the card and put a first-class stamp on the envelope than the four cookies are worth.

A few weeks later I wrote another article and mentioned the cookies again. That time I got just two free cookies. No one can ever accuse Mrs. Fields of bribing reporters.

For those who find an ordinary chocolate chip cookie too tame, here is what some consider the ultimate chocolate chip cookie, reprinted from a book filled with winners of a chocolate chip cookie contest held in 1980, the fiftieth anniversary of the Toll House cookie. It really is quite spectacular.

BRANDYWINE CHOCOLATE CHIP COOKIE*

½ cup unsalted butter
2 squares unsweetened chocolate
½ cup firmly packed brown sugar
½ cup granulated sugar
1 teaspoon pure vanilla extract
½ cup sour cream or buttermilk
1 egg
1½ cups flour
½ teaspoon baking powder
½ teaspoon baking soda
½ cup finely chopped pecans
1 cup semisweet chocolate chips
Additional granulated sugar for dipping
Coffee Brandy Frosting (see recipe)
Chocolate Glaze (see recipe)

1. Melt the butter together with the unsweetened chocolate and cool. Beat into the cooled mixture the brown sugar, granulated sugar, vanilla, sour cream and egg.
2. Stir into the liquid mixture the flour, baking powder, baking soda, pecans and chocolate chips.
3. Drop by heaping tablespoons, 2 inches apart, on ungreased baking sheets. Dip a wet-bottomed glass into granulated sugar and flatten the balls of dough.
4. Bake at 375 degrees for about 10 minutes. Do not overbake. Cool, frost, sandwich and glaze.
5. Store in an airtight container in a cool place.

YIELD: 20 "Sandwiches"

COFFEE BRANDY FROSTING

½ cup unsalted butter
2 tablespoons unsweetened cocoa powder
2½ cups confectioners' sugar
1 tablespoon instant coffee powder dissolved in 1 tablespoon water
1½ teaspoons brandy

*From The 47 Best Chocolate Chip Cookies in the World, copyright 1983 by Larry and Honey Zisman, reprinted with permission of St. Martin's Press, Inc.

1. Cream the butter and cocoa. Add the sugar, coffee and brandy. Beat until fluffy. If the mixture is too stiff, add a few drops of water to give it a better spreading consistency.
2. Spread the mixture on half of the bottoms of the cookies. Place the remaining halves on top of the frosting to make "sandwiches."

CHOCOLATE GLAZE

> 2 *squares semisweet chocolate*
> 1 *tablespoon brandy or coffee*
> 3 *tablespoons unsalted butter*

1. Melt chocolate with brandy in a small saucepan over hot water until smooth. Stir in the butter a tablespoon at a time.
2. Drizzle the glaze on sandwich cookies. Let cool and set.

Cookie Wars: David vs. Goliath
January 17, 1987

The chocolate chip–cookie wars that have pitted Mrs. Fields, David's and Famous Amos against one another are moving to new battlefields.

The latest skirmishes are being fought in the supermarket, where David is taking on Goliath. David Liederman, the New York entrepreneur who has 180 David's Cookies stores all over the country, is playing himself. Goliath is the Pillsbury Company.

Seven weeks ago squat little tubes of David's cookie dough appeared in the refrigerated sections of 1,100 supermarkets within a fifty-mile radius of New York City. There, they sit side by side with the longer and narrower tubes of Pillsbury's cookie dough. David's cookie dough is also available at Macy's Herald Square and in some supermarkets in the Albany area.

Each company has more than one variety, but the cookie over which the real battle will be fought is a version of the chocolate chipper.

Both brands come in twenty-ounce cylinders: Pillsbury's are called Natural Chocolate Flavored Chocolate Chip Cookies;

David's are called Chocolate Chunk Cookies, reflecting one of the characteristics for which they are famous—chunks of imported chocolate in place of chocolate chips. That is only one of many differences between the two cookie doughs.

Pillsbury's sells for $1.79 to $2.49 a package; David's for $3.69 to $4.39 a package. The questions, then, are what makes David's so much more expensive? And is it worth almost twice as much?

One of the first clues, of course, is in part of Pillsbury's name—"Chocolate Flavored." That means the chocolate used in the cookies is not all-natural, pure chocolate. And according to the Pillsbury ingredient statement, the "chocolate flavor chips" are made with sugar, hydrogenated vegetable oil (both cottonseed and soybean), cocoa, chocolate liquor, lecithin and artificial flavor. David's cookies are made with pure chocolate.

Primary Ingredients

There are other significant differences as well. The primary ingredient in David's dough is the chocolate, followed by unbleached white flour, sugar, grade AA 93 score butter, fresh eggs, natural nut flavoring, salt, pure vanilla and baking soda. All of which sound like the kind of ingredients you might use at home.

The primary ingredient in the Pillsbury dough is bleached enriched flour, followed by sugar, chocolate-flavor chips, hydrogenated vegetable oil (soy, palm, cottonseed) with BHA added to protect flavor, water, molasses, eggs, salt, baking soda, natural and artificial flavor.

So it's easy to see that the David's dough is not only made with more costly ingredients but that it also doesn't contain preservatives such as BHA or any artificial ingredients.

For people addicted to chocolate chip cookies, however, the only true test is taste. So I baked the cookies as instructed on the package, tried a few variations and sampled.

As a taster, I will admit to certain prejudices, the most important of which is that I have never been an admirer of David's chocolate-chunk cookies sold in the cookie stores. Lapses in quality control have been a problem, and while some of the cookies from the stores are all right, others have been very greasy and, on occasion, underbaked. If I wanted to eat raw cookie dough, I would ask for it.

But when cookies are baked at home, the degree of doneness is up to the baker. In addition, if you want to eat them hot from the oven, you can do so.

That, in fact, is how the Pillsbury cookies taste best—after about two minutes of cooling. After that, they lose any appeal they might have had. Not only are they devoid of the richness and flavor of real chocolate chip cookies, but also once they cool, the chemical aftertaste, which probably comes from the artificial ingredients, becomes quite pronounced.

So if you are looking for a chocolate chip cookie that is oozing with chocolate and rich with butter, that doesn't disappoint even when it is thirty minutes out of the oven, David's cookies win hands down.

However, if you want a big, fat cookie, you will have to ignore the baking directions on the David's package and prepare them like this: Cut off inch-thick slices, and place them about three inches apart on a baking sheet. Bake for about ten or eleven minutes and check. The edges should be browned, the center very soft—gooey would be an apt description. Cool the cookies until they firm up enough to remove from the baking sheet with a spatula.

When I don't feel like making chocolate chip cookies from my own recipe, David's are certainly a worthy substitute.

Fajitas: In Texas They Love Them
August 4, 1984

People here are getting tired of hearing about *fajitas* and hope that something else will catch on to take their place. Though Texas is in the throes of the fad for what started as mesquite-grilled meat in tortillas, the rest of the country doesn't even know what they are. Talk about turning a sow's purse into a silk ear!

The *fajita*—the word means "little belt" in Spanish—was once the food of poor Mexican ranch hands who worked in the border region. Today *fajitas* are a food fad, served not only in Mexican restaurants and in fancy restaurants frequented by young professionals but also at parties given by the well-to-do. Some of the variations that have been appearing are only distantly related to the ranch hand's food.

Born of Necessity

The original *fajitas* were created out of necessity, not a desire to have something new. Ranchers, who usually butchered their own meat, kept the steaks and roasts for themselves and gave their hands what they considered the less desirable cuts, including the so-called skirt steak, which is a section of the diaphragm. The long, narrow, beltlike strip would be marinated overnight in lime juice to tenderize it. The next day it was grilled over mesquite, a cheap, plentiful wood that itself has become a cooking fad. The meat was then cut into thin strips, each diner filling a flour tortilla with it and with *pico de gallo,* a spicy relish of onions, green chilies, tomatoes and cilantro.

Those familiar with Mexican dishes may notice the striking similarity between *fajitas* and *tacos al carbón* and *carne asada.* But *tacos al carbón,* a fad that preceded *fajitas,* are made with a better cut of meat that does not need to be marinated, and they reach the table already rolled in tortillas. As for *carne asada,* it is grilled meat and vegetables.

The view around here is that *fajitas* made their way north from the border to Austin about five years ago and began arriving in Dallas two years ago.

As was the case with croissants, the spread of the trend saw the variations become increasingly outrageous. Croissants used to be plain or with chocolate; now they come with everything from ham and cheese to ratatouille.

Today *fajitas* are available with shreds of chicken and pork, and in one restaurant I visited, they were serving shrimp-filled *fajitas.* When I reported that brand-new idea to food professionals in Dallas, they laughed at the absurdity of it. They also think that serving *fajitas* with guacamole is pretty amusing because ranch hands living in scrub country were as likely to see an avocado as a shrimp.

Alison Cook, an editor of *Texas Monthly,* is not surprised at anything she hears about *fajitas.* "People are getting really baroque with their perversions," she said in a telephone interview. "There are *fajitas* cookoffs just like chili cookoffs, and I've seen recipes calling for Coca-Cola and Dr Pepper instead of lime juice for the marinade."

Soy sauce and Worcestershire sauce are also frequently used, along with liquid smoke, orange juice, pineapple juice and garlic. The *fajitas* are served with guacamole, grilled onions, green peppers, even fried potatoes.

Cook, who is from Houston, said she had never had decent *fajitas* in Dallas. "The ones I've had there are like pot roast, braised rather than grilled," she said.

A Gravy of Cream

She acknowledged that she had seen chicken-fried *fajitas* in a Houston restaurant—a concept that makes pot roast *fajitas* seem positively mouthwatering. The Houston variation copies that famous Texas dish, chicken fried steak, in that the *fajitas* are served with cream gravy poured onto them.

If Texas food lovers are not happy with the distortions of a once simple dish, those who raise and distribute beef are delighted. Skirt steak used to bring less than $1 a pound here; now, at over $2 a pound, it no longer need be sent to New York, where there has always been a market for it (in better butcher shops in New York fully trimmed skirt steak is $4.98 a pound).

One beef provisioner is planning an invasion of the North with skirt steaks premarinated in a soy mixture and packed in Cryovac. A newspaper photographer in Houston hopes to strike it rich bottling his secret *fajitas* marinade in his backyard and selling it across the country.

New York City is ripe for a new trend, and it has all the ingredients to make its own authentic *fajitas:* mesquite, skirt steak, flour tortillas, limes, onions, hot chilies, cilantro, tomatoes. Even if guacamole was not part of the original dish, would it be so terrible if it were included?

Fajitas

Two years after my first encounter with *fajitas*, a return visit to Texas proved that these modern variations on *tacos al carbón* are alive and well and living all over the country, from New Mexico and California to Colorado and New York.

There are even more variations than there were in 1984. In Texas one Mexican restaurant is serving them accompanied with refried beans instead of guacamole. Someone else had added grated Cheddar cheese, almost as famous a Mexican ingredient as soy sauce. But perhaps the newest *fajita*, which almost matches the chicken-fried variety, is one called *moo shi fajita*. I only heard about it; I never saw it, so I can only guess its contents. No doubt the tortilla is spread with hoisin sauce, and the beef marinated in soy sauce and garlic; in place of the *pico de gallo* perhaps there are chopped cucumbers and green onions. The variations are endless, restricted only by the imagination of the cook. But when do *fajitas* become spring rolls or blintzes, for heaven's sake?

Here's a version that combines my recipes with one from the restaurant Pancho Villa in New York City.

FAJITAS

2½ pounds skirt steak
1 tablespoon finely minced garlic
1½ tablespoons lime juice
Freshly ground black pepper to taste
12 (10-inch) flour tortillas
Guacamole (see recipe)
Pico de Gallo (see recipe)

1. Trim the skirt steak of external fat. Cut each steak crosswise into three or four pieces, each about 5 or 6 inches long.
2. Place meat on a flat surface, and holding a knife parallel to the cutting surface, cut each piece of meat, sandwich-style, into two thin rectangles.

3. Blend the garlic, lime juice and pepper in a small bowl. Using your hands, mix the meat with the garlic mixture.

4. Cook the meat over charcoal about 2 minutes on each side, or broil close to the source of heat in the oven.

5. Stack the tortillas and wrap them in aluminum foil. Heat them at 350 degrees for 10 to 15 minutes. Keep them hot wrapped in foil.

6. To serve, arrange the grilled meat on a preheated serving dish. Serve the guacamole and *pico de gallo* in separate bowls.

7. To eat, place the meat in the center of a tortilla. Spoon on some guacamole and *pico de gallo* and roll up, folding over the bottom edge to prevent dripping.

YIELD: 6 servings

Note: If you cannot buy skirt steak, you can use a better cut of meat, such as sirloin or strip steak. Trim and cut into 4- or 5-inch-long strips, about ¼ to ½ inch wide.

GUACAMOLE

    2 *very ripe, medium avocados*
    2 *ripe, medium tomatoes*
    1 *small onion, finely minced*
    1 *or 2 serrano chiles, minced*
    1 *teaspoon each lemon and lime juice*
       Freshly ground black pepper to taste
    ¾ *teaspoon ground coriander seed*

1. Mash the avocado slightly with a fork.

2. Add the tomatoes, onion and chiles and chop finely.

3. Add the remaining ingredients; adjust the seasoning and serve.

YIELD: 3 cups

PICO DE GALLO

    4 *jalapeño chiles, finely chopped*
    1 *pound tomatoes, seeded and finely diced*
    ½ *cup finely chopped red onion*
    ½ *cup finely chopped fresh cilantro*
    2 *tablespoons freshly squeezed lime juice*
       Freshly ground black pepper to taste

Combine all ingredients and serve at room temperature.

YIELD: About 2 cups

A Chili, by Whatever Spelling, Adds Spice to Life

January 5, 1985

Chiles, chilies or chilis: No matter how these peppers are spelled (my preference is for the Spanish spelling, chile), they are confusing to those both north and south of the Mexican border. There may be as many as two hundred varieties, and according to authorities, at least one hundred can be found in Mexico.

Even the highly regarded expert on Mexican cooking Diana Kennedy confesses to confusion. In her book *The Cuisines of Mexico* (Harper & Row, 1972), Kennedy writes: "From my own experience, wandering through the markets of Bajio alone—where many chiles are grown—I soon became confused by the numerous types, shapes and colors, all almost alike but not quite, many of which I had seen before."

To further confuse the issue, chiles from the same plant can vary from mild to hot, although, in general, the smaller the chile, the hotter. What is more, some chiles have two names—what is called poblano in Mexico and New York is called pasilla in California.

Until recently the mad, mad world of chiles was not of burning interest to people outside the Southwest, but with Mexican restaurants firmly taking root, interest in Mexican ingredients all over is soaring. For those who do not like hot food, the question whether a dish contains a fiery serrano chile or a poblano, which is mild to medium hot, can make a vital difference.

Despite the popularly held belief that jalapeño chiles are synonymous with hot, far more fiery chiles are commonly available.

Here is a primer of Mexican chiles.

Among the fresh chiles, these are the most popular:

Serrano. Small and usually rounded at the end. Color is between forest and grass green. About 1½ inches long and ½ inch wide. Very hot. Used in guacamole and *salsa ranchera.*

Jalapeño. A bit larger than the serrano, and darker green. About 2½ inches long and ¾ inch across at its widest part. Hot, sometimes very hot. Often found canned. Often stuffed with fish or cheese and frequently served pickled (escabeche).

Poblano. Sometimes known as pasilla and sometimes as ancho. Plump, wide at the top and middle and tapered to a point at the bottom; about 3 by 5 inches. Dark green. Mild to medium hot. Most often stuffed, as in *chiles rellenos.*

Anaheim. Also known as California, after its state of origin. Long and medium green in color. Quite mild. Usually used in *chili con queso.*

Guero. Not readily available. Pale yellow. Size can vary greatly, but usually 4 or 5 inches long and about 1 inch wide, with a pointed end. Quite hot. Often used in a salad or in stews.

These are among the most popular of the dried chiles:

Ancho. The name for the dried version of the poblano chile (although the fresh poblano, confusingly, is sometimes called ancho also). Deep reddish-brown. Like the poblano, it is often stuffed.

Guajillo. About 4½ inches long and 1¼ inches wide, with a brownish-red skin. Very, very hot.

Chipotle. Light brown with a smoky taste and aroma; 2¼ inches by ¾ inch. The dried version of the jalapeño. Available in cans; often canned in vinegar or used in a red *adobo* sauce.

Mulato. Shaped like an ancho (the dried poblano), but sweeter and more brownish-black than reddish-brown. Used in *mole poblano.*

A Warning on Handling

For those who have been tempted to try a dish or two using chiles, the most important information concerns their handling. Do not touch your face, especially your eyes or lips, after handling a hot chile; the stinging sensation takes a long time to disappear.

The popular misconception about chiles is that the seeds are the hottest part. They are hot, but the veins are hottest of all.

Some Mexicans reduce the heat in chiles by soaking those that have been peeled and roasted in salt water for several hours. But an easier way to cut down on the heat is to use less, substituting green bell pepper for part of the hot chile.

In Quest of the Real Tex-Mex
June 7, 1986

By common agreement, the best Tex-Mex food in the United States is found in San Antonio. But where the line is drawn between Mexican food and Tex-Mex is beyond a northerner's comprehension.

Compounding the difficulty is the fact that Texans can't agree themselves on a definitive list of authentic Tex-Mex foods. It has been variously called "food from our parents who have been here for one hundred years or more," "food cooked by people in Texas who didn't know how to cook Mexican food" or "poor people's food." It is probably all those and more.

The list of Tex-Mex foods certainly includes tacos and enchiladas with red sauce, pinto beans, tamales with pork, chili con carne, *chile con queso, chiles rellenos,* nachos and *chalupas.* But does it also include grilled sweetbreads, mesquite-grilled steak, Texas hamburgers with refried beans, crushed tortilla chips and *pico de gallo,* a relish of green chiles, onions, tomatoes and cilantro?

No matter the length of the list, if you know where to go in San Antonio, you can taste some of the best examples of a food that warms body and soul. Here it is eaten without regard to hot weather.

You will not find many tourists in places like Rosario's or El Mirador. These are restaurants with Formica-topped tables, paper napkins, the original overhead fans, walls painted in high-gloss enamel and bowls of either red or green salsa on the table, sometimes both. The first thing the waitress brings, before you order, is a bowl of freshly made saltless chips to dip in the salsa. After you have been in Texas for a while, you learn that salsa is the ketchup of the Southwest: It's put on everything from cottage cheese to eggs.

Don't eat all the tortillas, save room at Rosario's for a black bean soup that is rich without being thick and for quesadillas oozing with cheese.

At El Mirador try the red enchiladas. They make them red by adding red chili to the masa (corn flour). Or order the combination plate. After eating it you will know the difference between what passes for one in New York and the real thing. On a single plate you will be served a meat-stuffed corn flour turnover, chicken enchilada and green sauce, cheese enchilada with chili con carne, rice, refried beans and guacamole.

The very best chips and salsa I tasted were served at the Liberty Bar, which is yuppie Texan rather than Tex-Mex. To my mind, chips and salsa are best with beer, but the owner of the Liberty Bar, Drew Allen, maintains they taste great with Châteauneuf-du-Pape.

Food from Tycoon Flats

Tex-Mex is also described by Billie Bledsoe, a San Antonio food writer and consultant, as the kind of food they serve at Tycoon Flats. Tycoon Flats looks like a truck stop, a rundown one at that. But the clientele would wear three-piece business suits in New York City.

A very good version of the hamburger with crushed tortilla chips is served here. The standard lunch is a margarita, the hamburger and nachos. These are not nachos made with Velveeta, says Kathy Coiner, the wife of one of the owners, rather indignantly. "We use real cheese, and we don't put them in a microwave," she said. "The margaritas cut the richness of the refried bean hamburgers."

Tex-Mex, according to many observers, includes mesquite-grilled steak, and one of the best places to savor it is at the Grey Moss Inn, a 200-year-old house in a lush green forest in the foothills of the Texas hill country. Though forty minutes from downtown, the inn still has a San Antonio address.

Tex-Mex, Texan or Mexican, is what people call comfort food here. "You have to remember," one friend said, "that around here you can go to an event where people are wearing $4,000 gowns, and they'll serve nachos."

Tex-Mex

There is new Tex-Mex and old Tex-Mex.

Black Bean Relish is adapted from a recipe from Dean Fearing, chef at The Mansion on Turtle Creek in Dallas. It is the new Tex-Mex.

BLACK BEAN RELISH

6 *ounces black turtle beans, soaked in 3 to 4 cups chicken stock*
1 *small red bell pepper, cut into small dice*
1 *small yellow bell pepper, cut into small dice*
1 *garlic clove, minced*
1 *small jalapeño chile, minced*
2 *tablespoons chopped fresh cilantro*
2 *tablespoons white wine vinegar*
  Salt, lemon and lime juice to taste

1. Cook the soaked beans in stock to cover generously for 45 minutes, until al dente, not soft. Drain.
2. While the beans are still hot, stir in the remaining ingredients and toss. Serve at room temperature.

YIELD: 6 to 8 servings

Chile con queso is old Tex-Mex.

CHILE CON QUESO

2 *tablespoons vegetable oil*
1 *large onion, chopped*
2 *garlic cloves, minced*
4 *fresh Anaheim chiles, roasted, peeled and chopped*
1 *or 2 serrano chiles (depending on heat desired), roasted, peeled and chopped*
1 *teaspoon ground cumin*

½ pound plum tomatoes, finely chopped
 8 ounces Monterey Jack cheese, coarsely grated
 8 ounces longhorn cheese, coarsely grated
 Freshly made tortilla chips for dipping
 Jicama sticks for dipping.

1. In hot oil sauté the onion and garlic until the onion is soft.
2. Add the chiles, cumin and tomatoes and stir, cooking for 1 to 2 minutes.
3. Stir in the cheeses and set aside until serving time.
4. At serving time cook over very low heat until the cheeses melt.
5. Serve with freshly made tortilla chips and sticks of jicama for dipping.

YIELD: About 3 cups

Note: Any other mild chile may be substituted for the Anaheim if it is not available, including those that come canned.

Jalapeño may be substituted for the serrano.

Salsas: Easy and Versatile
March 15, 1986

This is an auspicious time to let in a little light on the slightly mysterious world of salsas, because cumin, cilantro, tomatillos and chiles are replacing andouille, tasso and roux in the lexicon of New Yorkers who keep up with the latest trends in food. Southwestern food is superseding Cajun, and salsas are an integral part of southwestern cuisine.

The simplest of the salsas, *salsa cruda,* is on the table in Mexican homes at all times of day. Made with tomatoes, cilantro, hot chiles and salt, it finds its way onto everything from breakfast eggs to broiled fish.

Mexican salsas are, in fact, all rather simple sauces requiring no long preparation and no complex techniques or ingredients.

Not all salsas contain tomatoes, but when they do, they are made either with the red tomato or the green tomato known as the tomatillo, *miltomate* or *tomate de cáscara*. Unlike an unripened green tomato, the tomatillo, which comes in a papery husk, is meant to be eaten while it is still green. When it ripens, it turns yellow. Except for salsas of northern Mexico, most have hot chiles in them.

Some Variations

For variety, the sauce may be raw or cooked, the chiles in it fresh or roasted.

Pico de gallo, which has gained some fame as an accompaniment to *fajitas*—the steak, tortilla and avocado dish—often has other vegetables in it, such as cucumbers and radishes.

A *salsa borracha,* or drunken sauce, is made with orange juice, onion, chiles and tequila.

The other night I had some plum tomatoes left over from making salsa for salmon hash, so I made another bowl of it and served it over broiled swordfish. The contrast of the richness of the hot fish with the acid coolness of the fresh sauce was perfect.

Salsas are certainly one of the reasons Mexican food is perceived as healthy. No rich beurre blancs or cream sauces were needed to make the swordfish special.

Meat Loaf, Loved and Loathed
April 20, 1985

The most unusual meat loaf I ever sampled was prepared for me (and several dozen other people) by Joan Crawford.

I'm still not sure that Crawford could cook, but she made a stab at it during the 1960s for a Pepsico promotion; she was then a member of the company's board of directors. Pepsico owns Frito-Lay, whose corn chips were the reason for the screen star's cooking appearance—before an audience, of course.

Her performance began with a long walk down the center aisle. She had come, she said, to prepare "her" meat loaf recipe. Not surprisingly, it contained corn chips. She stirred the mixture of chopped meat and corn chips two or three times, turned the partly mixed ingredients over to someone else to complete, washed her hands and departed to a round of applause.

Meat loaves made with the same ingredients had already been prepared, and samples were fed to the audience. The corn chips added a peculiarly inappropriate texture to the meat loaf, but I suppose they were preferable to meat loaf made with Pepsi-Cola. At any rate, I have never been tempted to re-create the recipe.

I love meat loaf in many of its varieties, but there are some that really turn me off. My mother's surprise meat loaf, for example: It had a hard-cooked egg inside. It had cooked so long that the yolk turned gray-green. She made it only once.

And there was one that contained a little meat and a lot of oatmeal, and unfortunately I was responsible for it. Pinching pennies, I had gotten carried away with finding out the maximum of oatmeal that a half pound of ground beef could sustain.

Repository for Leftovers

Meat loaves can contain almost anything and often do. When the combinations work, it can be a wonderful, tasty, moist surprise. But, while meat loaf may make a good repository for some leftovers, cooked vegetables are not among them.

Scanning the old-fashioned, serviceable cookbooks, I found recipes for meat loaves with beef, veal, pork, ham and lamb. And they call for a variety of ingredient combinations: horseradish, barbecue sauce, ketchup, cream, curry, sage, chili sauce, garlic, celery, green pepper, raw carrots, thyme, oregano, cloves, basil, marjoram, Worcestershire sauce, tomato juice, tomato sauce, onion soup mix, walnuts, potato chips, onion, bacon, salt pork, beef suet and, of course, the fillers such as crackers, cornflakes and rice.

An old edition of *Joy of Cooking* calls for arranging a partly cooked meat loaf in biscuit or pie crust dough—the poor man's version of beef Wellington?—and baking it until the crust is golden. A more updated version suggests using refrigerated crescent rolls for the dough.

This wonderful meat loaf comes from Bob Jamieson. Bob, a correspondent for NBC and a connoisseur of both food and wine, says he likes it as well as roast beef, and his wife, Janet, agrees that his version is as good as her mother's. "It's ideal," he says, "with baked potatoes and canned peas."

BOB JAMIESON'S MEAT LOAF

1½   pounds ground beef
⅓   pound ground veal
⅓   pound ground pork
3   tablespoons Worcestershire sauce
1   large onion, finely chopped
1   tablespoon butter
2   eggs, lightly beaten
2   tablespoons Dijon mustard
¼   cup ketchup
3   tablespoons cracker crumbs
   Salt and freshly ground black pepper to taste
5   tablespoons ketchup for glazing
2   strips bacon, optional

1. Allow the beef, veal and pork to come to room temperature. Combine with the Worcestershire sauce.

2. Sauté the onion in the butter until quite soft and golden. Add to the meat with eggs, mustard, ketchup, cracker crumbs and salt and pepper.

3. Spoon into a 9- by 5-inch loaf pan and pat gently. Spread the remaining ketchup on top and lay the bacon slices across the loaf, if desired.

4. Bake at 350 degrees for 60 minutes. Remove from the oven; remove the bacon and drain off the fat. Slice and serve.

YIELD: 6 servings

Meat Loaf Revisited

In addition to the usual requests for copies to replace those that were tossed out, one reader suggested the addition of savory to Bob's recipe for meat loaf—a worthy suggestion. Use about one teaspoon of dried savory.

Another reader, from New York, volunteered the information that his grandmother used meat to stuff a turkey. "Grandma used to do it using only chopped meat," he wrote. "I mix it with stuffing."

One very complimentary reader from New York City said the meat loaf column was my very best column. Except for one thing. I had not printed my favorite recipe. "So perhaps," he wrote "you'll be kind enough to print it in a follow-up column, 'Meat-loaf Revisited.'" I would except that Bob Jamieson's meat loaf is now my favorite.

A Most Remarkable Pancake
January 11, 1986

When they closed the doors of Reuben's Restaurant in 1966, the only thing left to commemorate the sixty-year-old institution was its justly famous cheesecake. It can still be purchased by mail.

The Reuben's apple pancake, however, disappeared, the recipe locked away in the files of Arnold Reuben, Jr., son of the restaurant's owner. Such a loss did not go unnoticed.... Today there are still those of us who mourn the passing of that rich, sweet creation that was somewhere between a crepe and a regular pancake—even though concerns about health may preclude eating it more than twice a year. Savoring it one snowy midnight more than thirty years ago is one of my cherished gustatory memories.

My college friend Pam Markel (now Goldman) invited two of us to join her, her father and grandfather for a weekend in Manhattan. Because of the weather we had to take a train from Boston and arrived too late to eat anywhere but in a restaurant open twenty-four hours day.

While I remember a great deal about the restaurant's decor, I remember nothing about the food except the twelve-inch pancake.

Italian marble, gold-leaf ceiling, lots of walnut paneling and dark red leather seats—to a small-town girl it was the quintessential New York City restaurant. Today nothing remains of the marble Art Deco facade on 58th Street near Fifth Avenue, where Reuben's moved in 1935.

Its cheesecake was better known than its apple pancake, in part because the cheesecake could be ordered by mail even in the early days. (Reuben's cheesecakes may be ordered from Arnold Reuben Jr.'s Cheesecakes, 15 Hillpark Avenue, Great Neck, New York 11021, 516-466-3685.)

Others have made good cheesecakes. But who else has produced such a pancake—bursting with apples and raisins, encased in a coating of caramelized sugar? It remains in memory the best pancake I ever ate, surpassing more delicate crepes, even the Austrian raisin-filled extravaganza, *kaiserschmarren*.

Not long ago my friend, who now lives in New Jersey, and I were reminiscing about that New York trip and about the pancake, and I decided to try to track it down.

Because Arnold Reuben, Jr., still sells the cheesecake, it was possible to find him and talk by telephone about the apple pancake. His first words were moderately encouraging: "I've made them a couple of times at home, and they come out all right." But then he added, "Most people don't want to fiddle with them."

Five pancakes, thirty eggs, 2½ pounds of butter and five cups of sugar later, I understood what he meant.

"We had a specialist make the pancakes," Reuben explained. "We had special, well-seasoned big iron skillets, and we never washed them." Reuben was not very specific about the method for making the pancake, though he had the exact ingredients for the batter. He was not quite right about the pan either. It is French steel, not iron. But it is special: It must be a seasoned pan, and it must be twelve inches in diameter on the bottom. It also requires two strong wrists to lift.

After trying the pancake in skillets ranging from cast iron to heavy aluminum and finding that the batter stuck each time, I bought the proper equipment, seasoned it and no longer had a problem with sticking.

But there are still two hurdles to overcome: one is trying to flip a twelve-inch pancake; the other is proper caramelization of the sugar. The solution to the first problem was to cut the recipe in half and prepare it in a smaller skillet. The proper method and amount of sugar for caramelization took some experimentation. The recipe can be doubled to make the original twelve-inch apple pancake or it can be made in an eight-inch well-seasoned French steel pan. For brunch or late supper, there is nothing more satisfying.

REUBEN'S APPLE PANCAKE

   1 *large green apple*
   2 *tablespoons raisins*
1½ *tablespoons sugar*
   ½ *teaspoon cinnamon*
   3 *eggs*
   ½ *cup milk*
   ½ *cup flour*
   ⅛ *teaspoon pure vanilla extract*
   ¼ *pound butter*
       Scant ½-cup sugar

1. Peel, quarter and core the apple and slice it into ¼-inch-thick, quarter-moon-shaped slices. Place it in a bowl with the raisins, 1½ tablespoons sugar and cinnamon. Mix well; cover and allow to marinate for at least 24 hours; longer if possible. Stir occasionally.
2. Beat the eggs with the milk and beat in flour and vanilla to make a smooth batter.
3. In a well-seasoned 12-inch French steel skillet with sloping sides and a long handle heat 2 tablespoons of the butter until it sizzles. Add the drained apples and raisins and cook over medium heat, stirring, for about 5 minutes, until the apples soften.

4. Add another 2 tablespoons of butter and melt. Pour in the batter evenly and cook over medium-high heat, pulling the sides of the pancake away from the edges and allowing the batter to flow under and cook. Keep lifting with a spatula to keep it from sticking. When the pancake begins to firm up, sprinkle ¼ to ⅓ of the sugar evenly over the top.

5. Add another few tablespoons of butter, slipping it underneath the pancake. Then flip the pancake and cook, allowing the sugar to caramelize. When it begins to brown, sprinkle the top with another ¼ to ⅓ of the sugar. Add more butter if needed. Flip the pancake again and allow the sugar to caramelize on the bottom.

6. Sprinkle ¼ to ⅓ of the sugar on top. Add more butter to the pan if needed. Flip the pancake once again and continue caramelizing.

7. Sprinkle the top lightly with sugar and place in a 400 degree oven for 20 minutes, to caramelize further.

YIELD: 2 servings

Reuben's Apple Pancake

Even though I had searched for a recipe for the pancake in *The New York Times* morgue, I had been unable to locate it. If it existed, I was certain a reader would supply me with a copy after the column appeared.

Not one, but three copies arrived. My friend Jean Hewitt, who had worked for the *Times* and is now food editor of *Family Circle*, had written about the pancake in 1964. The recipe she had gotten from the chef could not have been more different from the one I had. For one thing it had no raisins. For another it did not call for marinating the apples.

Despite the differences, when I tried Jean's version, the results were almost as good, though there was not as much caramelized sugar.

Then came a note from Libby Hillman, a cookbook author and

cooking teacher who has a cooking school in Whitingham, Vermont. She wrote, "Before I wrote my first book (1963) I was invited into the kitchen to witness the apple pancake from beginning to end.

"Everything you said was absolutely correct, but Arnold Reuben, Jr., forgot one important fact. The caramelization was accomplished by setting the entire pancake in flames. Plenty of butter and sugar produced a great flame and heavy candy coating. Oddly enough I do not remember raisins."

Other lovers of the legendary apple pancake reminisced about their encounters with it. And, of course, there was the usual naysayer, in this case a former newspaper colleague from the *Washington Post*, Victor Cohn, who had this to say:

> *I have two nits to pick about your otherwise smashing piece about apple pancakes recently.*
>
> *One, Reuben's didn't hold a candle, well, it wasn't as good as the old Lindy's. Also it was unaccompanied by Lindy's flip waiter-philosophers.*
>
> *Two, at the end of the recipe, you say, Yield: 2 servings.*
>
> *Not for a real apple pancake eater. A standard meal when I would get to New York in the late '40s and '50s, before Lindy's went out of business, was (at 9 P.M., they wouldn't make an apple pancake until then) a bowl of chicken noodle soup followed by one apple pancake, eaten one-third as is, one-third with sour cream, one-third with whole-cherry preserves.*
>
> *THAT was an apple pancake.*

The most encouraging news, however, came from two New Yorkers who have spent some time in Chicago. Both recommend a trip to Walkers in Wilmette, a northern suburb of Chicago, where they say the apple pancake sounds just like the one Reuben's used to serve.

I couldn't wait to go. But...

The pancake was O.K., but it can't hold a candle to the late, lamented Reuben's version.

Strawberry Shortcake
July 5, 1986

Given the intense scrutiny old-fashioned American food has been accorded of late, it's no wonder that people are arguing about the authentic versions of just about everything from mashed potatoes to strawberry shortcake.

"I feel shortchanged if I get strawberry shortcake on a biscuit," said one Manhattan native.

"Sponge cake is not real strawberry shortcake," said another, from the Midwest.

So even if food historians agree that true strawberry shortcake is made with a biscuit, that will hardly stop some Americans from eating their strawberries on top of a sponge cake.

An early version of this uniquely American dessert appears to have been on the scene from the time the colonists found wild strawberries. Roger Williams, the founder of Providence, Rhode Island, in 1636, wrote of the possible forerunner of strawberry shortcake in *Keys to the Language of America*. About strawberries, he said, "The Indians bruise them in a morter [*sic*] and mix them with meal and make strawberry bread."

Perhaps when cakes made with baking powder became popular, people began to gussie up this earthy dessert by putting berries on top of sponge cake. Even the *Joy of Cooking,* that chronicler of American food styles, suggests in its most recent edition that strawberry shortcake can be made with "fluffy biscuit dough, scone dough or any of the plain sponge cakes."

The English food writer Jane Grigson writes in *Jane Grigson's Fruit Book* of using sponge cake as "a peaceful unhurried solution as the cake can be made in advance and filled at leisure."

"It's a rather soft solution," she acknowledges. "I am not sure I don't prefer the American shortcake, which is a grand form of scone, for its crispness and butteriness. The snag is that it tails off the longer it waits."

The shortcake, she writes, is "an impromptu affair for unexpected friends, for unexpected sunny days in the cool of the trees."

I'm not sure I know many cooks who whip up a strawberry shortcake when unexpected company comes. However, strawberry shortcake can be made, at least partly, in advance.

Even biscuit-dough adherents, however, have more than one recipe from which to choose. Should it be the ordinary baking powder biscuit or the more elaborate scone dough?

Is the heavy cream whipped or is it "pour cream"—simply heavy cream in a pitcher? Should the topping be what Fannie Merritt Farmer suggested as an accompaniment in the 1922 version of the *Boston Cooking School Cookbook*? Cream Sauce II is a sauce made with cream, milk, powdered sugar, vanilla and an egg.

Mother Served Sponge Cake

I might as well confess that my mother never served strawberry shortcake on biscuit dough, but my mother never baked biscuits. So I grew up in the sponge cake school of strawberry shortcake, and it was not until I began to read cookbooks that I discovered the other kind. I have been addicted ever since.

I make my own version of Bisquick, a combination of the dry ingredients with shortening that can be kept, tightly covered, in a cabinet for at least six months. The day I plan to serve shortcake, the dry ingredients are mixed with the liquid, refrigerated and set out half an hour before baking time.

In search of the perfect combination of biscuit dough and strawberries, I learned at least one trick modern-day cooks don't bother with—to warm the berries on the back of the stove to enhance their flavor before putting them on the cake.

My biscuit dough is enriched with half-and-half and egg—no one said it was approved by the American Heart Association.

STRAWBERRY SHORTCAKE

2 cups sifted unbleached flour
4 teaspoons baking powder
1 tablespoon sugar
4 tablespoons unsalted butter or vegetable shortening
1 large egg
½ cup half-and-half
1 quart strawberries
½ pint heavy cream
Additional butter at room temperature to spread on cakes, about 2 tablespoons

1. Sift the flour with the baking powder and sugar.
2. Cut the butter into small chunks and blend it into the flour mixture with a pastry cutter or two knives until the mixture resembles coarse cornmeal.
3. Beat the egg to mix well and stir in the half-and-half. (You can substitute cream or milk if desired.)
4. Drizzle the liquid over the flour and stir well. If there are still some dry ingredients left in the bowl, drizzle in a little more half-and-half, but just a small amount at a time. The dough should just hold together when pressed.
5. Turn the mixture out onto a lightly floured board and shape it into a ball, pressing lightly. (It is important to avoid handling the dough too much.) Cut the ball in half with a sharp knife and shape into two smaller balls, using floured hands.
6. Butter two 8-inch cake pans and press the dough with floured fingers to fill the pans.
7. Bake at 425 degrees in the middle of the oven for 12 minutes, until medium golden in color.
8. While the cakes are baking, wash, dry and hull the strawberries. Slice the berries and crush them slightly with sugar to taste, reserving several of the best-looking berries for the top. Warm the crushed berries slightly.
9. Whip the cream to form very soft peaks.
10. When the cakes are ready, turn them out on wire racks and brush the tops with soft butter, about 1 tablespoon for each top. Place one cake on a serving plate and top with half the berries. Top with the second cake and spoon on the re-

maining berries. Either spoon on the whipped cream or serve it on the side. Decorate with the reserved berries.

YIELD: 6 servings

Note: To prepare in advance, follow directions through step 5. Wrap the balls in aluminum foil and refrigerate. The dough can be prepared up to 8 hours in advance. To bake, leave the dough at room temperature for ½ hour. Then continue with step 6. The berries may also be prepared several hours in advance.

Strawberry Shortcake

Nice to know that it was not only New Englanders who were deprived of strawberry shortcake with biscuits as children. A former midwesterner, now of New York, says he'd never heard of baking powder biscuits with strawberries until he had grown up.

"When I later asked my mother (who was an excellent baker) why she never made them, she said the rest of the family—I came along much later—preferred sponge cake. During the Depression she used biscuits as a base for braised meats and gravies quite frequently, and apparently it seemed a bit much to have them for dessert too. I suppose, as a result, I was ingrained with this concept also. Even today, I prefer a sponge because it *seems* more like dessert."

Another reader had a quibble over the use of the word *short-cake:* "While I'm with you in preferring biscuit shortcake, I have no quarrel at all with those who prefer sponge cake. What I do object to is confusing the two by calling them both 'shortcake.'

"Sponge cake is, by definition, made without shortening, while the very word *shortcake* indicates that shortening is a necessary ingredient."

Mention of homemade Bisquick brought dozens and dozens of requests. Here it is, once again.

BISCUIT MIX

   9 *cups sifted flour*
   ⅓ *cup baking powder*
   1 *cup plus 2 tablespoons nonfat milk solids*
   4 *teaspoons salt*
   1¾ *cups vegetable shortening*

1. Sift all dry ingredients.
2. Cut the shortening into the flour until the mixture resembles coarse cornmeal.
3. Store, well covered, in a cool dry place.

YIELD: 13 cups

Note: This can be used for waffles, pancakes and biscuits. Use it for anything for which you use packaged biscuit mix.

   Add 1 tablespoon sugar, if desired, for each shortcake recipe.

Mexican Treat for Holidays

May 25, 1985

Mexican cooking and its variations, Tex-Mex, California-Mex, New Mexico–Mex, have a large following in this country. It long ago left the confines of the Southwest and traveled north and east, where guacamole and tortilla chips have become favored treats.

Avocados, beans, sour cream, cheese, tomatoes and tortilla chips are among the most popular ingredients in north-of-the-border cooking today. Put together and seasoned with garlic and cumin, chili powder and coriander to create guacamole tostadas, the combination provides an hors d'oeuvre that is likely to disappear moments after it hits the table and is perfect for this holiday weekend and all summer entertaining.

A Maryland friend of mine, Mollie Dickenson, makes guacamole tostadas with canned beans and a package of taco seasoning mix, and it is very good. I make it with beans made from scratch and my own combination of seasonings to replace the package of seasoning mix. In this version, I reduce the amount of fat in the beans because I don't fry them first and eliminate the salt from the seasoning.

This is not as difficult as it sounds. In order to make such changes in this or any other recipe the cook need know only what the basic recipes for the convenience products are. Recipes for refried beans can be found in any Mexican cookbook. And while not all the spices are listed on a package of seasoning mix, anyone familiar with Mexican cooking knows which ones are appropriate.

As warm weather approaches, bringing luscious local tomatoes and readily available fresh cilantro, guacamole tostadas are at their best.

Here is a recipe to brighten Memorial Day festivities.

GUACAMOLE TOSTADAS

   1 *cup dried pinto beans*
 3/4 *cup chopped onion*
   1 *large garlic clove, pressed*
1 1/2 *teaspoons ground cumin*
2 1/2 *tablespoons mild pure chili powder*
   1 *tablespoon white vinegar*
 1/4 *cup unsalted butter, softened*
   3 *ounces tomato paste*
 1/4 *teaspoon ground coriander seed*
   8 *drops hot pepper sauce*
      Freshly ground black pepper to taste
   2 *ripe avocados*
   2 *tablespoons lemon juice*
   1 *cup sour cream*
   2 *large tomatoes*
 3/4 *cup chopped scallions*
   1 *cup pitted chopped black olives*
   2 *cups coarsely grated sharp white Cheddar cheese*
 2/3 *cup coarsely chopped fresh cilantro*
      Good-quality tortilla chips

1. To prepare the beans either cover with water and soak overnight or cover with water and bring to a boil; boil 2 min-

Kim Munson

$19.95
942-4121 hand
PNP. 541
mi Mama 885-3050

utes and allow to sit in the water for 1 hour. After soaking the beans, drain off the soaking water. Cover the beans with fresh water and cover the pot. Bring to a boil. Add ½ cup of the chopped onion, garlic and ½ teaspoon of the cumin. Cover and simmer until the beans are tender, about 1 hour. Drain.

2. Place the beans in a food processor with the remaining onion, ¾ teaspoon of the cumin, 1½ tablespoons of the chili powder, vinegar, butter, tomato paste, coriander and hot pepper sauce. Process until the mixture is smooth. Adjust the seasoning and add salt and pepper to taste.

3. Peel the avocados and mash coarsely with the lemon juice, salt and pepper to taste.

4. Mix the sour cream with 1 tablespoon of the chili powder and ¼ teaspoon of the cumin.

5. Chop the tomatoes.

6. To serve, place a layer of the bean mixture in a shallow serving dish. Top with the mashed avocados, then with the sour cream mixture. Sprinkle the tomatoes evenly over the sour cream; sprinkle on the scallions, olives and cheese and top with fresh cilantro.

7. Serve with tortilla chips.

YIELD: 16 servings

Note: The beans may be cooked a day or two ahead and mixed with seasonings. Remaining ingredients, with the exception of the avocado, may be prepared early on the day of the party. No earlier than an hour before, the avocado can be mashed and the dish put together.

The Luxury of Lobster Makes a Summer Feast
August 3, 1985

The 1622 version of bread and water was lobster and water. According to *Eating in America* (William Morrow, 1976), the fascinating history of food by Waverley Root and Richard de

Rochemont, "When a group of new colonists arrived in Plymouth, Governor William Bradford was deeply humiliated because his colony was so short of food that the only 'dish they could presente to their friends was lobster...without bread or anything els but a cupp of fair water.'"

Lobsters were so plentiful in Colonial times that after a storm they would pile up "windrows two feet high on the beach."

As recently as the mid-1960s they were inexpensive enough for backyard summer lobster feasts for about forty people. The lobsters were ordered from Maine for 59 cents a pound. Now that lobsters are $5.99 a pound, my summer feasts feature crabs; lobsters are saved for special occasions.

But for those summer evenings that call for a special treat, nothing quite compares. Summer is the best lobster-eating time for two reasons. They are at their most reasonable during the warm months, and they are definitely a messy bib-and-finger food that lend themselves to the informality of the season. Outdoors is best for the feast; the kitchen table would be second choice. The dining room is a mistake.

Preference for Steaming

Although I have eaten lobsters boiled, broiled, baked and steamed, I much prefer steaming, and most people from Maine agree. Maine lobsters are just about the best in the world, because the waters off the coast are the right frigid temperature for breeding the sweetest lobster meat. After steaming, in descending order of preference, I recommend boiling and baking. Broiling is last resort because it invariably dries out the lobster and toughens it.

Steaming a lobster is simple except for those who are squeamish about handling the crustaceans live. The lobster is placed on a rack above steaming water and cooked for fifteen to twenty minutes, a process that turns the dappled dark green shell to vivid red.

Some experts say larger lobsters, those over two pounds, are tough. It has been my experience that lobsters of any size can be tough: Perhaps it has more to do with the cooking than the lobster. For just the right amount of succulent rich meat, a 1½- to 2-pound lobster should be sufficient for most adults.

Females Are Prized

Although one-pound lobsters, called chicken lobsters in the trade, often cost less per pound than the larger ones, it is really worth the difference in money to buy the bigger size. The small lobsters just don't have enough meat. Female lobsters are more highly prized by connoisseurs than male lobsters because they contain the coral or roe, which should be eaten, not discarded. If a female is about to lay eggs, the coral turns from red to dark greenish-black, like caviar, and is even more delicious. The French call the developed roe *paquette.*

Female lobsters can be identified by the last pair of small claws, sometimes called swimmerets, on the underside. They are located where the chest meets the tail. On the female the swimmerets are soft, hairy and crossed; on the male they are hard, pointed and straight.

The other part of the lobster that novices are tempted to discard is the greenish-yellow liver called the tomalley. Like the roe, it is to be savored.

The only parts of the lobster that are inedible, besides the shell, are the hard sack near the top of the head, the dark vein and the spongy tissue. Even the meat in swimmerets is available to the persistent aficionado who extracts it by sucking on it. It is not unlike taking the last slurps through a straw from the bottom of an ice cream soda.

There is nothing dainty about eating lobster. With melted butter and lemon, corn on the cob and perhaps some tomatoes vinaigrette, there is no better summer meal.

Should you, by some strange quirk, have leftover cooked lobster meat, it would be excellent in this salad, where the sweetness of the meat contrasts with the sharpness of the olives:

LOBSTER AND OLIVE PASTA SALAD

 ¾ *pound mixed fresh yellow and green fettuccine*
 1 *jar (2 ounces drained weight) pimiento-stuffed olives, chopped*
 ½ *cup pitted Greek olives (calamata)*
 1 *large garlic clove, minced*
 ¼ *cup minced fresh parsley*
 ½ *cup homemade mayonnaise (made with part olive oil)*

½ cup plain yogurt
3 tablespoons white wine vinegar
1½ tablespoons good-quality olive oil
1 pound cooked lobster meat, cut into bite-size pieces
1 ripe avocado

1. Cook the fettuccine in boiling water about 30 to 60 seconds after water has returned to a boil.
2. Combine the olives, garlic, parsley, mayonnaise and yogurt. Whisk the vinegar with the oil and combine it with the mayonnaise mixture. Gently stir in the lobster and add the fettuccine to mixture. Refrigerate until serving time.
3. Just before serving, cube the avocado and mix in carefully.

YIELD: 6 servings

Lobster

There was one transplanted New Englander, now a resident of Tennessee, who said the column made her very homesick. But the rest of the correspondents devoted their discussions to the humane way to cook a lobster, and a lot of them had taken offense at the idea of steaming a live lobster. Excerpts from this letter are typical:

"Perhaps you will smile when I protest that your statement that 'steaming a lobster is simple except for those who are squeamish about handling the crustaceans live' strikes me as being despicable in its unthinking cruelty.

"Do you have no compunction in boiling, steaming, broiling an animal alive?

"I am disgusted at this inhumane practice and can only hope and pray that one day in the U.S., as it is now in Britain (and has been for about fifty years), it will be banned by an enlightened society."

Another New York reader suggested that I find out the humane way to cook lobster by getting in touch with the ASPCA. While one reader suggested putting the lobsters in fresh water for ten to fifteen minutes before cooking. "I'd rather be drowned than boiled or broiled," she added.

"The fastest and most efficient and humane way to kill a lobster before boiling it: a blow with a heavy knife on the area between the body and tail severs the spinal cord. We are taking the creatures' lives. Can't we, at the very least, do it as painlessly as possible?"

So the recommendation of a reader from Houston makes a lot of sense. A copy of a *New Yorker* cartoon by George Price was enclosed. It shows a steaming kettle of water on the stove. The lady of the house is holding a lobster with a pair of tongs in her left hand. In her right hand she holds a revolver, pointed at the lobster.

This would be a good place to close the chapter if it were not for the letter I received from Dr. Daniel S. J. Choy of Manhattan. He attached a copy of an article about cooking lobsters that he had written for a magazine. It suggests hypnotizing the lobsters, not necessarily because it is more humane but because it produces a better-tasting lobster. Excerpts from the article were printed in a later column.

This is what you do: "Turn the lobster upside down to stand on its head, yoga-fashion, bend its tail inward, then stroke the dorsal surface of the tail. The lobster is balanced on its snout and its two claws. After eight to ten strokes, the legs stop waving about, the lobster quiets down in the most uncanny way, and one can leave it alone until the water comes to a boil."

The doctor goes on to say: "Lobsters prepared in this manner can be dropped into the pot without struggling. The resultant improvement in taste is amazing. My personal theory is that the adrenaline secreted by a frightened, struggling lobster changes the taste. The tranquilized lobster is devoid of adrenaline."

Dr. Choy's letter brought the following response from some New Yorkers who were visiting friends in Maine.

My husband came in bearing four lobsters. Then, with the rest of us falling about screaming with laughter, he proceeded to stand the creatures on their heads on the kitchen counter and stroke their little backs. He claimed on the basis of your September 14 article that they would go to the boiling pot in the state of blissed-out acquiescence and that their relaxed state would make them taste better.

I was convinced that your informant, Dr. Daniel S. J. Choy, is a world-

class practical joker. I guessed he'd made a bet with some colleagues that he could get The New York Times *to print this preposterous suggestion and that all over the country people would then be engaged in standing lobsters on their heads.*

But lo! Either Maine lobsters are clearly superior to those we've been getting in Manhattan or the exercise worked. They were the sweetest, the tenderest, the most succulent lobsters in memory.

Mashed Potatoes:
Some Like Their Lumps

July 7, 1985

An unscientific survey of twenty-six people proves that the vast majority prefer smooth mashed potatoes to those with lumps. Only four of those asked said they liked lumps, and only one gave a rational explanation. "With lumps," she said, "I know they are real."

It wasn't until about a year ago, when the revival of mashed potatoes, along with such other oldies as meat loaf and crème brûlée, turned them into trendsetters that I first learned there were some people who actually preferred lumpy mashed potatoes. Perhaps they like lumpy gravy too.

The subject hadn't come up much for the past thirty years— ever since the reconstituted potato, served in K-rations during World War II to soldiers in foxholes, joined the civilian world and almost drove real potatoes out of the supermarket. With dried potato flakes it is probably impossible to produce lumpy mashed potatoes.

However, before their advent smooth potatoes were the sign of an accomplished cook. Or so I thought. At the very least they were a sign of a cook who took the time to put the potatoes through a ricer or mash them thoroughly with a potato masher.

But Jane and Michael Stern, authors of *Square Meals* (Alfred Knopf, 1984), a nostalgic look at American food, who admit they are pro-lumpers, have a different view. Pro-lumpers, they say, are a category of people who "view the little nubs of unmashed potato in the same light as the small flaws that Renaissance artists consciously put into their masterpieces—symbols of humility, a nod to the imperfection of man's handiwork." Anti-lumpers, according to the Sterns, consider lumps "a red flag that the potatoes have been made by a slattern, a slugabed with no respect for domestic science."

Pro- and anti-lumpers aside, there does not seem to be much agreement on the best way to make mashed potatoes. The Sterns counsel mashing the potatoes with a hand-held mixer, potato masher, heavy wire whisk or wooden spoon. Myrna Davis, who wrote *The Potato Book* (Morrow Quill Paperbacks, 1973), a resident of Long Island, home of some of the most famous potatoes in the United States, advises using a food mill, electric blender or fork. If she had written the book after the food processor had become more popular, she probably would have suggested one of them. But the author of *Potatoes*, Inez M. Krech (Primavera Books, 1981), says the best mashed potatoes are made by hand, using a bettle (a wooden pestle) or potato masher. "For best flavor and tenderness," she says, "do not use an electric mixer, a blender or a food processor." Blenders and food processors are especially harmful to the texture of mashed potatoes.

Next comes the thorny question of what to put in them: cream, half-and-half, milk, butter, salt, pepper? These questions weren't so thorny before Americans were so interested in health. While we never put cream in our mashed potatoes—milk was the liquid of choice—we never stinted on the butter. Simply enough to make the potatoes taste creamy and buttery.

Mashed potatoes are a comfort food for which most children have a ritual, whether using them to disguise disliked foods or combining them with favorites. The most interesting combination I ever heard comes from Jane Carr, who grew up in Maine. In Carr's family they are eaten this way, to this day: Half of the mashed potatoes are carefully smoothed out with the tines of the fork. A mixture called Pottsfield pickles—chopped relish of cabbage and green tomatoes—is spooned over and then covered with the remaining half of the potatoes, the tines of the fork once again pressed evenly into the potatoes to look like so many railroad tracks.

Mashed Potatoes

After the mashed potato column appeared, the pro-lumpers came out of the woodwork. The ratio of twenty-two anti-lumpers to four pro-lumpers changed dramatically. Those preferring lump-free potatoes were still ahead, but now by less than 50 percent. The ratio became thirty-five to fifteen.

My colleague Pierre Franey announced that he preferred his potatoes with lumps. People stopped me in the corridors to claim their undying fealty to lumpy potatoes, and when I served mashed potatoes to guests at a black-tie dinner—without lumps—several of the guests said they wished there had been lumps.

There was a note from Jane and Michael Stern, who wanted to pass along an advertisement they had seen in a restaurant trade journal for " 'instant mashed potato flakes...with lumps'—for that homemade texture in ersatz spuds. That's the kind of moral (or is it immoral?) support pro-lumpers don't need."

A New York reader made my mouth water with a description of her mother's mashed potatoes, circa 1935: "She mashed them with a fork, then added one whole raw egg, and some homemade chicken fat, salt and pepper. Extremely high in cholesterol, true; but the real reason she used the fat instead of butter or milk is that we were a kosher family, and one could never mix potatoes with milk products if one intended to eat these potatoes with meat."

Another reader from Florida suggested the addition of sour cream. Then a reader from New Jersey corrected a mistake repeated in the column, that potatoes contain gluten: They do not. So that is not what toughens them when they are beaten in the food processor, but they still get tough.

A woman from New Hampshire who sells a truly low-tech kitchen gadget called My Mother's Potato Masher sent a picture of it. Virginia Nicoll of Meredith said there are still a lot of people who advocate hand mashing, and the replica of her mother's old potato masher fills the bill. It is made with a birch handle, brass pins and a high-carbon-steel mashing plate. It is also good for mashing avocados, turnips, bananas, carrots, deviled egg yolks, applesauce and strawberries for strawberry shortcake.

If you are tired of mashing potatoes by hand with a fork, send $10.95 to POB 300, RFD 1, Meredith, New Hampshire 03253.

Emily Post and the Art of Enjoying Asparagus

April 11, 1984

I don't know what came over me the other evening as I peered down at a plate of crunchy, spring-green asparagus. I put down my fork, picked up a stalk in my fingers and ate it in several bites, telling myself all the while that my table manners were deteriorating.

As I reached for my knife and fork to cut the second stalk of asparagus, I had a flash from past perusals of Emily Post's book on etiquette. I recalled that the doyenne of all arbiters of manners had once long ago written that it was perfectly proper to eat asparagus with your fingers. I put down the fork and knife and picked up the next stalk with my fingers, smug in my knowledge that Emily Post was on my side.

Not in a Fancy Restaurant

When a little of the vinaigrette dripped on my blouse, I decided that even if the latest edition of Emily Post still says asparagus may be eaten with the fingers, I probably wouldn't do it in a fancy restaurant anymore, especially if I had on a silk blouse.

Out of curiosity the next day I picked up the most recent copy of *The New Emily Post's Etiquette* in the office. But this 1975 edition is pretty wishy-washy on the subject of asparagus table manners.

"By reputation this is a finger food," Post writes, "but the ungraceful appearance of a bent stalk of asparagus falling limply into someone's mouth and the fact that moisture is also likely to drip from the end, cause most fastidious people to eat it—at least in part—with the fork. That is, cut the stalks with the fork to where they become harder, and then pick up the ends in the fingers if you choose. But don't squeeze the stalks or let juice run down your fingers."

Post (actually it is her granddaughter-in-law, Elizabeth L. Post, who is writing the books; Emily Post has been dead for many years) goes on to say: "Asparagus that has no hard end is eaten entirely with a fork. All hard ends should be cut off asparagus before serving it at a dinner party, since picking up stalks in the fingers is scarcely compatible with formal table manners."

Elizabeth Post has apparently never had properly cooked asparagus. If she had, she would know that when the stalks are cooked correctly there is no limp part. The entire stalk is crisp, crunchy and firm. That it drips is another matter.

Asparagus in vinaigrette ought to drip and probably shouldn't be picked up in your fingers. And certainly asparagus topped with a hollandaise or an orange-flavored *maltaise* sauce should be eaten with a knife and fork.

Along with its wishy-washiness the etiquette book leaves unanswered a lot of questions that come up at this time every year, at the height of the asparagus season. Even though under certain circumstances it may be all right to eat asparagus with your fingers, what about those stalks that are so young they are pencil-thin and almost impossible to pick up with a fork? And how does Post feel about asparagus tips in a dish of stir-fried beef and asparagus? You can't pick them out with your fingers, can you?

Vegetables: There's Crisp, Crunchy and Firm

April 28, 1984

A recent column on the etiquette of eating asparagus with the fingers instead of a knife and fork moved a number of readers, including Julia Child, to comment. Most of the mail described a third alternative to fingers and forks, a utensil known as asparagus tongs. And Judith Martin, author of *Miss Manners' Guide to Excruciatingly Correct Behavior,* sent a copy for reference the next time I want etiquette information on any subject, especially the proper way to eat finger foods.

Child said she did not wish to become embroiled in a discussion of etiquette but wrote, "I have one bone to pick (I should probably say stalk to peel!)."

She took issue with my comment that properly prepared asparagus should be "crisply cooked asparagus—the whole stalk of which is crisp, crunchy and firm."

"In my opinion," Child went on, "you can't say 'crisply cooked asparagus,' because the only crisp asparagus is a raw asparagus. Perfectly cooked asparagus, for my tooth, has undergone the subtle change from raw to cooked—the stalks bend only a little bit, the asparagus has definite texture—but it is not crisp. If it is still crisply crunchy, you have not attained nirvana, you're not getting that delicious taste of carefully and perfectly cooked asparagus."

Then Child warmed to her subject: "Perfect cooking, of course, requires full attention, and I suspect the nouvelle restaurants of having put this 'crunchily undercooked' business over on the public. It's so easy: Dump the vegetables into the pot and pull them out again, no need to pay attention at all—the ultimate chic of crunchily undercooked. A more accurate descriptive phrase for that method would be 'hot raw.' "

Those who have patronized the ultimate nouvelle cuisine restaurants know just what Child is talking about. When everyone at the table is eating broccoli at the same time, it is difficult to hear anything but the crunching.

Child continued: "It's time for a public discussion of this aspect of vegetable cookery—a real definition of terms. I don't think 'crisp-tender' is correct either. It's certainly better than crunchily undercooked, but tender is not crisp and crisp can never be tender. An interesting semantic challenge, certainly."

Certainly. And I plead guilty to an imprecise use of words. When I cook asparagus, I do not want them crunchy, but I do want them firm. Whether I want them crisp depends on which definition of crisp is used. The first, older definition of crisp in *Webster's New World Dictionary* is "stiff and brittle; easily broken, snapped or crumbled." But the second definition—"fresh and firm"—is closer to an accurate description of perfectly cooked asparagus and myriad other vegetables such as broccoli, green beans, brussels sprouts, beets and carrots.

Child said over the telephone from her winter home in California that her definition of properly cooked vegetables applied to "any vegetable that is mushy when it is overcooked and crunchy with it is undercooked."

Perusing several modern cookbooks that I admire in pursuit of some easy definition for properly cooked vegetables, I had little luck. In one book asparagus were described as done when they were "tender but still retained their crunch." In another they were cooked "if they barely droop" and were "crisp-tender, not hard-crunchy." Still another book described perfectly cooked green beans as "bright green but still crunchy," while a fourth insisted that cauliflower and brussels sprouts were done when they were "fork tender at the stem end."

Most books use the word *crunchy* in an effort to describe the proper condition for a well-cooked vegetable. Even Child has used it in the past; in *Mastering the Art of French Cooking* she explained how to test broccoli: "It is done when a knife pierces the stalks easily. Taste a piece as a test: It should be just tender, with a slight crunch of texture."

No Substitute for Sampling

Cooks confused by the terminology ought to keep in mind Child's admonition: "Perfect cooking requires full attention." She also says that cutting them with a knife or piercing them with a fork is not enough. There is no substitute for sampling.

As for Miss Manners and the etiquette question, she agrees that asparagus can be eaten with the fingers. One of her readers took exception, writing, "I have it on good authority that one's fingers should never be eaten with any other food." To which Miss Manners replied: "How right you are. But after the fingers convey the asparagus to the mouth, the fingers may then be eaten with whatever remains of the hollandaise sauce."

Asparagus, the Taste of Spring, Is Back in Town

February 3, 1985

Every year at this time, when we have all had more winter than we can tolerate, the sight of the first asparagus of the season is as cheering as the sight of the first tentative green tips of tulips as they push their way up through the cold ground in the middle of Park Avenue in New York City.

No matter how fat and tender and expensive out-of-season asparagus are, they never seem as succulent and sweet as spring asparagus. Perhaps it is only in the mind, but the long, tender stalks taste better, look better and have a verdant aroma they lack in November.

Beginning to Appear

In California harvesting can begin as early as January. The peak season for asparagus is March 1 to May 15, but they are already beginning to appear in stores on the East Coast.

When I was a child, asparagus were not expensive, yet they always seemed like a treat to me. They were served only with Sunday roast chicken in our house and for company meals.

My mother never put anything on them but a bit of salt, and I think, by today's standards, she probably overcooked them. Still, I could never get enough of them. Cleaning them was one of the chores I actually looked forward to.

Today preparing asparagus hardly seems as time-consuming because there is seldom much sand to wash off. And although I think peeling asparagus is one of those refinements that make the spears even more elegant, like peeled tomatoes, I don't have the time for them.

Some people carefully select only the fattest spears at the market; others choose the slimmest. One is not really better than the other as long as the spears are young, fresh and, for their size, plump. They should also have tightly furled tips.

As asparagus age, their natural sugars become woody, so shriveled, ridged spears or flabby spears with unfurled tips or outcroppings along the sides—all signs of age—should be left in the store.

Though many people use a knife to cut off the woody parts, I have always found it more accurate to break them off because the asparagus will naturally break at the point where it becomes tender.

Many recipes call for boiling the spears, but the result is better if they are steamed. Any kind of steamer will do, and average-size spears are ready in five to seven minutes. Pencil-thin spears take a little less time; the jumbo size take a trifle longer. Whether fat or thin, the spears should be the same size for uniform cooking.

White asparagus, just gaining popularity here, are so beloved in certain European countries that festivals are held when the first ones of the season arrive. Entire menus feature asparagus, including asparagus ice cream. But that's where I draw the line.

White asparagus are green asparagus that have been grown under a mound of dirt to shield them from sunlight. They are much more expensive than green asparagus because of the labor involved in growing them. If they are not fresh, white asparagus are bitter; even fresh stalks must be peeled. On the whole I prefer green asparagus, which taste sweeter.

Though the spears are excellent just steamed until they are tender, a bit of melted butter, lemon butter, black butter and capers or hollandaise never hurts them. Toasted pecans sprinkled on top provide a marvelous contrast of textures.

Slice, Then Stir-Fry

Sliced on the diagonal, asparagus take nicely to stir-frying when seasoned with a bit of ginger and a touch of soy sauce. Often served with ham, asparagus are also a delightful accompaniment to grilled fish or chicken.

Cold they are excellent with vinaigrette, but they should be sauced just before serving or the spears will turn yellow. They also make a great midnight snack, served cold.

And though they are seldom seen in arrangements of crudités, asparagus tips are wonderful raw.

Asparagus

I got taken to the grammarian's woodshed on this one:

"In your 'De Gustibus' piece in today's *Times* (2/3/85) you write the word *asparagus* as though it were plural. It is *not*—it is singular, according to three dictionaries I have consulted, and I should be most grateful to know how you received the plural form. I am making a short study of popular usage as opposed to dictionary definitions and have never seen asparagus in the plural before this use of yours.

"I imagine the terminal 's' sound confuses people in the same way that they speak of my appendix have been removed," said a Cambridge, Massachusetts, reader.

If you knew how careful the copy desk that reads my copy is, you would know why I was so shocked to receive this letter. The desk had checked *Webster's New World Dictionary, Second College Edition,* which gave the following definition: Any of a genus of plants of the lily family, with small, scalelike leaves, many flat or needlelike branches, and whitish flowers.

Reporting on this in a later column did not silence the critics, and this letter came from New Haven, Connecticut: "On the subject of the grammatical number of asparagus, I must agree with the reader from Cambridge that your plural usage is bizarre, notwithstanding your defense published this Saturday. I cannot agree with your reading of it. According to the second definition, the (singular) noun asparagus means (i.e., equals) 'the tender shoots, that is, it refers to a collection of shoots; cf. the second definition of lettuce, which I cannot imagine you take to be a plural noun, but which similarly refers to 'the leaves' (plural)."

My Cambridge critic also had another comment. "Why is it correct to dangle spears of asparagus in the fingers and eat thus when we in America never do this? I have seen it done in London—by people who are supposed to know the correct thing to do at table."

Maybe they don't eat asparagus with their fingers in Cambridge, but they do in New York City and Washington, D.C., so I referred the writer to my column of the previous year on the proper method for eating asparagus.

Filling Phyllo (Strudel) with Surprise Stuffings
October 15, 1983

The freewheeling spirit that has characterized American cooking in the past few years has reached into Middle Europe and the Middle East for one of its newer inspirations. The translucent sheets of pastry known as phyllo in Greece, *yufka* in Turkey and strudel in Central Europe are being used to wrap things that had never seen the inside of the dough until Americans began experimenting with them.

Caramelized fruit, sausages and apples, and spears of asparagus are taking their places alongside the more traditional fillings of cheese, spinach, lamb and rice, dried fruits and nuts and the most glamorous phyllo dish of all, Moroccan *bastelle*—chicken with saffron, cinnamon and coriander. In fact, almost anything that can be put in pie crust, brioche or croissant dough will be equally good wrapped in phyllo.

Commercial production of the leaves (phyllo comes from the Greek word for leaf) has put such dishes within the reach of any moderately dexterous cook. But I don't know if my Aunt Bess would approve. She always made her strudel dough from scratch, which means she painstakingly stretched the dough with her hands.

After the filling was made but before the dough was mixed, she took off her rings and washed the white enamel kitchen table. The table was somehow exactly the right size for the amount of dough that had been made. The dough was worked with clenched fists so that fingernails could not poke holes in it. In my aunt's strudel dough there could be no holes. How she knew to what point it could be stretched without tearing remains a mystery to this day.

Years later I watched a Yugoslav woman make the dough. Hers had a few holes in it but she patched it. I went home and tried it. I guess I didn't have the right kitchen table. But even my uneven and hole-ridden dough produced a wonderful crust.

Since Greek girls start to learn the art of making phyllo when they are five years old, it is probably too late for most of those reading this column to become proficient. Fortunately it is possible to buy handmade phyllo in some Greek pastry shops.

Handmade phyllo is a lighter, more tender pastry than the leaves made commercially by machine. But many of the commercial doughs are of such high quality, especially if they have not been frozen, that it is possible to produce wonderful dishes using them.

After years of working with phyllo I have developed a ritual from which I try never to deviate. The few times I have, I have regretted it. The most important step is the purchase of the dough. I would rather do without than buy it frozen because no matter how I thaw it—three days in the refrigerator, a few hours at room temperature—the results are always the same: The leaves stick together and tear.

Before I take the leaves out of the airtight plastic pouch in which they are packed, I ready the filling and the work surface and melt the butter. The leaves are placed on waxed paper and covered with more waxed paper. Then a damp towel is laid over them.

Because the dough is so thin, it must be kept damp at all times or it will dry up and crumble like ancient papyrus leaves. Covering it with the towel makes it possible to work at a more leisurely pace than might otherwise be possible. One woman I know, worried that the dough would dry out if she were interrupted, used to lock her doors and take her phone off the hook when she made *tiropeta,* the cheese-filled phyllo.

After the leaves are arranged, the width of the strips is determined with a ruler and the strips are cut with a large, sharp knife. Then as many as can be laid on the counter in a single line are arranged. At this point speed is of the essence. The sheets must immediately be generously brushed with melted butter. I prefer a two-inch paintbrush.

The final buttering of the tops of the phyllo packets, whether triangles, rolls or squares, is done after a baking sheet has been filled with them. At this point they can be frozen without ill effect—if they will not be used within a day or two—before or after baking.

No matter what any cookbook says, phyllo should be baked at 400 degrees, not less, if they are to brown properly. The advantage of baking them before freezing is that they will be ready to serve after just a brief reheating.

After years of filling, wrapping and rolling cheese, spinach, nuts and raisins in phyllo, I have branched out. Recently I tried a mixture of chopped *weisswurst* and apples and before that I made phyllo triangles filled with shrimp, crab and basil. Next on my list are coronets made from phyllo and filled with fruit and liqueur-flavored whipped cream.

I may never be in my Aunt Bess's league, but I'm having a good time trying. I wonder what she would think if she could see me rolling the sheets of phyllo without even taking my rings off?

Phyllo

This strudel-phyllo column brought a fascinating suggestion from a Greek woman who has been baking with phyllo for thirty years. It is so interesting that it is worth sharing because it is so much simpler and quicker than the traditional method.

The correspondent, from Troy, New York, does not cut strips. Here are her directions:

Take an entire sheet of phyllo, short side at the top and bottom. Brush the left two-thirds of it with melted butter. Fold one-third of the right over to the left. Then brush the part that was just folded over with butter. Fold the left third over the right third. You should have one long strip with two folded sides.

Place the filling at the bottom in the usual fashion and fold in the customary American-flag manner. Cut each triangle in half to make cocktail-size triangles; butter the tops and bake as usual.

Phyllo Stuffed with Goat Cheese and Prosciutto

    1/2 pound medium-sharp soft goat cheese
     3 tablespoons cream cheese
    1/2 cup large-curd cottage cheese
     2 teaspoons fresh chopped thyme leaves, or 1/2 teaspoon dried
       Freshly ground black pepper to taste
     2 medium eggs
     3 ounces prosciutto, sliced thin, cut into 1/8-inch-thick strips and
       then into 1/2-inch pieces
    1/2 pound fresh phyllo dough, approximately
    1/4 pound unsalted butter, melted

1. In a food processor whirl the cheeses with the thyme, pepper and eggs until smooth. Stir in the prosciutto.
2. On a work surface lay out the phyllo, one sheet at a time, keeping the remaining phyllo covered with a damp cloth. Cut the dough lengthwise into 1¾-inch-wide strips. Brush the

strips with melted butter and fold over ¼ inch of the bottom edge.

3. Put less than a teaspoon of filling on the folded end and fold over one corner to make a triangle. Continue folding the phyllo from side to side in the shape of a triangle, just as you would a flag. Place seam side down on a baking sheet. Repeat the procedure until all the filling is used.

4. Brush the tops of the pastries with melted butter and bake at 400 degrees about 15 minutes, until golden brown. Serve warm or at room temperature, not hot.

5. If desired, the baked phyllo may be refrigerated or frozen and reheated at 350 degrees for about 10 minutes.

YIELD: 50 to 60 triangles

Healthy Dining: Do Guests Know the Difference?

October 13, 1984

The last time I served a standing rib roast with roast potatoes to company was twelve years ago, and then it was on request. Today when I really want to impress my guests, I use boneless chicken breasts instead. Or, possibly, veal, occasionally fish or lamb.

I suppose that, in a way, I am imposing my taste for light, healthful food on other people. But for the most part if I don't tell them it's good for them, they like it. Over the years I have altered my cooking techniques for family meals to reflect an increased appreciation for fresh vegetables and a desire to reduce fat and sodium in our diet. Without my realizing it, some of those techniques have spilled over to company cooking as well.

Absence That Isn't Noted

I don't salt food when I cook it except for the bit added to baked goods, where it is essential. Still, force of habit causes me to put salt cellars on the table, though guests seldom pick them up anymore. It is amazing that even those who have not reduced their salt consumption don't notice the lack of salt in the food I serve—and that includes those who come for a brunch at which omelets are featured. Since an omelet always has a filling, usually one of mushrooms, onion, tomatoes and whatever else is in the refrigerator, along with herbs such as thyme or cilantro or spices like cumin, salt doesn't seem necessary. At dinner a new-potato and broccoli vinaigrette salad served without salt was not salted by the guests.

If a recipe calls for browning in oil or butter, I automatically reduce the amount. Eggplant, just like a sponge when it comes to mopping up oil, doesn't need as much as I once thought. While following an old recipe for caponata for twenty-five people, I started with one cup instead of the usual 1½ and never added more; one was sufficient. Even so, as a guest was spooning it onto black bread, she said, "This is so wonderful I suppose it has a lot of oil in it." Only about two teaspoons a serving.

At that dinner a salad of red peppers, mushrooms and scallions was dressed with a mixture of equal parts of olive oil and red wine vinegar, plus freshly ground black pepper. The traditional ratio of oil to vinegar is three to one, but a mellow vinegar allowed the use of less oil. And there was no salt. The salad was the hit of the evening, several people asking for the recipe.

Most people will happily eat healthful food as long as it tastes good, but when they go to dinner parties, they would just as soon not be reminded of the fact. It is also true that most of them will eat whatever is set in front of them unless it violates a dietary restriction for religious or health reasons. But offer people a choice, and they are as likely to choose the fattening as the healthful food.

Leftovers for an Army

No matter how often I serve crudités because "everyone" says they want them, the next day, invariably, I could feed an army with the leftovers. If I also serve phyllo filled with cheese and oozing butter at the same dinner party, there is seldom enough to give the dog a treat.

When it comes to dessert, if guests are given a choice between pears poached in red wine with basil or rosemary and a mousse cake called double chocolate threat, they usually opt for both.

Last week the chef at the Golden Door, a spa in Escondido, California, was visiting New York. He prepared a low-calorie, low-fat, no-salt-added lunch that all my twenty-three guests agreed was delicious—and filling. But four of them were spotted afterward eating at the Délices Guy Pascal bakery around the corner.

Spa Food

Correction. They were not eating chocolate cake. They were eating something *worse!* And better!

It is the signature dessert from the bakery called Délices Guy Pascal, and it consists of layers of hazelnut meringue, divided from one another by chocolate *ganache*, mocha buttercream filling and *crème Chantilly*.

It is one of New York City's most devastating desserts. And I include the recipe for it, which you must promise you will not try until after you have had this recipe for hot broccoli and potato salad, which illustrates how reducing the amount of oil substantially in a salad dressing can produce a wonderful dish.

HOT POTATO AND BROCCOLI SALAD

> 1 *pound tiny new potatoes*
> 1 *pound broccoli, trimmed of tough stems, heads cut into florets*
> 4 *tablespoons olive oil*
> 4 *tablespoons cider vinegar*
> 1/2 *teaspoon dry mustard*
> 1/4 *teaspoon paprika*
>   *Freshly ground black pepper to taste*
> 1 *garlic clove, minced*
> 2 *scallions, finely sliced*

1. Scrub the potatoes and cook them whole in their jackets in a covered pot in water to cover until tender, about 20 minutes. When the potatoes are done, drain and cool slightly. Cut into quarters.

2. Steam the broccoli florets over hot water until just tender, about 7 minutes.

3. While the vegetables are cooking, whisk the oil with the vinegar, mustard, paprika and pepper. Stir in the garlic and scallions.

4. Gently stir in the potato quarters and broccoli and serve warm.

YIELD: 4 servings

And now, death by dessert.

LE DÉLICE GUY PASCAL

> 4 *Meringue Disks (see recipe)*
> 4 *cups La Ganache à la Suisse (see recipe)*
> 8 *cups coffee buttercream (see recipe)*
> 3 *cups* Crème Chantilly *(see recipe)*
> ¾ *pound blanched, sliced almonds, toasted*

1. Lay one meringue disk on a serving dish and spread 4 cups of *ganache* over it.

2. Lay a second meringue disk over the *ganache* and spread it with half of the coffee buttercream, leaving enough to cover the top and sides of the finished cake.

3. Lay a third meringue disk over the coffee buttercream and cover it with *Crème Chantilly.* Top with a final meringue disk.

4. Spread the top and sides of the dessert with the remaining buttercream. Coat the cake with the toasted almonds. Refrigerate until well chilled.

YIELD: 10 to 12 servings

MERINGUE DISKS

> *Unsalted butter for greasing baking sheets*
> *Flour for dusting baking sheets*
> 5 *ounces blanched almonds, ground*
> 2⅓ *cups superfine sugar*
> 2 *tablespoons cornstarch*
> 1½ *cups egg whites, about 12 large eggs*

1. Preheat the oven to 275 degrees.

2. Butter and lightly flour two baking sheets. Trace 2 eight-inch circles on each sheet.

3. In a large bowl, mix the ground almonds, 2 cups of the sugar and the cornstarch. Set aside.

4. In a large bowl, beat the egg whites until they are frothy. Gradually add the remaining sugar, beating constantly, until the whites are stiff.

5. Fold the whites into the almond mixture.

6. Fill a pastry bag fitted with a Number 4 round tip with the meringue. On the baking sheets, squeeze the meringue around the rim of the traced circle. Work toward the center in a circular motion until the entire circle is filled in. Repeat with the remaining circles.

7. Bake 45 minutes or until the meringues are golden and crisp. Do not let the meringues become too brown.

YIELD: 4 eight-inch meringue disks

LA GANACHE À LA SUISSE

10 ounces sweet dark chocolate, cut into small cubes
3½ cups heavy cream
1 vanilla bean

1. Place the chocolate in a large bowl and set aside.

2. In a saucepan over medium heat, combine the cream and the vanilla bean and bring just to a boil. Remove from heat immediately. Remove the vanilla bean and pour the cream over the chocolate, stirring to dissolve the chocolate pieces.

3. Refrigerate the chocolate cream for one hour, or until the mixture is completely chilled, stirring occasionally and carefully, checking the consistency. If the chocolate cream becomes too cold before whipping, the end product will be grainy. If it is not cold enough the cream will not whip.

4. Beat the chocolate cream until it holds a peak. Do not overbeat or the mixture will separate. Refrigerate again for half an hour, or until ready to use. The chocolate cream will harden as it stands.

YIELD: About 4 cups

COFFEE BUTTERCREAM

2 *tablespoons powdered instant coffee*
2 *tablespoons boiling water*
1 *cup egg whites, about 8 large eggs*
1 *pound confectioners' sugar*
1 *pound unsalted butter, at room temperature*

1. Dissolve the instant coffee in the boiling water. Set aside.
2. In the top of a double boiler over simmering water, beat the egg whites and confectioners' sugar just until the mixture is slightly warmed, creamy and smooth. The temperature should not exceed 90 degrees on a candy thermometer. Remove from heat.
3. Continue beating until the mixture has cooled and is thick and white.
4. Add the butter, a little at a time, and continue beating. The mixture will look as if it is about to separate. Continue beating until the butter is well incorporated and the mixture becomes smooth.
5. Fold the coffee into the buttercream. Beat thoroughly. Cover and refrigerate until ready to use.

YIELD: 8 cups

CRÈME CHANTILLY

2 *cups heavy cream*
1/4 *cup confectioners' sugar*

1. In a large bowl beat the cream until it begins to thicken.
2. Gradually add the sugar, beating constantly, just until the cream holds stiff peaks. Refrigerate until ready to use.

YIELD: About 3 cups

For Colds Around the World, It's Chicken Soup

February 8, 1986

"Jewish penicillin" is made by the French, the Italians, the Greeks, the Hungarians, the Vietnamese and people of countless other nationalities who know that chicken soup has mystical therapeutic properties. Science has never been able to isolate them, but not for lack of trying.

Three physicians at Mount Sinai Medical Center in Miami Beach performed an experiment that is described by Joe Graedon, a pharmacologist, in a self-help book called *The People's Pharmacy II*. He says in part:

> We decided to assess whether chicken soup might have a therapeutic rationale other than its good taste. We measured nasal mucus velocity, since transport of nasal secretions serves as a first line of host defense in removal of pathogens (nasties like viruses). It was not possible to design a double-blind study because the placebo could be distinguished by taste from the chicken soup, but we did randomize the various treatments.

For Acute Rhinitis

> Drinking hot chicken soup either by sipping or by straw increased nasal mucus velocity compared to the sham procedure. An increase in nasal mucus velocity should be beneficial in acute rhinitis (stuffy nose) since the contact time of a pathogen on the nasal mucosa would be shortened, thereby minimizing its penetration and multiplication. Finally, the delayed suppression of nasal mucus velocity thirty minutes after drinking cold water suggests that hot rather than cold liquids might be preferable in the recommendations for fluid intake in patients with upper respiratory tract infections (colds).

In other words, chicken soup is good for colds.

In addition, the survey found that volunteers who drank hot

water also showed an increase in velocity, but not nearly so great as that experienced by the chicken soup imbibers. Could the difference be the aroma?

Not all chicken soup is the same, of course. Mother's is best (although there are some families in which grandmother's may be better). And every mother makes it differently.

What is striking is that broth, whether made with chicken or veal or beef, is the medicine of choice for a cold or flu almost everywhere.

In Hungary it is called *becsinalt leves,* which roughly translates, according to Paulette Fono, as a *gemischt* soup, which roughly translates to a soup with a lot of different things. Fono, a restaurateur in San Francisco who was born in Hungary, says it is a "vegetable soup done the same way as chicken soup." The vegetables are sautéed with chicken wings or little pieces of veal, then are dusted with flour, put in a pot with water and cooked. Fono said that for the really sick, the soup was made with the whole chicken.

For Greek children, the traditional chicken soup, made with carrots, celery, onion and garlic, is further enriched with lemon juice and eggs, according to Tessie Chrissotimos, who lives on Staten Island.

The French, however, do something slightly different, according to Marc Sarrazen, owner of DeBragga & Spitler, a wholesale meat company. When he was a child in France, he got beef consommé with bits of very lean cooked hamburger in it. But Sarrazen said his children were brought up in this country and "we gave them Jewish penicillin."

Those used to European-style chicken soup would consider the Vietnamese version quite exotic. And quite delicious. According to Germaine Swanson, who was born in Vietnam, the chicken soup there is made with fresh ginger and an onion that has been grilled over charcoal to give it a burnt flavor. After the fat is skimmed off, the soup is seasoned with *nuoc mam*—fish sauce— and fresh coriander, green onion, rice noodles and the meat of the chicken. "It's also good for hangovers," said Swanson, who owns Germaine's, a restaurant in Washington, D.C.

The Vietnamese and Italian variations are among the most interesting. Carole Lalli, a senior editor at Simon & Schuster, remembers chicken broth made thick with pastina.

The Canned Version

Just as this column was being written a can of Mount Sinai Medical Center Clear Chicken Soup arrived in the mail! The literature that accompanied it reiterates the researchers' earlier findings about the benefits of chicken soup. Packed for the medical center by Manischewitz, and kosher for Passover, it can never compete with mother's. For one thing, it contains monosodium glutamate.

The bottom line is that everyone loves soup when a cold strikes. It is so highly regarded that a Jewish Penicillin Connoisseurs Association has sprung up. According to a press release from the Stage Delicatessen on Seventh Avenue at 54th Street in New York City, the association is "a consortium of Jewish mothers, grandmothers and related perpetrators of 'old wives tales.'"

And in this season of colds and flu, the Stage Deli is prepared to offer a bowl of free chicken soup any Thursday this month from 11 A.M. until closing to anyone, "man or woman, who brings in proof of their spouse's status as a doctor, in addition to proof of their own identity as husband or wife of the doctor."

The restaurant is doing this, it says, because the physicians in question have to work overtime during the flu season and their loved ones may feel lonely and neglected.

Chicken soup is good for that too.

Chicken Soup

The day after the chicken soup piece appeared, one reader was sent a calendar put out by the people who sell St. Joseph's aspirin. Along with helpful hints and a recipe for roast pork, the calendar made reference to the study at Mount Sinai and added this piece of startling information: "In the twelfth century, Rabbi Maimonides recommended hot chicken soup for illnesses."

MY MOTHER'S CHICKEN SOUP

> 4 cups water
> 3 to 4 pounds chicken, cut up
> 2 or 3 carrots, washed
> 3 celery stalks, washed
> 1 onion, sliced
>   Salt and pepper to taste

1. Combine the ingredients in a large pot. Cover and bring to a boil. Reduce the heat and simmer for 45 minutes. Strain.
2. For fat-free soup, refrigerate until it congeals. Remove the fat layer.

Note: Because so little water is used, this is a very rich broth. If you want more broth and less flavor, you can add 2 more cups of water, but no more than that.

YIELD: About 4 cups

Making the Most of Shad Roe
March 31, 1984

Usually it is on one of those late-February days when the world has turned to slush that I see the first sign in a fishmonger's window offering shad roe. It is as pleasant a harbinger of spring as forced hyacinth or paper narcissus. Although spring will be a little late this year, the shad do not seem to have noticed the recent awful weather and have made their presence felt all over town. Not as keenly, however, as in the part of the world in which I learned most of my cooking, Bethesda, Maryland, where the best seafood comes from Chesapeake Bay.

It is difficult to believe that my first cookbook instructions for preparing shad roe directed me to remove the membrane—the sac that encases the eggs—after poaching. I tried it once, and after hours of fruitless peeling I vowed never to cook shad roe again. And I didn't until a more experienced cook assured me that the membrane was both harmless and tasteless and should be left on.

That was my first lesson on shad roe. The second, self-taught, was that before the roe are sautéed or broiled, the membrane should be pricked or it is likely to burst (it takes a great deal of time to remove bits of tiny eggs from the surfaces around the range).

Since the roe and I have come to terms, I have waited eagerly for the first sign of spring at the fish counter.

Shad were once so abundant along the East Coast that the wealthy would not eat them, fearing that they would be mistaken for poor folk. In former times, when the fish returned to fresh water from the ocean to spawn, the waters teemed with them. Today shad roe are considered an expensive delicacy.

The first shad in New York come from Chesapeake Bay, where shad roe and the first spring asparagus are an immutable combination. The roe are usually poached, then sautéed and served with crisp bacon strips. This simple preparation cannot be faulted. Sautéing intensifies the essence of the shad, highlighting its sweetness. But Maryland, which prides itself on its blue crabs, can be forgiven for insisting on a dish that combines the roe and crabmeat, especially since it is so delicious.

New Ways of Preparation

Only in recent years have cooks begun to experiment with new ways of serving shad roe. The flavor is so delicate that assertive sauces and seasonings will overwhelm it. La Caravelle offers excellent poached roe with two caviars in a *beurre rouge,* the caviar and sauce complementing the beautifully poached roe. Though cream sauce or hollandaise, melted butter or a light garlic mayonnaise is excellent with shad roe too, my favorite method of preparation is to sauté them and serve them with brown butter and toasted almonds. Gilding the lily a little never hurt anyone.

The roe do not have to be poached or blanched before being sautéed, but poaching is recommended for the cook inexperienced with them because it firms the egg masses and makes them easier to handle. Roe come in pairs, or sets, which must be carefully split after poaching.

Overcooking and high heat will toughen the roe. To poach, lower the washed roe into gently boiling water that has been acidulated with a tablespoon of lemon juice. Reduce the heat so that the roe simmer and cook only until they turn opaque. To stop the cooking process plunge the roe immediately into a bowl of ice water; drain on paper towels and then split carefully. The roe are now ready for further cooking.

To make the dish with brown butter and toasted almonds— one small set is enough for a person—dust the roe lightly with flour and sauté them slowly in butter, about two tablespoons per set, on both sides until they are nicely browned. Meantime, melt two tablespoons of butter and add a tablespoon of sliced almonds. Cook until the butter and almonds begin to brown. When the roe are done, place them on a warm plate, pour on the brown butter and almonds and serve with steamed asparagus.

Cooking for One Made Easier
March 23, 1985

It has been a long time since singles have had to open a can of pork and beans and call it dinner because they hated cooking for one. With carryout food available on almost every block in Manhattan and salad bars threatening to take over the center aisle of corner vegetable stands, the single diner now has lots of choices.

Salad bars appeal especially to frugal weight watchers, but even they tire of cold or marinated vegetables, varied only by the choice of toppings and dressings, night after night.

To bring some diversity into their menu planning the creative cooks have been putting the salad ingredients to a new use— they are cooking them. The most popular dishes are stir-fried, but a good many lone diners are steaming the vegetables. Since all the preparation has already been done, it takes very little more effort to have a cooked meal in place of a cold salad.

Progressive shops in other cities, aware of this trend, have begun offering additional nonsalad ingredients that fit right in with stir-fry cooking. Some supermarkets are providing bowls of marinated strips of chicken and beef alongside the chick-peas and three-bean salad, bacon bits and radishes.

For those whose markets do not yet offer such amenities, there are some simple alternatives. A small package of chicken breasts or a suitable cut of beef such as round steak can be purchased in the supermarket, marinated and frozen in appropriate portions. Or, for those who prefer a vegetarian meal, a single block of tofu, available at most markets, can be cut up and added to the stir-fried dish. If a fish market is nearby, a few shrimp, scallops or a small fillet of salmon or other flavorful fish might also be added.

There are two things to consider when you wonder whether it is worth paying someone else to slice the vegetables: waste and stamina. Cut-up red peppers, broccoli florets, bok choy and sliced mushrooms can be purchased in just the right amount, avoiding waste, and it's a lot easier at the end of a hard day just to dump them in the pan, wok or steamer. That's still less expensive than eating out or buying a carryout salad. And there's a certain satisfaction in cooking something, however simple, even if it's just for one. Beyond that, there won't be those little mysteries wrapped in tinfoil or plastic discovered weeks later in dark corners of the refrigerator.

Cooking for One from a Salad Bar

When the salad-bar-in-supermarkets-and-greengrocers piece was first written, salad bars were infrequently found in Manhattan and perhaps not at all in most other cities. Today they are on almost every street corner, and instead of selling twenty or twenty-five items they now have as many as one hundred, with many prepared salads and hot dishes.

And after doing a story about the best salad bars in New York City and sampling from twenty of them, I got food poisoning, the kind that lasts 2½ weeks. I can never prove that it came from a salad bar, but I steer clear of them now except for the raw ingredients that can be turned into a cooked dish. I won't eat anything from them raw anymore.

The raw ingredients can be a great boon to the single cook. They perform the task of an assistant cook, preparing the *mis en place*.

Here is a recipe for one that takes advantage of the salad bar. Of course, the meal can be made with whole vegetables too.

TEX-MEX PIZZA
FRUIT SALAD

This is a very simple and light meal, so fruit salad or some other dessert is suggested. Or you could make three pizzas for each serving!

    2 10-inch flour tortillas
    3 ounces red onion, sliced or whole
    1 tablespoon olive oil
    6 to 8 ounces zucchini, slices or whole
    ½ pound red bell peppers, slices or whole
    3 shiitake or other wild mushrooms, or ordinary white mushrooms
    ½ to ¾ cup tomato puree
    1 ounce Parmesan cheese

1. Preheat the oven to broil.
2. Heat a 10-inch heavy skillet. When it is hot, place the tortillas, one at a time, in the ungreased skillet and heat until each begins to blister on one side; turn and repeat. The total cooking time for each tortilla is about 1 to 1½ minutes. Repeat until all the tortillas are heated; set aside but do not stack, in order to keep the tortillas crisp.
3. Meanwhile peel and slice the onion in a food processor if it is not sliced.
4. Heat the oil and sauté the onion in it.
5. Wash the zucchini and red pepper and slice if they are whole. Add to the onions and continue to sauté.
6. Wash, stem and cut up the mushrooms; add to the vegetables and continue to sauté until the vegetables are tender.
7. Spread the tomato puree evenly over the top of each tortilla.
8. Arrange the vegetables on top of each tortilla.

9. Grate the cheese and sprinkle over the vegetables.

10. Cover the broiler pan with aluminum foil and broil the pizzas close to the heat for 1 minute or less, just to melt the cheese. Watch carefully as they burn easily.

YIELD: 1 serving

Frying Chicken: Ask Five Cooks, Get Five Answers
March 2, 1985

If, as each fried chicken expert insists, there is only one right way to fry chicken, why are there so many recipes for it?

A glance at the recipes provides the explanation. No one can agree on anything about making fried chicken except the four basic ingredients: the chicken, flour, salt and pepper. Even the frying medium is open to dispute.

Which produces the crispest skin: vegetable oil, vegetable shortening, butter, bacon grease or lard?

Should the chicken be soaked in something before it is floured? If so, what? Milk, buttermilk, lemon juice or vinegar and water?

Must the fat cover the chicken?

Is a cast-iron skillet essential?

Should the skillet be covered or uncovered?

Is it still fried chicken without the gravy?

And, the inevitable question, should anyone be making fried chicken with all its fat and calories?

Ask five Southern cooks the answers to those questions, and you will find yourself with five answers.

As a matter of fact, Lindy Boggs, the congresswoman who represents the French Quarter of New Orleans, doesn't make fried chicken anymore. She prefers hers oven-baked.

Edna Lewis, who has spent a lifetime interpreting Southern food for the rest of us, prefers frying in butter. She also insists on letting the chicken rest for an hour after flouring to make it "crisp and evenly browned."

Frances Hooks says an old cast-iron skillet is essential and recommends hunting one up at a garage sale rather than trying to season a new one. She soaks her chicken in water that has been acidulated with lemon juice and vinegar. Hooks's husband, Benjamin, now executive director of the National Association for the Advancement of Colored People, once worked for the Minnie Pearl fried-chicken fast-food franchise, and it was his wife's chicken he thought the company should reproduce.

Liz Carpenter, former press secretary to Lady Bird Johnson and a native Texan, however, says all the talk about technique and equipment for frying chicken is beside the point. "You either know how to fry chicken or you don't," she says. "You're either born with it or you aren't." Liz says, "It's a mortal sin if you don't serve hot biscuits, turnip or mustard greens, and rice" with the chicken.

But that doesn't stop the less fortunate from trying.

Liz Wolferman Haupert, a native Arkansan, from whom I learned to fry chicken thirty years ago, never soaked it, never insisted on a cast-iron skillet, but said bacon grease was essential. And in the days when I thought bacon grease was something to treasure and save in a coffee can, I fried some pretty good chicken for a New England native.

For those who have been worrying about the crispness of their southern fried chicken and for those who have thought about frying it but have never dared, there are a few elemental rules that are essential.

1. Fried chicken is never deep-fried. It should be made in a deep frying pan with a cover.

2. Fried chicken must never be coated with anything except flour mixed with salt and pepper. Whether the cook wants to add paprika, nutmeg or cayenne pepper is up to the cook. But forget the eggs, bread crumbs and crushed cornflakes.

3. Fried chicken can be shaken in a bag with seasoned flour as long as there is enough flour to coat every nook and cranny of the pieces.

4. Fried chicken should be eaten warm, not hot. It needs time to cool down. On the other hand, fried chicken that has seen the

inside of a refrigerator is not really fried chicken anymore. Cook enough for only one meal at a time.

Liz Haupert's recipe will make a Rebel out of any Yankee even though it has been revised to use corn oil in place of the bacon grease. What corn oil lacks in flavor it makes up for by easing guilt feelings about saturated fat and cholesterol.

And for those who have given up fried chicken, there is Lindy Boggs's recipe for oven-fried chicken.

LIZ HAUPERT'S FRIED CHICKEN

3 to 3½ pounds chicken, cut into equal-size serving pieces
1 to 1½ cups flour
Salt and freshly ground black pepper to taste
Corn oil

1. Wash the chicken pieces and drain but do not dry them.
2. Place the flour in a plastic bag, add salt and pepper to taste and shake to mix. Add a few chicken pieces at a time and shake to coat the pieces thoroughly all over with flour. Place the coated pieces on waxed paper and repeat until the chicken is floured. Add more flour if necessary.
3. Pour enough oil into a deep, heavy skillet to cover the chicken pieces almost entirely and heat until the oil begins to ripple. The skillet should be large enough to accommodate all the chicken pieces in a single layer.
4. Place the chicken pieces into the hot oil skin side down and cook over high heat 10 minutes or until golden. Turn and cook 10 minutes more or until golden. Turn and reduce the heat to medium; cover and cook for 5 minutes. Turn and cook 5 minutes more.
5. Remove the chicken from the pan and drain on several layers of paper towels on both sides. Serve warm, not hot.

YIELD: 4 servings

LINDY BOGGS'S OVEN-FRIED CHICKEN

¼ cup butter
⅓ cup flour
2½ pounds chicken, cut into equal size serving pieces
2 eggs
 Salt to taste
1 tablespoon paprika
2 tablespoons lemon juice
1 cup cracker crumbs

1. Place the butter in a 13 × 9 × 2-inch baking dish and place in a 350-degree oven to melt the butter.
2. Flour the chicken pieces and set aside.
3. Beat together the eggs, salt, paprika and lemon juice. Dip the chicken pieces, one at a time, in the egg mixture, then in the cracker crumbs. Arrange the pieces skin side down in the baking dish with the melted butter and bake for 45 minutes at 350 degrees, turning once.

YIELD: 2 to 3 servings

Soft-Shell Crabs: Simplest Is Best

May 4, 1985

They are called busters and peepers in Louisiana, peelers in the Chesapeake Bay. For the cognoscenti, those terms denote the most succulent stage in the life of an Atlantic blue crab: when it is molting. And the molting season is upon us.

Crabs are *the* American shellfish, especially as soft shells. If soft-shell crabs are part of the culinary repertory of any other country, it is a closely guarded secret. Here they are not well known outside the East Coast and the Gulf states. The blues are found in salt and brackish waters along the Atlantic and Gulf coasts, though there is general agreement that the best come from the Chesapeake Bay. In the South the males are called jim-mies and the females sooks.

Except for about forty-eight hours two or three times a season the blue crab is well protected by a blue-green shell that turns fire engine red upon cooking and can be penetrated only with the aid of a mallet. To some people the meat is not plentiful enough to be worth all the mess involved in extracting it. Those people eat picked crabmeat from cans.

But from March or April until November blue crabs become exceedingly vulnerable as they shed their armor-like shell. And for lovers of crab, who want all the pleasure without any work, there is nothing as satisfying as a soft-shell crab, preferably a plate piled high with them. As wonderful as picked crabmeat may be, it just does not have the same allure, the same romance or the same succulence as crab in its shell, soft or hard.

People who live along the water where the crabs retire to shed often collect them just before they are ready to lose their shells and keep them caged in the water, waiting for them to shed.

In the soft-shell stage the crab can be eaten in toto after a bit of trimming and cleaning. It contains more meat when it is in the peeler stage than when its carapace returns.

Until recently most people who prepared the crabs didn't fuss too much with them. A light coating with flour, a little salt and pepper, and the crabs were either deep-fried or sautéed and gar-nished with a lemon wedge. The first break with simplicity and tradition came when someone added sautéed almond slices to the crabs. A worthy addition. Then someone suggested a touch of garlic, a bit of cayenne. Not bad either.

Now the floodgates have been opened, and soft-shell crab is being served with linguine in a tomato-based sauce; with spinach fettuccine, pine nuts, basil and cheese; with mushrooms, fennel and tomato-anchovy sauce; with hot chile oil and sesame seeds.

It is being marinated in vinegar, accompanied by chopped cor-nichons, sautéed with pesto and wrapped in phyllo. And the suc-culent sweet taste of the crabs, not to mention the delicate texture, disappears under these overpowering and not especially appropriate ingredients.

Before you try any of the newfangled soft-shell crab concoc-tions, try them the simple way: sautéed. Maybe for a little glam-our, add a few almonds.

SAUTÉED SOFT-SHELL CRABS

16 medium-size soft-shell crabs
½ cup sliced almonds
   Flour for dredging
   Salt and freshly ground black pepper to taste
8 tablespoons unsalted butter
3 tablespoons vegetable oil
   Lemon wedges

1. To clean the crabs: With a small knife cut off the apron at the rear of the body. Turn the crab and cut off the face at the point just behind the eyes. Lift each point of the crab at the sides and with your fingers clean out the feathery gills. Wash under cold water.
2. Toast the almonds until golden.
3. Season the flour with salt and pepper and dredge the crabs lightly in it. Heat the butter and oil in 1 or 2 skillets large enough to hold the crabs in a single layer and sauté about 3 minutes on each side, until golden. Top with the almonds and serve with lemon wedges.

YIELD: 4 to 6 servings

Note: Cayenne pepper can be added to the flour. If crushed garlic is used, add it to the pan with the crabs.

Secret Weapon for Attacking Hard-Shelled Crabs

August 2, 1986

After 25 years of eating hard-shelled crabs in Washington, D.C., crab houses, up and down the Maryland and Delaware coasts and on the shores of the Chesapeake Bay, I considered myself a pro at extracting the sweet, white meat in the hard red shells. But last Tuesday night I learned something about the art of picking a crab in the most unlikely of settings, a restaurant in the heart of Manhattan.

It happened at the American Festival Cafe in Rockefeller Center, which has imported the owners of Baltimore's best crab house, Obrycki's, to cook hard-shelled crabs the way Marylanders have learned to love them over the centuries: steamed in a mixture of hot spices that cry out for a pitcher of beer.

Rose and Richard Cernak trucked an enormous pressure steamer up from Baltimore to turn Maryland's beautiful blue crabs into gorgeous red creatures. True aficionados can eat a dozen of them in one sitting. Last summer at a crab feast in Bethesda, Maryland, Sarah Brady, the wife of the White House press secretary, James S. Brady, did just that. She was still picking her twelfth crab while the rest of us, who had consumed no more than six, were on dessert.

Not Even a Nutcracker

For those who don't know the proper picking technique, it can take just as long to eat one crab as it takes Sarah Brady to eat a dozen. Novices think that the mallet usually provided is meant for bludgeoning the crab into giving up its meat. All that does is mix in particles of the shell. In fact, it isn't necessary to use the mallet directly on the crab at all. It isn't even necessary to use a nutcracker. A small paring knife is the secret utensil that the Cernaks used with such dexterity the other night. When I mentioned it to Sarah Brady, she laughed knowingly.

But my ignorance is nothing compared with the Cernaks' experience when a group of "sophisticated New York food people confronted the crab for the first time," Rose Cernak recalled with an amused smile. They demanded cocktail forks to remove the crabmeat from the shell, unaware that informality is the watchword for a crab feast. The steamed crabs are dumped unceremoniously in the middle of a table covered with brown paper or newspaper. There are no forks. Wash-and-wear clothing is a must.

The American Festival Cafe will be serving Obrycki's steamed crabs through Aug. 24. Directions for attacking the crabs are printed on a paper place mat that accompanies the meal. For those like me who know almost everything about eating crabs but not the knife trick, follow these directions: "Place knife edge on white concave side of shell just above pincers. Tap back edge of blade with mallet to break shell. Break claw in two and remove meat attached to pincers. Break second joint the same way."

Hard-shelled crabs are not for the lazy. Obrycki's menu quotes James A. Michener's book *Chesapeake* on the subject: "A crab provides little food, so he is not easy to eat. But the little he does offer is the best food under the sky. To eat crab you must work, which makes you appreciate him more. He is the blessing, the remembrance. And no man or woman ever ate enough."

Hard Crabs and Obrycki's

Not everyone in Baltimore, it seems, thinks Obrycki's crabs are the best: "I have to protest your calling Obrycki's the 'best' crab house in Baltimore: 1. It isn't. 2. No one in Baltimore thinks it is, except for a few upper-middle-class transplants who would be scared to go to the good ones. How can any place claim to be even a good crab house when they serve their crabs on tables so fancy that in some rooms you aren't even supplied with a mallet? That's the kind of double reverse snobbery Obrycki's deals in: Snooting you because you don't know the knife trick; then snooting the occasion by presenting the crabs in their pseudo-Colonial setting."

And there's more!

"The mere fact that the American Festival Cafe brought them to New York should have tipped you off to their desire for the ersatz approval of cocktail-fork-demanding non-Baltimoreans. I could tell you my own 'best' Baltimore crab house, although maybe I prefer to keep *Times* readers in the dark."

This letter came from Los Angeles, California, from a man who lived in Baltimore for eight years. What he didn't know, because I didn't write it in the story, was that a native Baltimorean, Ruth Epstein, who lives and works in New York in public relations for the American Festival Cafe, chose Obrycki's because she had always loved it when she lived there. And I didn't consider it snooty at all to be taught the knife trick. A number of other native Marylanders had never heard of it either.

On a friendlier note came a letter from Ruth Epstein saying that shortly after the article appeared she was at the American Festival Cafe when she saw "a couple from Baltimore who had just ordered their third dozen crabs and had just remembered that they had your article with them, so, with much wiping of fingers and licking of wiped fingers, the man drew it from his coat pocket and read the directions to his wife. They were both amazed that they had never known how to open the claws either. Then they went table-hopping and showed your article to crab eaters sitting nearby and told everyone that, by golly, this was the way to open the claws."

I think the California correspondent would feel a lot better if he could get a Maryland hard-shelled-crab fix.

Assuming that most people prefer to purchase their hard-shelled crabs already steamed, here, instead, is a wonderful recipe for crabcakes, that is short on filler and long on crabmeat.

MARYLAND CRABCAKES

    1 *pound lump crabmeat*
    ½ *cup cracker crumbs*
    2 *tablespoons mayonnaise*
    1 *tablespoon prepared mustard*
    1 *egg, beaten*
    1 *tablespoon chopped fresh parsley*
    1 *teaspoon Worcestershire sauce*
       Butter for sautéing

1. Pick over the crabmeat and mix with the cracker crumbs.
2. Combine the remaining ingredients except the butter and gently mix in with the crabmeat. Do not break up lumps of crabmeat. Form into 6 patties. Refrigerate, if desired.
3. To serve, heat the butter in a skillet and sauté the crabcakes on both sides until golden brown.

YIELD: 3 servings

If a Garlic Clove Isn't Enough, Bake a Whole Head
May 12, 1984

The first time a newspaper published a recipe of mine calling for a head rather than a single clove of garlic, I received several letters from cooks correcting me. But there was no error.

The thought of putting a whole head, or bulb, of garlic into a dish strikes horror in the hearts of most cooks. The reaction to actually eating a whole head of baked garlic is one of amusement and disbelief. "I've never heard of it and I'd never try it, I'm sure," a friend said. But long, slow cooking removes the sting and the pungency of garlic, something to keep in mind because baked garlic may be the next rage.

Garlic has come a long way since the days when a few bold cooks—who were not preparing Italian dishes—tentatively inserted thin slivers from a single clove into a leg of lamb. This July the fifth annual Garlic Festival will be held in Gilroy, California. Gilroy, in the Santa Clara Valley south of San Jose, is a town in which the predominant aroma is garlic.

Despite the vast quantities of garlic used in the cooking contest during the festival, there were no recipes for baked whole heads. That has been left to trend-setting restaurants, especially in California but in New York too. Recently I had a whole head of baked garlic at the Gotham Bar and Grill, in Greenwich Village. The garlic, not thoroughly baked, was not as sweet as it should have been, and the lingering aftertaste kept vampires and friends at a distance for several days.

As James Beard notes in his book *Beard on Food:* "After garlic has been cooked slowly for a certain length of time, it loses its harsh rawness and becomes something completely delicate and refined." To prove his point Beard offers two recipes using copious quantities of garlic: one for garlic soup that calls for six to eight cups of chicken stock and thirty cloves of garlic and another for chicken with forty cloves of garlic. He also recommended a Julia Child recipe for potatoes with thirty cloves.

In each of these recipes the cloves must be separated and peeled. The great advantage to baked heads of garlic is that the cloves remain intact and are not peeled until it is time to eat them. By then the sweet, creamy flesh pops out of the dried skins.

At Chez Panisse, the Berkeley, California, restaurant that some consider the fountainhead of new California cooking, Alice Waters serves whole baked heads of garlic. In her *Chez Panisse Menu Cookbook* she includes several recipes using garlic measured in heads rather than cloves. One for fish with a garlic *confit* that serves six calls for four large heads; another, for garlic soufflé, has two heads. A recipe that requires no separating and no peeling is for baked heads with goat cheese and peasant bread.

The Santa Fe Bar and Grill in Berkeley also serves baked garlic, as do the Zuni Cafe and Little City Antipasti Bar in San Francisco. Most recipes recommend it with roast meat, including chicken.

Those who are worried about how an insatiable love for garlic may ruin their social lives should take heart from Ford Madox Ford, who wrote about a model and her love of garlic in *Provence*. Though at first she used small amounts, say half a clove, in her salad, her co-workers could barely stand to be around her. But she, unable to live without garlic, decided to give up her modeling career instead of changing her tastes. During a week of vacation before she resigned she ate garlic to her heart's content, including *poulet béarnais*, the main garniture of which is a kilogram—two pounds—of garlic. When she offered her resignation after eating garlic for a solid week, not a soul protested the effects of her indulgence. Ford explained: "She had solved the great problem; she had schooled her organs to assimilate, not to protest against, the sacred herb."

Here, for the adventuresome, is a recipe.

BAKED GARLIC

 8 *whole heads fresh garlic*
 2 *tablespoons butter and 2 tablespoons olive oil*
 4 *sprigs fresh rosemary or oregano, or 2 teaspoons dried*

1. Remove the outer layers of skin from the garlic, leaving the cloves and head intact. Place on a double thickness of foil; top with butter, oil and herbs. Fold up to seal.
2. Bake at 375 degrees for about 1 hour. The garlic should be extremely soft when done.
3. Serve one whole head per person. Squeeze the cooked cloves from their skin onto cooked meat and vegetables or onto French or rye bread.

YIELD: 8 servings

Hot on the Trail of the Fish Cooked Medium Rare
August 23, 1986

It began, no doubt, with nouvelle cuisine. Chefs were running pieces of fish past the flame, serving them almost raw. If they had been beef, they would have been described as blood red. Those who slavishly admired everything nouvelle insisted that they adored inch-thick pieces of fish virtually uncooked.

Arguing with Waiters

Those who didn't like it and were unafraid to say so argued with the waiter—who usually responded that the fish was cooked the way the chef wanted it done, implying that the patron was a boor for demanding anything else. Eventually, more rational behavior prevailed, and raw fish steaks went the way of liver with blueberry *coulis*.

We are speaking here of half-inch-thick fish steaks or fillets, not the translucent slices of fish that are part of a sushi or sashimi plate. There is an enormous difference in texture, and the difference is significant.

I happen to be an admirer of raw fish prepared in the Japanese fashion. I am also very fond of raw fish that has been "cooked" by immersion in acidic compounds, such as seviche, as well as raw fish that has been marinated, as is gravlax. But again, the texture of the fish has been dramatically altered so that it actually tastes cooked.

But something quite wonderful has emerged from the raw-fish fetish, as has been the case of so many of the excesses of nouvelle cuisine: an alternative to fish that has been cooked within an inch of its life until, as the old instructions say, "it flakes easily with a fork and is no longer translucent." This shorter cooking time for fish—which produces a moist and succulent dish that needs no sauce—requires impeccably fresh fish.

It is often a problem describing what you want to waiters. There is no universally understood name for the technique. I have tried asking for my fish either underdone or medium rare.

Translucent in the Middle

Sometimes, when there is a quizzical look on the waiter's face, I add that I would like the fish cooked so that it is still translucent in the middle. In the better restaurants the waiter knows exactly what I am talking about. When I have to explain what it is I am after, the chances are even money that my fish will be cooked to a fare-the-well, the way the chef has been cooking it for the past twenty-five years. The result is not only dry, it is usually tasteless.

Using the term *underdone* to describe how the fish should be cooked is pejorative: It implies that it is not being properly cooked. But to people who have abandoned the prejudice that fish must be cooked thoroughly, there is no better way to eat it than when it is still translucent in the middle.

Depending on the variety, the interior color may not differ noticeably from the outside, but it will be shiny while the exterior is dull. In a piece of whitefish the color is not especially different, but the interior of a piece of salmon is a deeper pink, and the interior of a piece of tuna is redder.

Like a properly cooked steak, the interior of this medium-rare fish is not cold; it is slightly warmed, though still much cooler than the exterior. That's why the term *medium rare* seems appropriate, because that, to my taste, is how beef and lamb are best.

The problem is how to make medium rare apply to fish as it does to beef and lamb. It is likely to happen if restaurant patrons band together to use the term whenever they want a piece of fish that has not been cooked to a dry flakiness.

Chefs, Beef and Fish

But work must also be done on the chefs. They will have to learn that some people like fish medium rare just as some people like beef well done. They may not approve, no more than they approve of customers who order their food without sauce.

Most of the chefs have learned to cope with sauce-free, salt-free, fat-free dishes, even if they are less than gracious about it. So it shouldn't be too difficult to accede to the wishes of the lovers of medium-rare fish, if we just stick together.

Raw Fish

An alternative to medium rare, suggested a Connecticut reader, would be "dry flake for well done, medium flake for medium rare and soft flake for chef's attention." The reader went on to explain chef's attention to mean "not well done or medium rare." He said eventually, if the system were to be adopted, it could be abbreviated to DF, MF and SF.

A Brooklyn reader suggested "lightly broiled." "I had been fooling around with other terms with very little luck," he wrote, "until I simply told the waitress that I don't like my fillet of sole to be overcooked. The words *lightly broiled* just tumbled out of her mouth and were properly transcribed on her guest-check notepad. The fish was perfect, light, moist, juicy and tender. I have tried this tactic in other restaurants, and it seems to work most of the time."

Another Connecticut reader offered her interpretation of the Canadian cooking technique for fish to get it medium rare at home. The Canadian technique recommends cooking the fish ten minutes per inch of thickness, using the thickest part of the fish as a guide. To make the fish moister the reader cooks it eight minutes to the inch instead.

The owner of Alabama Seafood, a restaurant and market in Birmingham, wrote to say thanks for the article. He is delighted for the reinforcement to the bumper sticker he gives out which says TO OVERCOOK FISH IS CRIMINAL.

Just when everyone seemed happy with the column, a letter arrived from California with an article enclosed from the July 15, 1986, issue of a magazine called *Emergency Medicine*. It deals primarily with the hazards of sushi and raw clams and oysters. I must confess I gave up raw clams and oysters about three years ago, after writing my third story in a year on the outbreak of gastrointestinal illnesses and hepatitis traced to polluted shellfish. But the article does touch on lightly cooked fish. It says that all bacteria "can be killed by normal cooking but a lot of recipes now out are for steaming or very light poaching and that may not be enough."

Well, I've already given up the raw bar. I'm going to stick with my medium-rare fish, at least for a while longer.

Pumpkins
October 20, 1984

My father always said the only part of a pig you couldn't sell was its whistle. Although I'm sure few people have given it much thought, pumpkins are nearly as versatile: The only part that is unusable is the stem.

But it was not the versatility of this vividly colored gourd that fascinated me at first as a child. It was its ability to turn into a fierce jack-o'-lantern. How could I have known that I was following a custom so ancient that it may have been reflected in the ancient Druidic practice of lighting bonfires on hills and making sacrifices to the moon god? The Druids were seeking protection against witches and spirits of the dead who haunted the earth on what, during the Christian era, came to be known as Allhallows' Eve or Halloween.

Preholiday Cajolery

As Halloween approached I began to cajole my mother to buy me the largest pumpkin I could carry. Tall ones were better than round, because they had more vertical space for carving a frightening face. The features were plotted with black crayon on the skin. But year after year, whether from lack of proper equipment or lack of talent, the jack-o'-lantern looked the same: crooked triangles for eyes, an inverted and equally crooked triangle for a nose and jagged teeth, at least one of which always fell off. I still bear a scar on my little finger from the year I tried to make circles for eyes.

I had mixed emotions about the next job: removing the seeds and the gooey stuff they were attached to. But if the seeds were not removed, they couldn't be washed and salted and toasted, and next to making the jack-o'-lantern, eating the seeds was the best part. Baking them in the oven was the first cooking I was ever allowed to do.

Sometimes around Halloween I still see toasted pumpkin seeds, but they never look quite right. They have to be very crisp and browned to have any flavor. Sometimes I hear people say the seeds should be hulled before eating, but that's hard to believe.

If our jack-o'-lantern had not rotted by November 1, the flesh could be turned into pumpkin pie, but as a very young child, I never cared if it was or not. And it was years before I learned that the pumpkin had to be cooked way down to get the flavor and texture of canned puree, and that the medium-size pumpkins made the best pies, if not always the best jack-o'-lanterns.

Like most children, many of whom carry the prejudice into adulthood, I was not fond of custard-style pumpkin pie. When the first chiffon pies made their debut in the small northeastern city where I lived, my mother switched to them, hoping that pumpkin chiffon pie in its gingersnap crust would gain more adherents than the old-fashioned custard variety. She was quite right. But she probably would have liked this pumpkin cheesecake just as well, my current Thanksgiving dessert.

Pumpkins Redux

Pumpkins are my nemesis, I guess. In one column I called pumpkin a vegetable, and as a reader was quick to point out, it is a fruit. The copy desk missed that one. In another column I missed an ingredient. An important one called sugar.

There were several complaints, as you can imagine. This was typical: "The cake looks beautiful and the baking time was fine. The problem is it has no flavor. To say the least!"

Once again I apologize and promise that this recipe is correct.

PUMPKIN CHEESECAKE IN NUT CRUST

4 eggs
3 egg yolks
2½ pounds cream cheese, softened
1 cup firmly packed dark brown sugar
½ cup granulated sugar
2 teaspoons cinnamon
1 teaspoon nutmeg
1 teaspoon ginger
¼ teaspoon allspice
2½ teaspoons finely grated lemon rind
3 tablespoons flour
1 cup heavy cream
1 tablespoon pure vanilla extract
1 16-ounce can pumpkin puree
Nut Crust (see recipe)
Coarsely grated lemon rind for garnish

1. Lightly beat the eggs and egg yolks. Add the softened cream cheese and sugars and beat until thoroughly mixed.
2. Beat in the cinnamon, nutmeg, ginger, allspice, lemon rind and flour.
3. Beat in the cream, vanilla and pumpkin.

4. Pour into the nut crust; place a pan of hot water in the bottom of the oven to keep the cake from cracking.

5. Bake at 400 degrees for 20 minutes. Reduce the heat to 275 degrees and bake 50 to 60 minutes longer. Turn off the heat and allow the cake to cool overnight in the oven for 8 hours. Then chill. Sprinkle with grated lemon rind.

NUT CRUST

2 *cups ground pecans*
2 *tablespoons brown sugar*
1 *egg white, beaten until frothy*
1 *teaspoon ginger*
1 *teaspoon finely grated lemon rind*

Mix the nuts with the brown sugar, egg white, ginger and lemon rind just until the mixture is bound together. Press into the bottom and a little way up the sides of a 10-inch spring-form pan.

YIELD: 12 to 16 servings

Holiday Turkey: The Feast That Won't Go Away
November 19, 1983

The definition of eternity, according to one wag, is a ham and two people. At this time of year, the Thanksgiving turkey might do as well. And to judge by some families the number of people could easily be increased from two to ten. Turkey may be an essential part of the traditional holiday meal, but most people would rather eat the trimmings. Like the little boy who, when asked if he would like more turkey, said ever so politely, "No thank you, ma'am. But I'd sure like more of what the turkey ate."

My cousin finally became so disgusted with her children's attitude toward turkey—every Thanksgiving and for days after they complained about having to eat it—that one year she served pot roast. When the perfectly presentable and ordinarily eagerly consumed piece of meat arrived at the table on the turkey platter, the family was dumbstruck. Then the children began to hiss and boo their mother!

Secretly she was delighted. She had made her point, and turkey has been served ever since.

No Luck with Substitutes

In our house we have tried to substitute other dishes for turkey—duck, Cornish game hens, even a goose—but nothing ever so deviant as pot roast. Still, we have not had much luck, and I finally gave up about ten years ago. When it's just our family, I order as small a turkey as possible, always fresh. For the past two years we have had Thanksgiving dinner with several friends. What they do with their turkeys the next day and the day after that and the day after that, I do not know, but I always refuse the offer to take some home.

Having made my peace with the necessity of upholding the turkey tradition at Thanksgiving and having perfected a method for roasting it, I never make changes. Instead I concentrate my efforts on the side dishes, and almost every year there is something new. Even the gravy has undergone several changes. I used to thicken it with flour, then I simply served the pan juices, now I reduce them and add a little butter.

The stuffing isn't static either, though I tend to favor bulgur with apricots, raisins, and almonds. We returned to that after trying stuffings with Italian (Parmesan cheese), Chinese (water chestnuts), and French (pork and brandy) accents.

Acknowledging that pumpkin must be present in some form at the feast, we moved beyond pumpkin custard pie to pumpkin chiffon pie, which even nonpumpkin eaters like. But I fell in love with the pumpkin cheesecake; I have been working on that for the past three years.

The equally essential cranberry relish has undergone a number of refinements since the days when I cooked the cranberries with the sugar. Years ago I stopped cooking the mixture and ground the raw cranberries with oranges and orange rind, sweetening the mixture with sugar. Now that I've added orange liqueur, I have reduced the amount of sugar and a few years ago started tossing in chopped walnuts. This year I have been toying with a cranberry chutney instead of a relish.

If I had my way, we'd have only brussels sprouts for dinner, just steamed and sautéed quickly with a little sugar. But I'm the only one who likes them, so they end up in the refrigerator next to the turkey. Now it's broccoli, steamed and paired with sautéed red peppers.

While the turkey, cranberries and pumpkin are sacred, the first course is not. Anything goes, from chicken pâté to consommé, from celery and black olives to poached oysters with ginger and saffron. But I'm not responsible for the first course this year, just the dessert and maybe the relish. And it will be pumpkin cheesecake with fresh fruit poached in wine for strong-willed dieters.

Preference for Fresh Turkeys
November 19, 1983

There are so many myths about turkeys that it is difficult to separate fact from fiction. And people who ought to know better help to perpetuate the myths.

The United States Department of Agriculture, for example, in its brochure *Talking About Turkey,* says, "There is no significant difference in quality between a fresh turkey and a frozen one." Any serious cook knows that is not true. Perhaps if a turkey was kept solidly frozen from the moment it left the processing plant until the moment the cook began to defrost it, the bird might be as good as a fresh one, but realistically that doesn't happen. And small fluctuations in temperature cause deterioration in poultry, just as they do in any frozen food.

Further on in the brochure, in another context, the department acknowledges the effects of temperature changes, saying that they "can affect the juiciness and flavor of the turkey."

Occasionally, as Thanksgiving approaches, supercautious home economists advise that to be completely free from harmful bacteria, a turkey should not be stuffed. While it is certainly inadvisable to stuff a turkey in advance, there is absolutely nothing wrong with stuffing it just before roasting. And there is nothing dangerous about preparing the stuffing a day ahead and refrigerating it until it is time to put it in the turkey.

The Perfectly Sanitary Way

It is not necessary, as the Department of Agriculture booklet advises, to mix the dry ingredients and leave them at room temperature and mix the perishables and put them in the refrigerator. All the ingredients are perfectly sanitary if they are combined and refrigerated.

On several points everyone is, or ought to be, in total agreement about turkey. Anyone who roasts a turkey at 250 degrees overnight is courting danger. It will take too long for the turkey and the stuffing to reach a temperature high enough to destroy bacteria. The method of partly cooking a turkey one day and finishing it the next is not recommended for the same reason.

If the crowd for Thanksgiving dinner is so large that a twenty-five-pound turkey is needed and no one is willing to get up at 5 A.M. to roast the bird for a 1 P.M. dinner, it would make more sense to have two twelve-pound birds.

And even though most of us have cooked turkeys in paper bags in the past, it is not a good idea to do so anymore. The chemicals used to make the paper bags are such that should they migrate from the bag to the turkey during cooking, the meat might contain ingredients unfit for consumption.

If people roasted turkeys as often as they roast chickens, this annual discussion would not be necessary. Despite all the obstacles—to paraphrase Jo in *Little Women*—Thanksgiving just wouldn't be Thanksgiving without a turkey.

Turkey and Stuffing

BULGUR STUFFING

3/4 cup unsalted butter
2 large onions, chopped
1½ teaspoons ground coriander seed
½ teaspoon ground cumin
1½ cups slivered, blanched almonds
1½ cups coarsely chopped dried apricots
1½ cups raisins
4 cups cooked bulgur
2 teaspoons cinnamon
½ teaspoon cloves
Salt and freshly ground black pepper to taste

1. Melt the butter in a large skillet. Add the onions, coriander and cumin. Cover and cook, stirring occasionally, until the onions are translucent, about 10 minutes.

2. Add the almonds, apricots and raisins. Cook, uncovered, stirring occasionally, until the almonds are golden. Transfer to a large bowl.

3. Add the bulgur, cinnamon, cloves, salt and pepper and mix well. Refrigerate the stuffing if it is not to be used immediately.

YIELD: 11 cups, enough for a 20-pound turkey

CRANBERRIES AND PORT WINE

12 ounces cranberries
7 to 8 tablespoons sugar
1 cup port
¼ teaspoon cinnamon
1 cup orange sections

1. Wash the cranberries. Place in pot with sugar and port and boil over high heat until the sugar has dissolved. Reduce the heat and boil, uncovered, until the cranberries begin to pop, about 5 minutes.

2. Stir in the cinnamon and orange sections. Remove from heat and chill. Refrigerate at least overnight.

YIELD: 8 to 10 servings

Thanksgiving Leftovers
November 30, 1985

Should anyone ever commission a study of the refrigerator in the average household, there is little doubt that immediately after Thanksgiving and perhaps Christmas the door is opened and closed more than at any other time of year. Even more than the hours between the end of the school day and dinnertime in families with teenage children.

Thanksgiving night and the night after and the night after that. Pick, pick, pick. The carcass of the turkey is slowly but surely denuded. There are many among us who actually prefer to eat cold turkey as it sits in the refrigerator under its foil tent, rather than in all its splendor on the buffet table, surrounded by a fragrant stuffing. We are people who prefer the trimmings at the Thanksgiving feast: The turkey can be dealt with later.

Besides, for dieters, anything that is eaten standing up doesn't count. This is true not only for turkey but also for leftover sweet potatoes, cranberry relish, creamed onions, brussels sprouts, oyster stew and all the pies: pumpkin, apple and lemon meringue. It is especially true if the food is consumed in a darkened kitchen late at night, when the only light comes from the open refrigerator door.

And that, of course, is how most leftovers disappear. In families in which there are pickers, or grazers in the current vernacular, there is no need to worry about leftovers. Such a solution is infinitely superior to the suggestion one newspaper food section made in the early '60s:

In an oblong casserole, layer turkey slices, cranberry relish, mashed sweet potatoes, creamed onions and stuffing. Repeat layering until all ingredients are used or casserole is full. Pour over leftover gravy (if there isn't enough gravy, add a can of mushroom soup) and bake at 350 degrees for 30 minutes or until ingredients are heated through. Serve hot.

Even though all those dishes had been eaten simultaneously on

Thanksgiving, they lost their charm when combined in a single casserole.

It's a miracle the author of the recipe, whose philosophy of eating is summed up in the thought that it all goes to the same place anyway, didn't suggest spreading the top of the casserole with the leftover pumpkin pie filling.

There are better things to do with leftovers if they haven't been picked to death by now. With almost no work the carcass will provide turkey stock that can be frozen and used in place of chicken stock for many recipes. Just cook the carcass in water with carrots and celery and onion and salt and pepper to taste until the broth is cooked down and is richly flavored. Strain it and freeze in portions suitable to your family's use. Turn the candied sweet potatoes into sweet potato soufflé, using more egg whites than the standard recipes call for to lighten the mixture.

An Elegant Sherbet

The cranberry-orange relish—not the jellied kind—becomes an elegant sherbet. For a cup or so of leftover relish fold in two stiffly beaten egg whites and freeze. To serve, if the mixture is frozen very hard, defrost slightly and beat to a sherbet consistency.

For leftover turkey, try a modern version of a turkey sandwich: On some nice crusty bread that has been lightly spread with mayonnaise flavored with a little cumin, arrange the turkey slices with smoked fresh mozzarella cheese and marinated sun-dried tomatoes. That sandwich is so good it's worth hoarding some of the leftover turkey to make it.

Tale of the Truffle:
Woe and Affection
November 12, 1983

First impressions, thank goodness, are not invariably lasting. If that were so, this column would not be about the glories of white truffles.

About twenty years ago some dear friends who care as much about good food as I do decided that the nicest present they could bring back to me from their trip through Italy and France would be white truffles. One of their last stops in Italy was made to purchase some truffles, which the seller assured my friends would last for ten days if they were kept in the straw in which they were packed.

Following instructions my friends tucked the truffles into their suitcase between the top and bottom of a pair of pajamas and set off for France. Each evening they unpacked them in their hotel room: During the day, as they traveled across the country, they left them in the suitcase in the car.

Early November can be warm in France, and it doesn't take much imagination to picture the greenhouse effect in a closed car with the sun beating down. Warming truffles decreases their life span noticeably.

Toward the end of the trip my friends couldn't sleep in the same room with the truffles and took to leaving them in the car at night along with the pajamas. They found a jar in which to put the truffles, but that didn't help. Still, they had devoted so much time to the truffles they felt they had to bring them back to the States, reasoning that just because the truffles couldn't be slept with didn't mean they couldn't be eaten.

A Tale of Woe

The day after they arrived home they brought the truffles to my house with their tale of woe. I don't think I betrayed the queasy feeling I had when they walked in the house with the malodorous package, but I rushed the truffles to the refrigerator to keep the smell from pervading the house. I can't remember when I finally confessed to my friends that I threw the spoiled truffles out almost immediately: They could not be salvaged.

It was five more years before I met my first fresh truffle, and it was love at first bite. Now, when asked how I like them, I steal a line from the French gastronome Curnonsky, who said: "In great quantity, Madame. In great quantity." He was talking about black truffles, but I am just as happy, perhaps happier, with white ones.

Even when the white truffle is freshly dug, the aroma of the gnarled little knob—which is more beige than white—has been described as earthy, nutty and musky. The musky description fits in neatly with the aphrodisiac qualities attributed to the truffle. *Science* magazine did nothing to destroy the myth when it published an article saying that truffles contain a steroid with a "pronounced musklike scent," the same steroid "synthesized by human males."

Brillat-Savarin, who wouldn't have known a steroid if he had met one, knew, however, that truffles "make women more tender and men more agreeable." Just a few shavings will perform such magic. And even though any truffle lover would prefer them in great quantity, it is quite possible to enjoy their delectable pungency with very few shavings. At current prices shavings will have to do.

An ounce of truffles can make four truffle lovers reasonably happy. Use a truffle slicer to shave them paper-thin. Four servings of pasta or *fonduta* (Italian fondue) will be generously perfumed by an ounce of truffles. To make the truffle go even further, it may be used for a simple but delectable hors d'oeuvre. Tiny shavings of truffles are sprinkled on thin slices of Italian bread that have been brushed with olive oil and toasted.

Truffles will last up to two weeks buried in cornmeal or rice in a closed container in the refrigerator. Cook the aromatic rice and make polenta from the cornmeal.

To make a *fonduta* for four, dice three-quarters of a pound of Italian Fontina into a bowl and cover with milk at least four hours before serving. Melt three tablespoons of butter in the top of a double boiler; add the cheese with about three teaspoons of milk. Stir and cook over hot water until the cheese melts. Remove from heat; beat in three egg yolks; return to the double boiler, stir and cook until the mixture is like thick cream. Season with white pepper. Cover the fondue with white truffle shavings and serve with toast.

Cumin Has a Place in More Than Chili
November 12, 1983

Herbs and spices, like clothing, go in and out of fashion. Basil, after all, was in vogue for several years. It is only since this summer that cooks who keep up with the latest fashions have begun to talk of it as they once talked of the kiwi: "I think if I see another kiwi..."

But other than in pesto, I think basil hasn't been overused, and the idea of being able to buy it fresh at so many markets is appealing.

If it is time to elevate another herb or spice to the level basil has reached, I nominate cumin. It is the fruit (though it is often called the seed) of an herb in the parsley family. Until lately most people thought of it as just one of the spices in a curry or chili. As recently as 1967 the author of a spice book wrote that cumin was not generally used by home cooks and was found only in commercially prepared products.

An Inspiring Aroma

But cumin can rest on its own laurels. I have some in my cupboard that is not stored, as it should be, in an airtight jar. Every time I open the door its heady perfume permeates the kitchen and acts as an inspiration. Last week its aroma inspired me to add it to an ordinary tuna and apple–salad sandwich. Tuna has never been so interesting.

Cumin, which is native to the Nile Valley and was used medicinally in Egypt as early as 1550 B.C., is surprisingly versatile. Strongly aromatic and yellowish-brown, it is described as spicy, sometimes bitter, especially if too much is used. There is no mistaking cumin's flavor in a dish. It is a vibrant pick-me-up.

Despite its relative obscurity in this country, it has been widely used elsewhere for hundreds of years. The Dutch, Swiss and Scandinavians use it in their cheese *kumminost* or *cuminost*. A German liqueur contains cumin along with caraway. It is routinely added to sauerkraut, soups, stews, pastries, breads, rice, chutney, sausages and pickles.

I never realized how enamored of cumin I had become until I looked over a collection of recipes I had compiled in the past three years. I have used it dozens of ways. It appears in combination with garlic, red wine, onion and cinnamon, as a delicious marinade for chicken breasts. Minus the cinnamon it makes a piquant vinaigrette for warm new potatoes. It adds zest to a bland boiled rice, which is mixed with pine nuts for an interesting textural contrast.

An Affinity for Chiles

Some of the dishes I have used it in are classics, like *picadillo*. Cumin has a natural affinity for chiles; in this Spanish ground beef dish, it is especially simpatico with fresh and dried chiles mixed with cloves, raisins, black olives and cheese. Corn and green-pepper salad takes on a Mexican flavor with chiles, red onion and cumin. Zucchini and tomatoes, ordinarily Italian in feeling, are totally different with cumin and ground coriander, an herb with which cumin is often paired. A bland vegetarian dish of kasha, corn and cottage cheese becomes exciting when oregano, chili powder and cumin are added.

I also added cumin to lamb sausages, beef pot roast, vegetarian chili, curried chicken, Cheddar cheese toasts and Greek meatballs, where it is the dominant flavor. It provides zest to a pie with a beef crust filled with corn and custard; to carrots and ginger; to guacamole tostadas, and to a Portuguese dish of clams and pork.

In bygone days cumin was used to keep lovers from becoming fickle and poultry from straying. Whether or not it was successful at those tasks, it has earned its keep as a stimulating addition to the contemporary cook's culinary closet.

Cumin

This reader tells me I goofed: "I can assure you that the Scandinavians do not usually use cumin. In Swedish, which is the case I am linguistically most familiar with, the word *kummin* means caraway. Indeed cumin is generally unavailable in Sweden except in exotic food shops."

CHICKEN WITH CUMIN AND CINNAMON

> 3 *medium garlic cloves, chopped*
> ⅔ *cup finely chopped onion*
> 1 *cup dry red wine*
> ¼ *cup olive oil*
> 2 *teaspoons cumin*
> 1 *teaspoon cinnamon*
> *Freshly ground black pepper to taste*
> 6 *small whole chicken breasts*
> 4 *tablespoons olive oil*

1. In a food processor combine the garlic, onion, wine, olive oil, cumin, cinnamon and pepper. Process until the mixture is liquefied.
2. Place the chicken pieces in a single layer in a shallow dish and pour the marinade over it. Marinate for several hours or overnight. If desired, the dish may be frozen.
3. To serve, scrape the marinade off the chicken and reserve the marinade. Heat the oil in a large skillet. Sauté the chicken pieces on both sides, beginning with the skin side. Reduce the heat and spread the reserved marinade on both sides of each

piece. Simmer about 20 minutes, turning once, cooking until the chicken is done.

YIELD: 6 servings

The Once Trendy, Now Passé Kiwi Is Still Tasty

December 1, 1984

Declaring myself a lover of kiwis is likely to lower my standing in the food world. Through overuse and misuse, kiwis have become pariahs among those who set the trends. Where once sparkling green little ovoid slices of kiwi graced every plate that came out of nouvelle cuisine kitchens, whether they were appropriate or not, kiwis are now relegated to sherbet, if they are used at all.

It's not as if kiwis have been around a long time. As Bruce Beck notes in his stunning new book, *Produce* (Friendly Press, $35): "Few edibles have had such a meteoric rise to international celebrity and it can only be hoped that this one will survive its fifteen minutes of stardom to become a kitchen staple. And many people who really like it pray for the day when it loses its trendy nouvelle cuisine stigma altogether so that they can enjoy it without embarrassment."

This stigma has been around a long time. Seven years ago James Beard told me he hoped he would never have to look at another kiwi again. I doubt that he got his wish, but it is a shame that he, and many other professional cooks, have become tired of kiwis. The problem is that they have been bombarded with so many kiwi concoctions they have forgotten what a pleasure it is to eat them out of hand. Like certain other fruits—cherries, white peaches and melons—nothing improves their flavor. They are best eaten without adornment.

While Beck says kiwis are probably not Chinese, the California Kiwifruit Commission says the fuzzy brown-skinned little fruit was known only in the Yangtze Valley of China, where it was called *yang tao* until 1847, when the Western world became aware of it. In 1906 it was introduced to New Zealand. I don't know when it came to the United States, but I had my first kiwi in the early 1960s at a lunch with the late Victor Bergeron at one of his Trader Vic restaurants. It was served in its skin, cut in half and eaten with a demitasse spoon. Then it was called a Chinese gooseberry. It has had many other names as well, including In-chang gooseberry, monkey peach and kiwiberry. As I look back on my first kiwi encounter, I realize that it was not as ripe as it should have been for best flavor.

According to several sources, the name by which this fruit is now known was the creation of some sharp promotion-minded New Zealanders. At the time they wanted to export the fruit to the United States, Americans had little use for things Chinese, so they created a new name, based on the national bird of New Zealand, the kiwi.

In addition to a wonderful balance of acid and sweetness, kiwis have other delightful attributes. They are in season year-round and keep for several weeks in the refrigerator. Unlike some fruits, they will ripen at home, a process that can be speeded by placing them in a plastic bag with a slice of apple. Rock-hard and very soft fruits should be avoided. Ripened kiwis yield to gentle pressure. Even those that are not completely ripened have a pleasing flavor, but when they are in their prime, they have a full-bodied winy taste.

The kiwi is healthful. Two have about ninety calories, only one gram of fat and 230 percent of the recommended daily allowance of vitamin C. They have smaller amounts of other important nutrients, too, and contain a significant amount of fiber.

At first kiwis arrived in the United States in a trickle and cost as much as $1 each. Today California has joined New Zealand in supplying most of the kiwis available in the world. I have seen kiwis for as little as 29 cents each in the market from time to time. It is a price that does not appeal to kiwi ranchers. And as supplies increase, there is more likelihood of lower prices.

According to the Kiwifruit Commission, proposed marketing orders will help to control the supply and therefore the price. If there is a glut, the orders could keep fruits that are too flat or too small off the market, even though size and shape have nothing to do with flavor.

Kiwi

Only one reader came to the kiwi's defense. "I was glad to see you defend the once adored, now maligned kiwi. One of your illustrious predecessors referred recently to the kiwi as lacking in flavor, or words to that effect. Far from that, the taste can suggest many fruits, sometimes honeydew, banana, strawberry, mango, depending, perhaps, on the ripeness.

"The problem, of course, is surfeit. Not being a professional food critic I have been spared the dreadful glut."

In fact, two years after the column appeared kiwi is no longer considered a glut on the foodie's market. It seems to have assumed its place in the kaleidoscope of fruits alongside what is trendy right now—mango, passion fruit and cherimoya.

That doesn't mean you have to like everything they put kiwis in, for example, kiwi vinegar. But if you are ready for something beyond sprinkling kiwi slices on top of fruit salad, or using them in a fruit pie in place of strawberries, a kiwi sorbet marries well with any other tropical fruit.

KIWI SORBET

2 pounds ripe kiwis
⅓ cup sugar
3 tablespoons Grand Marnier
1 kiwi, cut in slices, for garnish, optional

1. Peel the kiwis and remove the hard core. Cut in half and puree in a blender or food processor.
2. Heat the sugar with 1 cup of puree over low heat until the sugar dissolves. Return to the remaining puree and stir in the liqueur; chill.
3. Follow the directions provided with the ice cream maker, or if you are making the sorbet in an ice cube tray in the freezer, freeze until half firm. Beat with an electric mixer until smooth. Return to the tray and freeze until firm.

4. Serve slightly softened, topped with additional kiwi slices, if desired.

YIELD: 4 servings

Perfect Rice, Quickly Cooked
March 22, 1986

There are, perhaps, no more intimidating food ads than those that admonish cooks to stay away from regular long-grain rice. The ads imply that it is difficult, if not impossible, for anyone with average kitchen skills to cook it properly and that no matter what is done, the rice is bound to emerge in clumps of stuck-together grains. This is a sin equal to, if not worse than, greasy fried chicken and layer cakes that sink.

It is simply not true that ordinary rice is difficult to cook, and it is not necessary to use converted rice or instant rice to produce good results. Nor is it necessary to resort to the boil-in-the-plastic-bag rice.

Perhaps many consumers just assume that cooking rice from scratch—or anything, for that matter—takes too much time. And time is one thing that few people today have enough of. So, if the makers of Uncle Ben's rice or Minute rice or Success (the boil-in-the-bag variety) say it's easier to use their products, who's going to argue?

Any Cook Who Can Boil Water

But let the world know that any cook who can boil water can cook long-grain rice. And all it takes is seventeen minutes. Any cook who can boil water can also cook short-grain rice or Arborio rice or basmati rice or brown rice. And anyone can cook all of them successfully. Novices can also cook the delectable alternatives to rice that are increasingly available in the supermarket—bulgur, couscous and buckwheat groats, known to most aficionados as kasha.

Cookbooks often make a production out of preparing these ingredients, picturing them as much more time-consuming and complicated than they need to be. Take basmati rice, for example. Some directions suggest several washings and soakings. But a perfectly delicious dish of basmati rice can be yours simply by cooking it as you would cook ordinary long-grain rice. No rinsings. No soakings. Or brown rice. No one wants to bother with it, despite its superior flavor, because it takes at least forty minutes to cook. But just by soaking the rice overnight, in the same water in which it is to be cooked, it's possible to cut the cooking time to twenty minutes, making it almost as fast as regular white rice.

Often recipes calling for couscous describe all the steps necessary to prepare it, but, in fact, most of the couscous on the market today requires barely any cooking at all, and I'll bet it would take a native Moroccan to tell the difference between the so-called instant couscous and the old-fashioned variety.

The situation with bulgur has improved somewhat, and virtually no one believes it takes thirty minutes to cook bulgur (if it spends that long boiling on the stove, it will turn to mush). Bulgur can be properly cooked in fifteen minutes; in fact, it doesn't have to be cooked at all. For a superb tabbouleh salad, boiling water is poured over the bulgur, and the grains are allowed to sit until the water is absorbed. That same technique can be used for any dish calling for bulgur if it does not have to be hot. Kasha takes a little longer, but not much.

It would be nice to say that the secret to perfect rice or bulgur or couscous or kasha is simply following the directions on the package, but that is not always the case. Instead, try these suggestions:

Perfect Long-Grain Rice: Combine rice with twice as much water in a heavy-bottomed saucepan. Season with salt, if desired. Bring to a boil. Reduce the heat so that the rice simmers in a covered pot. Cook seventeen minutes, until the water is absorbed and the rice is tender and fluffy.

For perfect brown rice, soak overnight and then follow the same directions.

For perfect basmati rice, follow the directions for long-grain rice but cook thirteen to fifteen minutes instead.

Perfect Bulgur: Combine bulgur with twice the amount of

water. Bring to a boil, and cook covered for about twelve minutes, until the bulgur is tender and the liquid has been absorbed.

Perfect Couscous: For three servings, bring one cup of water and one tablespoon butter to a boil in a covered pot. Add one cup couscous; cover and remove from heat. Allow to sit for about five minutes, until all the water has been absorbed.

Rice

I still cannot believe the volume of mail this column produced. Everyone wanted to tell me how they boiled rice and why their method was better than mine.

It goes without saying that there were those who prefer to bring the water to a boil first and then add the rice. And I don't think there is anything wrong with that. Except... Except that when I am rushing around the kitchen making dinner, I forget that I've put the water on to boil. Sometimes when I finally remember, there is no water left. Then I have to start all over. When I put the rice and water on together, should I forget them, they boil over and remind me!

One reader from New Jersey wanted to know why I didn't recommend an Oriental electric rice cooker and then proceeded to tell me that the new ones aren't any good because they have "a direct electric coil and can burn rice." Another from New York said he didn't think "there exist any long-grain rice that can absorb twice the amount of water without ending up a soggy, mushy mess these days." He then gave me a recipe that I am sure produces gorgeous rice but requires an hour to cook.

A third from Virginia didn't like my method either and suggested soaking the rice first for fifteen minutes at least and then cooking it. He also recommended throwing in some powdered kelp to "reduce blood pressure."

Another Long Island reader suggested a double boiler, and I know they are great too, but do you know how long that takes! Someone from Minneapolis wrote in to say that you should never put the water and rice in together at the same time because the "chlorine in the water destroys the thiamine in rice." Boil the water first she said. I checked that one out with a biochemist-nutritionist who said not to worry about the chlorine destroying the thiamine. There isn't enough chlorine to make any difference.

One cook from Dedham, Massachusetts, wondered what she had done wrong: "I put two ounces bulgur then twice as much water, which would be four ounces, brought to boil, then covered and turned low for twelve minutes, but it stuck the first time. The second time I looked in at ten minutes and it had just about stuck that time. I did the same thing with rice and it stuck, so I went back to my old way." Two ounces of rice is not the same as one cup. The lady was cooking by weight, not volume, and it can't be done. The proportions were wrong.

Then, of course, there are those who cook their rice in the microwave oven. I can't. I don't own a microwave oven. And don't intend to buy one. One microwave champion, however, did approve of soaking the brown rice. She said that "a Japanese friend tells me soaking overnight releases the life energy of the rice, making it healthier and the eater more peaceful!"

After all these criticisms about my method for cooking rice I don't feel very peaceful!

A Houston reader who grew up eating brown rice suggested another rice that has a hint of pecan in it. It is a delicious rice, put out by Konriko, and is available in many specialty food shops. A Chicago woman wrote to say that the only kind of rice her husband likes is wild rice, except that it isn't a rice. It is a grass. "I'm not a cook—period—so I hope you can come up with a simple recipe for wild rice—or aren't you into saving marriages?"

I hope the outcome of the writer's marriage does not rest on her ability to cook wild rice, but it isn't complicated. Any package tells you how. Today most of the wild rice sold is actually cultivated and does not grow wild. It requires no soakings, just cooking. But it does take twice as long as regular rice.

In addition to the discussions about the proper method for cooking rice, there were several letters demanding to know what happened to the recipe for Perfect Kasha. It, in fact, was eliminated because of space. Most of those who wrote said they did not want to follow the directions on the box, which call for stirring the kasha with an egg first and then cooking it with water. There is nothing that says you have to use that method. For those who do not want to use a whole egg, the directions on the package may be followed using just the egg white. Kasha also may be cooked using the same method suggested for rice.

Another reader said kasha in the box was too expensive. For cheaper kasha I suggest a trip to the health food store where it is called buckwheat groats and is sold in bulk for less money. (Yes, there are some things in health food stores that are cheaper than they are in supermarkets.)

And finally, for the New York reader who wanted a recipe for tabbouleh, this is one of my favorites:

TABBOULEH

- 1 *cup bulgur*
- 2 *tablespoons virgin olive oil*
- 6 *tablespoons lemon juice, more to taste*
- 3 *medium, ripe tomatoes, chopped*
- 1 *bunch green onions, chopped*
- 3 *cups chopped parsley*
- 1/4 *cup chopped fresh mint*
  Salt and freshly ground black pepper
  Cinnamon

1. Pour enough boiling water just to cover the bulgur in a large bowl. Set aside for about 20 minutes, until the water is absorbed and the bulgur is tender. Drain any excess water and squeeze out the remaining water with hands.
2. Beat the oil and lemon juice together and mix with the tomatoes, onions, parsley, mint, salt and pepper.
3. Mix into the bulgur thoroughly. Serve on lettuce-lined plates and sprinkle with cinnamon. Or pass the cinnamon separately.

YIELD: 6 servings

Sweets for Valentine's Day: Ripe Red Peppers

February 11, 1984

They are red, they are sweet, and they are available. That makes them an appropriate, if unusual, subject for a column devoted to Valentine's Day. Unlike chocolate candy hearts, red velvet cake and cookies dyed red and cut in the shape of cupids, red peppers are very low in calories, sodium, fat and cholesterol, high in vitmin C, loaded with vitamin A and in addition offer some B vitamins, a little iron and fiber.

Red peppers were difficult to find except in specialty markets until two or three years ago. It is still hard to find them in supermarkets outside New York City, sometimes in New York City as well. That's because red peppers are nothing more nor less than ripened green peppers and thus do not keep as long as green ones. If, instead of picking the mature pepper while green, the farmer allows it to ripen on the vine, it not only turns red, it also becomes infinitely sweeter.

Explains Harold Seybert of Fairway Fruits and Vegetables in Manhattan: "Red peppers are just one step away from turning rotten, so there is more waste. But they are also at the peak of their flavor." Red peppers are also more expensive than green peppers.

Both red and green peppers were widely available in Europe before they became popular in the United States. Raising peppers commercially became big business here only about forty years ago. During the summer peppers sold in many markets are grown locally; the rest of the year they come from Florida, California and Holland. Those from Holland have thicker skins and are considered more desirable for salads or dishes that require long cooking because they will hold their shape better. The thin-skinned are best for pureeing and deep frying.

But don't worry too much about all these niceties. If you can find only the thin-skinned varieties, the dish will still taste wonderful and look beautiful. One of the varieties grown in the United States is suited to Valentine's Day. Called Perfection, it is heart-shaped, and is raised to become a canned pimiento.

Delicious as peppers are when used raw in salads or sautéed quickly with onions, they take on entirely different characteristics when roasted. Their flavor develops a smokiness, their texture becomes softer, and of course, their skin blisters and blackens and is easily removed.

When buying red peppers to use either raw or roasted, look for those that are bright red, crisp, shiny and firm. If you are planning to roast the peppers, it is better to choose those that are well shaped, free of too many nooks and crannies that make peeling more difficult.

If the only reason for roasting peppers is to remove their skins, it would be easier to drop them into boiling water and peel them just as tomatoes are peeled. But it's that roasted flavor that makes them so special. Roasting can be done under a broiler, over a gas flame on top of the stove or, during warmer weather, over a charcoal fire.

How to Roast Them

To roast peppers, wash and dry them thoroughly. To char them over an open flame, spear them on a long fork, preferably with a wooden handle. Keep turning them very close to the flame until they char and blister all over. Or place them on a broiler rack two or three inches from the source of heat. Watch carefully and turn the peppers, as they char and blister all over.

As each pepper is ready, place it in a plastic bag and seal. This makes removal of the skin easier. When the peppers are cool enough to handle, peel off the charred skin with your fingers and a small paring knife. Don't worry if some of the pepper itself is charred. Don't run the peppers under water to clean them further; they will just absorb the moisture.

Remove the seeds, stem and ribs, and the peppers are ready to be served or used in recipes.

They can be marinated in olive oil and garlic, sautéed, pureed or julienned, turned into a salsa, cooked with sausages and onions, added to homemade mayonnaise, used to season butter or to make soup.

Roasted peppers will keep several days in a tightly covered container in the refrigerator; if marinated in oil and vinegar, they will last ten days to two weeks. They may also be frozen.

Red peppers are a food I could happily nibble on in preference to chocolate chip cookies, if not all the time, at least some of it.

Red Pepper Puree

Purees were a very fashionable part of nouvelle cuisine. They were done to death, so now they have been banished, along with kiwis, to the land of clichés. It's a shame: They can be so wonderful, the freshness of the vegetable contrasting with the creaminess of the puree.

Cliché or not, here is a simple and flavorful red pepper puree. Use it as a sauce or vegetable.

RED PEPPER PUREE

> 6 *large red bell peppers*
> 2 *to 3 tablespoons high-quality olive oil*
> 1 *teaspoon chopped fresh thyme*
> *Freshly ground black pepper to taste*
> *Few dashes of cayenne*

1. This is the easiest method to remove the skin from peppers. Line a broiling pan with aluminum foil and place the peppers on foil 3 or 4 inches from the source of heat. Turn them on all sides, on top and bottom, as the skin blisters and blackens. When sufficiently blistered place the peppers in a plastic bag and close to allow the peppers to steam 10 to 15 minutes.

2. Using your fingers and a small knife remove the skin; seed the peppers. Cut each pepper into 5 or 6 pieces.

3. Heat the oil and add the thyme and peppers. Sauté about 2

minutes; season with the black and cayenne peppers.

4. Puree the peppers in a food processor with the steel blade or in a blender. Reheat to serve.

5. The puree may be refrigerated and reheated slowly.

YIELD: 6 servings

Doing Battle with the Tough-as-Nails Pomegranate

October 25, 1986

Pomegranates have their virtues. Neatness is not one of them. Anyone who has ever tried to cut them up and extract the seeds can attest to that.

The interior of the pomegranate has been described as four two-storied compartments, each filled with seeds. Hundreds of them. Each seed is covered by a sac of red pulp, and it's the pulp, with its sweet, slightly acidic berry flavor, that the eater is after.

What stands between the eater and the seeds is a bitter whitish-yellow pith and a tough skin. The pomegranate doesn't just lie there when it is invaded. It fights back. Hard.

It spits seeds the way a hand grenade spits metal—that, as a matter of fact, is how the grenade was purportedly named in 1590. And the city of Granada in Spain is supposed to have been named after the pomegranate because its design resembles the fruit cut in half.

So much for pomegranate lore. At eight o'clock this past Monday night I decided to do battle with a pomegranate, and cut it up in my 7-by 12-foot kitchen. As it turned out, I underestimated the enemy.

At 8:30 I cleaned up bright red juice spots on the floor and the countertop; then I went into my office. When I came back at nine, I discovered more spots—on the overhead cabinets and on the under-the-counter cabinets. I cleaned them up and went back into the office.

At 10:30, on my way out of the office through the kitchen, I noticed still more pomegranate stains in and around the burners on the stove and on the oven door. I decided I had better look around carefully. There were stains on the refrigerator door, on the wall behind the sink and, of course, on the apron I was still wearing. My pomegranate had exploded in silent anger.

By that time I had decided that whatever the virtues of pomegranates, they did not compensate for the trouble of eating them. I was reminded of what is said to be an ancient bit of Chinese wisdom: The only way to eat pomegranates is in the bathtub.

Pomegranate juice is better known under its other name, grenadine, but most brands of grenadine today are likely to be made not of pomegranate juice but of sugar, food coloring and chemicals.

And despite recipes in several books for homemade versions of grenadine that use pomegranate juice, it is not a recipe I am likely to try any time soon.

Pomegranates probably came from ancient Persia (no one is quite sure), and while they appear in several colors, ranging from green and white to gold, scarlet is the color seen in this country. The handsomely shaped fruit is a symbol of fertility, and it is held in high regard in the arid lands of the Middle East because of its thirst-quenching power and its keeping quality.

Between mid-October and January is pomegranate season. The best of these fruits have a leathery outer skin. The fruit is heavy for its size, the surfaces slightly flattened, the skin unbroken.

Pomegranates will keep for three months in the refrigerator. The seeds will keep in the freezer for three months packed in an airtight container, according to Elizabeth Schneider in her book *Uncommon Fruits and Vegetables.*

To open a pomegranate, put it in the sink (or bathtub), and score the skin in quarters, cutting from the blossom end. Lift off a piece with a knife. Then loosen the pith and pull it off.

With your fingers, bend the skin and pith back to expose the seeds, and pry them out with the tip of a knife, being careful not to prick them.

Whether to simply chew and swallow the seeds or suck the pulp from them and then spit them out is a matter of individual preference. It is certainly neater to eat the seeds, but not everyone thinks that is a good enough reason.

Most pomegranate fans eat them unadorned, but the seeds are often used for color and flavor in the Mediterranean and Middle East in soups and stews and in sauces for fish. Frequently, they are found sprinkled over salads, cold meats and desserts, and they add a piquancy to *baba ghanoush*, the rich Lebanese sesame-eggplant dish.

Pomegranates have their uses. But I don't think I want to fight with one again. Whoever said their only value is for display in a winter fruit basket knew whereof she spoke.

Pomegranates

The pomegranate column brought a first—my first letter from a swami. Swami Murugananda, whose return address on the envelope is as follows: Satchidananda Ashram-Yogaville, Route 1, Box 172, Buckingham, Virginia. My editor Nancy Newhouse tells me Swami Satchidananda is very famous.

From Swami Murugananda:

On pomme-granites. A hard apple indeed.

I am rather surprised you did not know the "cut and suck" method of consuming pomegranate juice. It is guaranteed non-messy. First gently roll the fruit on the table; this is to break up the seeds, releasing the juice. With a sharp paring knife cut out a small triangle about ⅛ inch on a side. Tilt back your head and place mouth at opening—gently squeezing fruit, sucking out the juice.

A less fun way (and even safer) is to squeeze the juice into a glass, but this does take all the adventure out of it.

Please print this letter so others can enjoy non-messy pomegranate juice.

The letter continues on the reverse side of the paper.

P.S. Some time ago you (or one of your associates) printed a recipe for egg creams. [A swami who knows about egg creams!]

Being an egg cream and ice cream maven for over forty-five years I must tell you that the method was not at all correct.

He goes on to explain the proper method for making an egg cream. A swami who is also a maven. Now that is what I would call ecumenical.

For some reason pomegranates attract religious leaders, so along came another letter from a priest.

"I was truly shocked to read your depressing report on the pomegranate," wrote a priest with the title of Very Reverend from Detroit. He enclosed a large step-by-step drawing of the proper way to extract the seeds. He is a very competent artist, but it still looks like a mess to me.

Since he is a priest, I am sure he is telling the truth when he said he has never had the slightest difficulty. "Why, I even taught a native-born Syrian how to eat a pomegranate, and you know how tough those terrorists can be," he wrote. "But to use a knife to remove pomegranate seeds? That's racist.

"Mrs. Burros, I think you owe someone or something an apology.

"I peel one or two and consume them while watching such journalistic drags as Nite Line [sic]. You can too.

"You can also make *baba ghanoush* with yogurt. Just eliminate the tahini."

That sounds like a great idea, especially for those who want to cut down on the calories.

Most of the other correspondents, and there were plenty, recommended the method for opening a pomegranate the swami had suggested, but I had tried it, more than once, and discarded it because I didn't find it any more satisfactory. I must have defective pomegranates. Each time I rolled one around, it burst open and spewed the juice all over the countertop.

One of those correspondents said the column brought "a mixture of joy and irritation.... The irritation was caused by the obvious fact that the author did not do her homework, thereby denigrating a delicious eating experience. The joy was the memory it stirred of my youth." The letter went on to explain the roll-and-suck method and ended on an obvious note of annoyance: "P.S. By the way, do you know how to eat a persimmon?" A copy of the letter was sent to Pomegranate Growers, U.S.A., Inc. I didn't know there was such a group.

One Brooklynite confessed to another problem with pomegranates, one I had not encountered because I didn't open enough. "Every crack in your skin, under-nails, nail moons turns an indelible red-black. And so, for the months I am eating almost nothing but pomegranates, my hands look awfully grubby, and I make excuses about being a dirt gardener and planting all those bulbs. However, do you know of a pomegranate de-stainer? Short of abstinence."

A caterer in Manhattan who has done battle with pomegranates so that certain dishes would be authentic added his bit: "One particularly nightmarish encounter involved seeding a huge number of them in order to garnish one hundred meat-stuffed *chiles en nogada*. The classic topping for that dish is pomegranate seeds."

His solution: "Fill a large bowl with cold water. Submerge the pomegranate completely into the water."

Follow the directions for cutting it open and removing the seeds and pith with your fingers. The seeds, he said, will sink to the bottom; the pith float to the top. It's true.

My friend Helen Witty, writer and cookbook author, wrote that she had found similar information when she was researching pomegranate juice in an old issue of *Sunset* magazine. "Know what you mean about pomegranates.... Pomegranates and I go way back to my California youth, and until fairly recently I didn't know a useful trick for separating the seeds from the pulp." The article suggests cutting the crowns off the pomegranates before scoring them and placing them in a bowl of cool water.

But I guess I just don't love pomegranates enough to bother, though I must admit the dish of pomegranate seeds flavored with a little sugar and rose water sent to me by Andrées Mediterranean Cuisine, a Manhattan restaurant, did tempt me. The rose water adds a tantalizing fragrance and flavor to the pomegranate seeds.

P.S. A month after the column appeared, a crate of pomegranates arrived from a grower with a notation that the best way to open them was under water.

Most of the pomegranates in the crate were cracked.

P.P.S. Another month passed before this postcard arrived from Bethesda, Maryland:

"I was reminded of your article about persimmons when I flew from Palermo to Rome a few days ago: Two German women had a crate of the fruit with them, and during the flight several persimmons dropped to the floor of the aisle and there ensued much cursing in Sicilian and a variety of other dialects as passengers scraped the stuff off their shoes, much like having stepped into dog droppings in the street."

Should I call the man and ask him if he meant pomegranates?

Cherimoya
February 2, 1985

To some it tastes like a piña colada without rum; to others, a cross between a strawberry and a pineapple. For natives of the Caribbean the cherimoya is a fruit that can be plucked from backyard trees for nothing. For New Yorkers it is one of the most expensive fruits on the market, topping even such luxuries as cherries in January and peaches in December. But it is delicious.

The outward appearance of this tropical fruit, native to the uplands of Peru and Ecuador, does not prepare one for its sensuous white flesh. Also known as custard apple and sometimes as sweetsop (though sweetsop is not the same), the fruit has a texture often described as custardy. To some it suggests sops, as milk-soaked bread was once called.

The Look of an Armadillo

Its flesh is encased in a dull greenish exterior that suggests an armadillo's skin. As it ripens, the green skin begins to brown. A properly ripened cherimoya is so sweet that very little sugar is needed when the fruit is combined with other ingredients.

But there is a drawback to the delicacy: large black seeds, which must be dealt with to get at the flesh. And some of the fruits have many more than others. When a cherimoya is eaten out of hand (best with a sprinkling of lime juice), the seeds can be removed with a spoon, and the flesh that clings to them slipped off between the teeth.

The Question of Disposal

How the seeds are disposed of depends on whether one is standing under a summer sun overlooking the ocean or seated at a damask-covered table. In any case, it is a shame to discard the seeds with the flesh still clinging to them. If the pulp is being collected to use in another dish, it can be slipped off the seeds with the fingers.

Most cherimoyas seen in this part of the country come from California, where they have been grown for one hundred years. They are also raised in New Zealand and Florida.

It is hard to believe that a California fruit could cost so much, as high as $6.50 each. Frieda Caplan, president of Frieda's Finest, a California wholesale specialty produce company, says there is a reason. For one thing, she says, the female cherimoya fruit must be hand-pollinated. In addition, Caplan says that the fruit is hand-picked and hand-sorted because it is very fragile. Even though cherimoyas are hard when unripe, if they are bruised, the spot will turn brown when they ripen.

All this care costs money. But despite the high cost of the fruit, sales are expanding.

Cherimoyas can be used the same way as such fruits as peaches, berries, plums and nectarines. Pureed, they are delicious in mousses, sorbets, ice creams, tarts and custards. But they do not take well to cooking; their sweetness seems to dissipate with the heat.

When purchasing cherimoyas, look for slightly soft, dull-green fruit that is beginning to brown, but avoid those that are bruised and mushy. To ripen, keep at room temperature for a few days, then refrigerate.

Cherimoyas are in season from December to February.

CHERIMOYA PARFAIT

1 cup heavy cream
1 cup sour cream
2 tablespoons orange juice
2 teaspoons lemon juice
4 teaspoons grated orange rind
1/2 teaspoon pure vanilla extract
1/4 cup sugar
1/2 cup cherimoya puree
2 cups cherimoya chunks

1. Beat the heavy cream with the sour cream to a froth. Add the orange and lemon juices, orange rind, vanilla and sugar and beat until stiff. Blend in the cherimoya puree.
2. Put half the cherimoya chunks, in equal portions, into eight parfait glasses. Spoon half the whipped mixture, in equal portions, over the chunks. Repeat with the remaining chunks and cream. Chill if desired.

YIELD: 6 servings

Cherimoya

Even the writer from New York who loved what I had to say about cherimoyas said I spelled the word wrong. "The Royal Academy of Spanish Language, and other responsible sources, clearly spell the name of this amazing fruit chirimoya. The popular consensus in Latin America supports the phonetic interpretation.

"Chirimoyas were offered to the Spanish conquistadores upon their arrival to the big Chief Zaque, not far away from Bogotá."

This reader has his work cut out for him because cookbooks and food reference books continue to spell the fruit cherimoya.

Another reader from New York recalled a similar fruit when she was growing up in Florida. "This is the same fruit I knew as the sugar apple when I was growing up in Florida where my grandmother, who was Bahamian, had a sugar apple tree. It is also called sugar apple on many of the islands in the Caribbean."

For This Bitter Italian Green, Quick Cooking Is Best

November 29, 1986

"Is that spinach?" asked one of the diners, pointing to a dish of cooked greens in the middle of our table.

"No," another guest replied with a sniff, "it's broccoli."

But the greens sitting in the middle of the table at Dieci, an Italian restaurant on the Upper East Side of Manhattan, were neither. They were a distinctively Italian vegetable that has more names than the Prince of Wales. Variously called broccoli rabe—the name given it in the southern Italian dialect—*broccoletti di rape, rape, cima di rape* and sometimes *rapini,* this bitter-flavored green is moving outside the Italian community into the ordinary American supermarket much as mozzarella did before it.

Joseph Franco, the owner of Dieci, says he is using fifteen cases of broccoli rabe a week. "We don't even sell fried zucchini anymore," he said. "It's played out because this is so much better for you."

People who have grown up on kale, collard, mustard, beet and dandelion greens find broccoli rabe's intense flavor and bitterness, which range from mild to strong, similar to those greens. And frequenters of Chinese restaurants will recognize the taste as well: broccoli rabe is related to choy sum.

As with its name, experts are also unable to agree on how to cook broccoli rabe. According to Giuliano Bugialli, one of the foremost teachers of Italian cooking in the United States, the vegetable should be soaked for an hour, boiled for 30 minutes and then cooked with garlic for 15 minutes. The authors of *The New American Vegetable Book* (Aris Books, $24.95), Georgeanne Brennan, Isaac Cronin and Charlotte Glenn, agree on long, slow cooking: "*Cima di rape* must be cooked slowly or it will acquire a bitter taste." At Dieci, however, they steam broccoli rabe quickly. "That's how I learned it when I was a child," said Franco. "If you cook it a long time you cook out all the nutrition and it gets mushy." Elizabeth Schneider, a cookbook author known for her meticulous research, is on Franco's side. Quick cooking preserves the freshness and bright green color of broccoli rabe, she says.

Does the length of time the vegetable is cooked affect its bitterness? "It may," says Franco, "but people who grew up eating broccoli rabe like the bitterness." Franco believes, however, that the bitterness is related more to the quality of the vegetable than the length of time it is cooked.

I decided to cook some broccoli rabe by both methods, although some, myself included, may ask why anyone would want to destroy the chief characteristic of the vegetable, its bitterness, by cooking it to death. Cooking the vegetable slowly does make it mellower, but it also produces an unappetizing steam-table green color. If novices prefer a milder flavor, there are other ways to achieve it, including blanching for a minute in boiling water, draining and proceeding with the recipe.

Because of its assertive nature broccoli rabe is superb for pepping up bland foods and for competing with strong ones, from sausages and roasts to pasta and creamy cheeses.

When buying broccoli rabe, look for crisp, green, fresh-looking leaves. Avoid wilted or yellowing leaves, although yellow flowers are fine.

LINGUINE WITH BROCCOLI RABE AFTER THE FASHION OF DIECI

　　1　pound broccoli rabe
　　2　tablespoons olive oil
　　4　teaspoons minced garlic
　12　ounces linguine
　　1　cup ricotta, whole or skim-milk
　½　cup or more freshly grated Pecorino-Romano or Parmigiano-Reggiano cheese
　　　Salt and freshly ground black pepper to taste

1. Wash the broccoli rabe and trim off thick stems. Cut each stem across into two or three sections.
2. Heat the oil in a skillet large enough to hold the greens. Add the garlic and cook 30 seconds. Add the greens, stir, cover and cook over medium-high heat 10 to 12 minutes, until greens are softened but still firm.

3. Meanwhile cook the linguine until al dente. Drain, reserving about ½ cup of the cooking water. Stir some of the water and the ricotta into the greens, mixing well; add more water if needed.

4. Stir the mixture into the linguine and place in a serving dish. Sprinkle with grated cheese, add salt and pepper to taste, and serve.

YIELD: 4 first-course servings

Broccoli Rabe

However the name of this vegetable should be spelled, one reader was disgusted with my use of the slang spelling and another from York, Pennsylvania, sent a wonderful story from a July 1985 issue of *Time* magazine that is indirectly related to the subject at hand. I reprint it in its entirety:

All contradictions implicit in the U.S. need for illegal Mexican farm laborers once produced a strange harvest on a truck farm near El Mirage, Ariz. The farm grew a vegetable called broccoli di rapa, a plant that needs lots of irrigation, so the surrounding fields were muddy.

This used to dismay the border patrol officers when they came tramping through the fields about once a week in search of illegal immigrants (they usually seized about five).

According to United Farmworkers Official Lupe Sanchez, who tells the story, the crew boss came up with a proposition: "Suppose I just give you five of them every week, and you don't have to do any running or get your boots muddy?"

A little peculiar, the border guards thought, but why not go along with somebody who wants to help out the law? Then the crew boss went to his workers, explained the deal and said everyone would make more money if work did not have to be interrupted by the raids. So the workers drew lots once a week to pick the five who would have to be shipped back to the Mexican border. Before the five victims left, though, the hat was passed for funds to help the unlucky five sneak back north across the border, a trip that usually started the next day.

RESTAURANTS

I spent one long, very hard, rather fattening year as restaurant critic of The New York Times. *It was exactly 51 weeks too long. But it did give me considerable grist for the De Gustibus mill. During that period I encountered every annoying, frustrating, infuriating, exasperating experience that befalls restaurant patrons and I also learned a thing or two about life on the other side of the menu.*

Those experiences and the restaurateur's side of the argument account for this section. I learned two things from my tour of duty:

1. Always cancel your reservations if you do not intend to honor them.

2. You could never pay me enough to run a restaurant.

Reservations:
Dealing with No-Shows
January 28, 1984

Not long ago a gentleman staying at the Waldorf Towers in New York City reserved a table for five at Lutèce for nine o'clock on a Saturday night. Lutèce is one of many restaurants that ask their patrons to confirm their reservations in order to cut down on the number of no-shows.

The gentleman confirmed, as requested, by Saturday afternoon, but at 9:15 he had not arrived. So André Soltner, chef-proprietor of Lutèce, called him. There was no answer. "I got so mad," Soltner said in recounting the story, "that I waited until three o'clock in the morning and I called.

"A lady answered the phone, and I told her who I was and that I wanted to speak to Mr. So-and-So about the reservation he had for nine o'clock. After three or four minutes the man came to the phone, and I said to him: 'My staff is still waiting to serve you dinner. Should we still keep on waiting?' "

The Chronic Offenders

Soltner is a believer in the old adage "Don't get mad, get even." Bad manners or not, the gentleman from the Waldorf Towers was not doing anything hundreds of other diners don't do every night. While most restaurants require confirmation of reservations to cope with the number of people who do not show up—restaurateurs say the figure varies from 15 to 30 percent— few of them have gone to the lengths Soltner did.

Some, however, have their own way of taking care of chronic offenders. At An American Place, the maître d'hôtel keeps a list of people who confirm but then don't call to cancel if they cannot make it. "It's difficult for them to get another reservation," the maître d' said, "and then only for six o'clock or ten o'clock."

289

At one time it was unusual for restaurants to request telephone numbers and to ask patrons to confirm their reservations. It is becoming more commonplace, not only because popular restaurants, thinking they are already filled, don't like to turn away customers but also because a few empty tables can make the difference between profit and loss. At DeMarco's, where there are sixty-five seats, "ten no-shows would definitely make a difference for break-even," according to the maître d'hôtel.

He said he could often tell on the phone if someone had made three or four reservations for the same evening. "They sound sort of vague," he said, "and are taken aback when you ask them to confirm and when you ask for a telephone number where they can be reached in the evening."

Quotas for Each Night

La Tulipe overbooks slightly to account for the number of people who confirm and still don't show up—between 5 and 10 percent according to John Darr, who owns the restaurant with his wife, Sally. The restaurant seats fifty, and theoretically it could accommodate one hundred diners each evening, but instead the Darrs aim for sixty-five. If everyone shows up, including all those who forgot to confirm, the restaurant can still take care of them. One evening everyone did, and there were eighty-four patrons.

"People don't realize," John Darr said, "that even if they are embarrassed to call at the very last minute, it helps a restaurant."

Asking people to confirm their reservations makes them more conscientious about honoring them, said one maître d'. But it also annoys some of them. "They don't like it, so they don't call to cancel out of spite," he said.

Soltner says no-shows are not a new problem: "It's always been very bad here and bad in France too. But we have a tremendous amount of people who call at the last minute, and sometimes I can accommodate them."

A Call of Apology

One person, however, he was not willing to accommodate was the head of a mission to the United Nations who failed to show up on three separate occasions. Soltner called him but could never get past his secretary, so he left a message. "Tell the ambassador," he said, "that my name is André Soltner and I am owner of Restaurant Lutèce, and as long as I am the owner, he will never, never get a reservation here." According to Soltner, within a few minutes the envoy called back to apologize, and a little later his chauffeur came by with a check, which the chef refused. "But," he said, "the ambassador always shows up now."

And what about those who forget to confirm but show up anyway? Most restaurants will try to accommodate them "if they are nice about it," Soltner said, "but they may have to wait."

Now, if we could just get restaurants to honor reservations and not to keep us waiting at the bar for forty-five minutes.

On Restaurants and Reservations
February 18, 1984

After a recent column described the problems caused by people who book tables at restaurants but fail to show up, readers who honor their reservations wrote to present their side. Their unpleasant experiences cover everything from a restaurant's refusing to honor a reservation or keeping patrons waiting for ages to treating early diners as second-class citizens.

One of the many readers who wrote said, "I suggest you follow up this article with the other side of the coin—the restaurateur who greatly overbooks." He went on to describe an experience at an Upper West Side restaurant in Manhattan.

He said that when his party of four arrived for an 8:45 reservation, he was told, "Dinner is running late, and the table will be available shortly." Shortly turned out to be forty-five minutes, and while he waited he watched two other foursomes and one couple being seated. To make matters worse, when his party finally got its table, many of the entrées were no longer available.

Getting a Better Table

Another irate reader said that several times she and a companion had been given undesirable tables, even though they had made reservations far in advance and better tables remained empty.

Unhappy at being seated next to a coffee urn at a fancy Italian restaurant on the Upper East Side, they asked for a better table but were told that all were reserved. Still unsatisfied, they got up and walked over to a better table. At that point, the management relented and seated them.

When dining out becomes a contest of wills between the management and the patron, no matter who wins the battle the restaurant usually loses the war. Not only are dissatisfied clients unlikely to return, they usually let their friends know about their unpleasant experiences.

One reader finds the custom of "seatings" especially distasteful. "If one makes a reservation for an early evening, say 6:30 P.M., the management immediately informs you you must be out by 8," she writes. "Why is the 8 P.M. reservation more important than the earlier one? Is it perhaps for a greater gastronome, bigger celebrity or just a bigger tipper?"

Then there is the restaurant that takes a reservation but neglects to write it down. In this instance, a reservation at one of the city's finest French restaurants was booked a month ahead, along with a room at the Hotel Pierre. The big New York City weekend, according to the reader, went as planned until she and her husband arrived for their 8:30 reservation at the restaurant. The woman who greeted them said they had no reservation and did nothing to rectify the situation.

Ten years later, this writer remains resentful. She says she often thinks about booking a table at the restaurant, but adds, "I just can't bring myself to call—I don't have any way of getting even."

Looking to the Future

Restaurants that give shabby treatment to patrons they don't know do so at their peril. They have every reason, of course, to take special care of regular customers. But very, very few restaurants are so popular that they may cater only to those they know —sooner or later they will need "new blood." In the long run they will do better to turn the disgruntled customer into a friend.

One popular cafe did. Among all the complaints, one reservation story had a happy ending. In this case, the couple were kept waiting for thirty-five minutes at the bar, where each consumed two drinks. They got up to leave.

"Just as we were leaving, we were told that our table was being prepared," the writer said. "But we were already in motion and our dander was up, so we kept on going. Overlooked in the contretemps was the fact that we had not paid our bar bill."

A Call from the Maître d'Hôtel

The next evening the restaurant's maître d'hôtel called, but not about the bar bill. Instead, he apologized and invited the angered patrons to return as guests of the restaurant.

The letter described the reception on the return visit: "We were shown to one of the better tables, and the waitress recommended one of the better wines on the list, which we took. Later on, when it was depleted, it was replaced with a second before we could muster the temerity to ask for it. The waitress recommended all the best items on the menu. It was a wonderful meal. Naturally, we left a gracious tip.

"It goes without saying," this customer concluded, "that we forgave them for their previous lapse."

Last-Minute Tables Do Exist

May 3, 1986

The complaints are familiar: Customers can't get reservations at New York City's most popular restaurants, and owners of the restaurants say they have empty tables because of no-shows.

Is planning always required to have dinner at Aurora, Le Bernardin, Lutèce and the Quilted Giraffe? Is there any point in calling at the last minute?

Wayne King, the maître d'hôtel at the Quilted Giraffe, who is also in charge of reservations, says, "Call three weeks in advance or at the very last minute." That, it seems, is good advice for almost every popular dining spot.

A week ago Friday night and on Tuesday of this week, calls were made to fourteen of the city's most popular restaurants to see if they could accommodate two for dinner the same evening. On Friday the calls were made at 8:30 P.M. and then again at 9:30. On Tuesday they were made at 9. The results are quite encouraging.

In general, if you are not fussy about how late you dine, you will have a host of possibilities. Not Le Bernardin or Lutèce, perhaps, but at any of the other restaurants there would have been room for two between 9:30 and 10:30. The Quilted Giraffe could have taken us at 9:45 on Tuesday evening.

Perhaps equally interesting is that only three of the restaurants reported having empty tables because of no-shows: Le Montrachet on Friday, Le Cygne on Tuesday and La Tulipe on both Friday and Tuesday.

Restaurant reconfirmation has become the rule rather than the exception at most of the city's best restaurants, and it has made a difference, says King. The procedure at the Quilted Giraffe is typical of most. Reconfirmation is required by the day before at four o'clock. Even so, King said, "Only 30 to 40 percent reconfirm." Those who do not are called by the restaurant. If there is no reconfirmation by four o'clock the day of the reservation, the table is rebooked. "We've cut our no-shows down to 10 percent or less," King said.

"We Always Fill Up"

André Soltner, chef-proprietor of Lutèce, says his no-show problem has not improved, but "people know they can call at the last minute so we always fill up right away."

On Friday night we could have had a table at The Four Seasons in the Grill Room at 8:30 and in the Pool Room (the preferred dinner location) after 9:45. Le Cirque could have taken us at 9:30, as could Le Montrachet. And Le Cygne had a table "any time."

If we had been willing to wait a little longer, we could have been accommodated at Arcadia, Aurora or Jams at 10 P.M. and even at the tiny Chanterelle at 10:30. There was room for us at An American Place at 10:30, and the River Cafe, which originally told us there was nothing until 11 P.M., had a table by 10:30.

"Just Unlucky"

Lutèce could not have been more sympathetic but could not help us at all, nor could Le Bernardin. Soltner said that we were "just unlucky."

Responses Tuesday evening at 9 were equally mixed, but there were still many possibilities. An American Place had a table for us immediately. Le Montrachet could have taken us at 9:30. La Tulipe had a no-show, as did Le Cygne, and both would have had room for us within the half hour. Aurora was able to accommodate us at 9:45, along with the Quilted Giraffe, and at 10 we could have gone to Arcadia or Jams. There was a table at 10:15 at the River Cafe.

The Four Seasons, Le Bernardin and Chanterelle had nothing. The line at Lutèce was busy from 9 to 9:30.

Everyone with whom we spoke was unfailingly courteous and seemed genuinely distressed that they could not help us until later in the evening.

The staff at Arcadia recommends calling close to six o'clock when they know if they have filled all their cancellations from the waiting list. Le Montrachet makes a "conscientious effort not to overbook," says Jack Gilbert, who takes reservations. "Our policy is to have a table or two open," he said. At the River Cafe, where reconfirmation is required by three o'clock on the day of the reservation, the best time to call is four o'clock.

But all the restaurants, with the exception of Le Bernardin, said it was always worth making a last-minute call. As long, that is, as you don't want to be in bed by eleven o'clock.

Reservations, No-Shows and Last-Minute Tables

Judging by the mail, the problem of restaurant reservations is a continuing one. The no-shows have gotten so serious in London that one restaurant, Inigo Jones, now charges twenty pounds if someone fails to keep a reservation.

According to a Washington, D.C., reader, an article in the May 1986 issue of the British magazine *Tatler* says that it is quite legal to charge someone for failing to honor a reservation because it is the same as breaking a contract. The author carries the analogy one step further: A restaurant is also guilty of breaking a contract if it does not have a table when one has been booked. Has anyone tried collecting the twenty pounds from the restaurant?

So far, in New York City, the only deposits required for reservations are those made for special occasions: New Year's Eve, for example, or when there is going to be a large party and special arrangements.

In a Chicago suburb one eighty-seat restaurant has an official ban list for no-shows. According to the trade publication *Restaurants and Institutions,* Cafe Provençal in Evanston has no trouble enforcing the ban because the offenders are put on a computer list. If they repeat the offense a second time, written beside their name is the damning phrase "No table ever again." Since the program went into effect, the restaurant reports a 50 percent reduction in no-shows.

As for the other half of the equation, a reader from Philadelphia made this suggestion: "When making a reservation ask for the name of the person taking it and note what time the call was made. Keep this information in a pocket calendar and, if necessary, whip it out if there is a problem." The writer says it works for him.

A three-page letter from a New York City restaurateur boiled down to this: Patrons who sit too long at their tables are the cause, at least 95 percent of the time, of a restaurant's inability to provide later customers with their tables on time.

"The astute diner," he wrote, "recognizes that he is contracting for a meal, ambience and service and is not leasing a parcel of real estate to be occupied and vacated at his whim. The person who takes 2½ hours for lunch? He's about as welcome as inspectors from the Health Department (who spend about an hour in each restaurant and cannot go back to their office without saying they found something wrong—even if it is only that the chefs are not wearing caps)."

Restaurant Frustrations

May 5, 1984

After a few rings, a machine answers the phone at Windows on the World. The tape recording says: "Thank you for calling Windows on the World reservations and information. Presently, all agents are busy. Your call will be answered by the first available telephone agent."

Agent? Is this a restaurant or Peoples Express? What kind of a message is that for a restaurant with white tablecloths and a spectacular view of New York City?

The disgruntled patron who called the message to my attention said it was only the spectacular view that persuaded him to go there with his out-of-town guests. "Otherwise," he wrote, "I would have been turned off entirely."

Manager Worked at an Airline

William Johnson, guest-services manager for the restaurant, said the sixteen reservations agents at the restaurant function "very much like an airline."

"Maybe it's because I once worked for an airline that the message sounds that way," he added.

Perhaps the next step is the advance purchase of a ticket for food service.

The increasing use of answering machines in busy restaurants, even when the messages don't sound like those of a business office, is an annoyance to many people. This is especially so when the machine says they have called at the wrong time and will have to call the next day. "No matter when I call," wrote one frustrated would-be patron of the Quilted Giraffe, "I never seem to call them at the right time."

Barry Wine, who owns the restaurant with his wife, Susan, says, "There is no sense in answering the phone twelve hours a day if all you have to say is 'no, no, no.' With the number of seats we have and as full as we are, the restaurant just fills up during that period of time."

Other Practices Are Bothersome

But the use of answering machines is just one of many restaurant practices that bother patrons.

The Oyster Bar and Restaurant insists that most members of the party be present before anyone in the group will be seated. One reader described the difficulty he had at lunchtime, when the restaurant is busiest. He arrived before the rest of his guests at noon and made his way to the head of the line by 12:05. He was told he would have to wait for the rest of the party.

In the meantime diners arrived in droves. When the rest of the man's party arrived at 12:07, he went to the front of the line and was told by the maître d'hôtel that he would have to go to the end and wait his turn once again. It's rather like losing your place in the supermarket checkout line. The man was not seated until 12:20.

Mario Staub, vice president of the Brody Corporation, which owns the Oyster Bar, said the rule was made because some customers say their party is larger than it really is in order to get a larger table. Staub asserted that this was a frequent occurrence. If so, the party should at least be seated immediately when all have assembled, instead of having to go to the end of the line.

Grace Period for Late Patrons

It is simply greedy to give a table to another party without allowing the original group a grace period of at least ten minutes. In this city, where traffic, especially at noontime, can reach gridlock proportions, fifteen minutes would be more civilized. After all, the same restaurants often make the patrons wait for their tables.

Once inside the restaurant, diners may have to contend with a variety of other unpleasant situations. A problem that I find more and more—one that is especially difficult to deal with—is what might be delicately called "the cleanliness problem." All too often I find myself cringing when certain waiters come near.

Whether the problem stems from too few baths, the absence of deodorant or a uniform that all the perchloroethylene in the world cannot clean, I do not know. But the only other olfactory problem that is guaranteed to ruin an otherwise good meal for me is a cigar smoker at the next table.

Perhaps the way to handle the situation is quietly to tell the maître d'hôtel or the owner at the end of the meal. The restaurant's management may not be aware of the problem and might be happy to correct it if told. Of course, if it involves an investment in a new uniform, the management may balk.

Frustrations in Restaurants

Well, whenever you think you have had the most annoying experience in a restaurant, along comes someone else with an even better story, such as an unexpected—and unwelcome—addition to the food.

"While having lunch with friends a few years ago," wrote a New York reader, "I discovered hair in my salad. Not wanting to spoil everyone else's lunch, I very quietly called the waitress aside and brought it to her attention. Holding the plate high, she proceeded to lift out a *very long, blonde* hair and loudly proclaimed: 'Well, at least it's not mine.'"

At least the woman who ordered a hamburger at the Museum Cafe in Manhattan had an honest server: "When the waitress put it down on the table, she took a good look at it and said with surprise in her voice: 'That looks good. It doesn't usually.'"

One man from Briarcliff Manor, New York, wanted to know if it is legal to insist on sitting people who are alone at the counter when there are tables available. Another from Albany complained because some New York City restaurants won't take reservations for one.

A Manhattanite offered the advice all of us have thought about many, many times but seldom, if ever, have the nerve to go through with. "Stiff" the server, she suggested. "It may not be the pleasant way to deal with this problem, but it certainly is a satisfying one! Someone once told me that if service is very poor, rather than leave no tip at all, leave only one penny."

A New Stamp: Made in America
December 31, 1983

Americans will be returning to their culinary roots during the rest of this decade, but they will not abandon ethnic foods, especially those that complement their lifestyle. There will always be a place for the elegant French restaurant, particularly on special occasions. But Italian restaurants featuring Tuscan food and Mexican restaurants that serve authentic cooking of the country will be as popular as places that offer regional American cooking.

Tuscan cooking is appealing because it fits our interpretation of healthful eating—fresh, uncomplicated food that relies heavily on the grandest carbohydrate of them all: pasta. It also features many grilled dishes, and grilling, an easy way of preparing food, is becoming popular.

Mexican food, in a sense part of our own regional cooking because variations of it are the cooking of the American Southwest, suits our informal way of living. But even as the taco parlors with their combination plates proliferate and give Mexican food a bad name, restaurants serving authentic Mexican cooking will begin to make their presence felt. Right now Mexican food in restaurants is where Italian food was thirty years ago: There is considerable room for exploring the cuisine and a desperate need for improvement.

One trend that I hope dies aborning is the Japanese restaurant serving Westernized Japanese food. Is this the next step, now that we have sushi parlors on every corner?

In the meantime, restaurants that offer regional American cooking continue to proliferate. Within a year or two, ribs and barbecue should peak, as southern and New Orleans restaurants begin to take over. As the decade wears on, cooking from other regions of the country will certainly capture our attention.

Much of this food, perhaps the best of it, will be cooked by young American chefs whose basic training has been in this country. The most ambitious and creative of them look forward to opening their own small places, where they can cook as they please and where quality, not quantity, is the measure of success.

These new restaurateurs, however, face serious staffing problems. Some of the problems can be overcome by changing the way the kitchen is organized and by judicious selection of the food that is served. If, for example, it is impossible to find a pastry chef whose work is up to the rest of the kitchen, new restaurants may turn to the increasing number of cottage-industry bakers who produce limited amounts of handmade pastries exclusively for restaurants. As a result, unfortunately, the frequent restaurant-goer will be faced with the same chocolate mousse pie in ten different places.

Staffing problems can also be alleviated by serving grilled foods. A cook need not be a graduate of the Cordon Bleu to know how to grill properly.

A current trend of serving some foods at room temperature, a very European custom, will also solve the problem of a less-than-efficient staff that cannot get food to the table while it is hot. Certainly there are dishes that taste much better if they are not piping hot or ice-cold, such as roasted meats and salads. But serving the appropriate foods at room temperature is no license for tepid stews, soups or french fries.

How restaurateurs in 1984 and the more distant future will solve the problem of staffing the dining room is too depressing to contemplate. Restaurant help becomes more and more unprofessional every year. In New York City especially, hundreds of out-of-work actors assume roles as waiters and do not prepare for their parts very well. Perhaps, just as young Americans have decided that cooking is an exciting profession, some will decide that being a professional waiter is equally rewarding.

In the new year, if one more waiter greets me with, "Hi, I'm Leopold, and I'm going to serve this evening," I hereby resolve to leave the restaurant and eat somewhere else.

Hi, I'm Joe, and . . .

The made in America column covered a lot of ground, but only one little corner of it struck a raw nerve: my resolution to leave any restaurant where the waiter introduces himself or herself to me by name.

"Is it snobbishness on your part that makes you want to leave a restaurant where the waiter introduces himself?

"Perhaps we'll have a better chance of getting professional waiters when each one is recognized as an individual with a name and will take pride in his/her ability," said one Brooklyn reader.

"Why do you resent having your conversation interrupted? The kid is just trying to please you. Is your conversation so brilliant?

"If you don't like Leo to introduce himself, complain to the boss. The boss is the one who told him to say it. As my husband says: 'Be nice to Leo. He may be your shrink soon.' "

Enough with, "Hi! I'm Waldo!"
January 31, 1987

For some, this is the Year of the Rabbit. For Patrick O'Connell, it is the Year of the Waiter. The chef and co-owner of the Inn at Little Washington in Washington, Virginia, is on a crusade to accord the people in the front of the house the same respect now reserved for those in the kitchen. "Waiters," said Mr. O'Connell "are in exactly the same evolutionary state the chef was eight or nine years ago."

In this country, being a waiter is not yet a profession: it is a job. And, said Gary Penn, owner of the Professional Waiters School in Los Angeles, it's a service job. "People with egos don't want to go fetch food," he said.

Like Mr. Penn, Mr. O'Connell wants to change that perception. Mr. O'Connell and the Society for American Cuisine, a group of restaurateurs, chefs and suppliers, plan to improve the status of waiters. Putting his money where his mouth is, Mr. O'Connell has made changes in his own restaurant. He has his work cut out for him. The French Culinary Institute in Manhattan offered a course last year called "Introduction to Professional Restaurant Service." Three people signed up for it.

"The Course Failed"

"The course failed," said Dorothy Cann, the school's director, "because today people feel they don't have to be trained for service since it's easy to get a job without training and still make a decent wage."

The course was not a total loss, however. When restaurant owners looking for professional waiters found the institute would be unable to supply them, they signed contracts to have their staffs trained by the school.

The situation is more advanced in Los Angeles, where Mr. Penn's school has been in operation for four and a half years. It has been so successful that it will begin franchising the concept next year, with the first clone opening in New York. Mr. Penn decided there was a need for this two-week course after years as a waiter: "When you see the level of incompetence," he said, "it's staggering."

Certainly there are restaurants in which service is excellent. These are usually places where training is more than teaching the new help where the ketchup is kept. At The Four Seasons, even experienced waiters must train for four weeks. The first week is spent in the kitchen, the second week is devoted to help-ing another waiter. During the last two weeks, the probationer works as a waiter under supervision. "During that time," said Paul Kovi, co-owner of The Four Seasons, "we decide whether to keep someone."

The Inn at Little Washington has instituted similar procedures. "We no longer hire anyone here as a full-fledged waiter even if they have been in the business for twenty years," said Mr. O'Con-nell. "We hire them as apprentices. It creates tremendous incen-tive." The quick studies can become waiters in two or three weeks; others can take as long as a year. The restaurant is pro-viding health insurance for the staff as well.

"For the first time, the system creates stages of advancement and it improves self-esteem," Mr. O'Connell said. Because Mr. O'Connell believes that the practice of tipping lowers a waiter's self-esteem, he plans to eliminate it. "People cannot take their jobs seriously if they feel they are being paid through the kind-ness and discretion of anonymous strangers," he said. "They have to be paid their full worth through the owner."

Mr. O'Connell hopes to banish tipping and replace it with a 15 percent service charge within the year. "The staff is looking for-ward to it," he said. "Now we have to feel out our clientele." Michael McCarty, the owner of Michael's in Santa Monica, and Barry and Susan Wine, who own the Quilted Giraffe and the Casual Quilted Giraffe in New York, have successfully eliminated tipping, replacing it with a service charge.

A Perfect Waiter

Mr. O'Connell is working on an essay contest in which the perfect waiter will be described. It will be open to American waiters (waitress is a word Mr. O'Connell wishes to eliminate) and will offer $50,000 in prizes. "I hope these essays will illustrate that these people are thinking, creative, intelligent and analytical and that they are in a position to educate the diner," he said. "I think it would make a sizable contribution to elevating their status in the eyes of the dining public."

The first step will be to abandon the recitation of this greeting: "Hi! I'm your waitperson and my name is Waldo."

Dining Out: The Woes of a Nonsmoker
March 10, 1984

Ask people who dine out often what bothers them most in restaurants, and ranked just below poor food and noise is smoking.

Many restaurateurs who never had to worry about the problem before are having to deal with it more and more frequently. They are being confronted by patrons who are annoyed by smoking, especially the smell from cigars and pipes.

"We have the problem every day," said Jean-Jacques Rachou, owner of La Côte Basque in Manhattan. "It is very uncomfortable for us. People ask to change tables. If I change someone's table because of a cigar," Rachou said with a sigh, "sometimes I offer a Champagne or an after-dinner drink."

Rachou, who sells cigars to his customers, has chosen to deal with each situation as it occurs rather than instituting any of the no-smoking policies many of his fellow restaurateurs have adopted. That includes everything from banning all smoking, a policy followed in very few restaurants, to establishing no-smoking sections or banishing pipes and cigars but not cigarettes.

In a recent nationwide survey conducted by *Restaurants and*

Institutions, an industry trade publication, over one-third of the respondents said smoking was a source of irritation. But none of New York City's high-priced restaurants have sections for non-smokers though some have an informal arrangement that creates nonsmoking sections on an ad hoc basis.

More and more of the city's restaurants are banning pipes and cigars. At Diva and at Jams, for example, pipe and cigar smoking are not allowed, and at Parioli Romanissimo cigar smoking is forbidden.

At Lavin's pipes and cigars are not permitted in the dining room until after 10:30 P.M.. But even then, if someone complains, the smoker is asked to extinguish the offending object. People who ask to be seated away from all smokers are shown to a part of the restaurant where they won't be bothered by fumes, according to the owner, Richard Lavin.

"I know the air patterns from the air-cleaning machines," Lavin said. He does not think a separate no-smoking section is necessary. "As long as you are sensitive to your guests, you can take care of them," he said.

A sign informs diners at An American Place that pipe smoking is not allowed. Cigars still are, but Reggie Young, the maître d'hôtel says, "I think we are probably going to have a cigar sign too. This is such a small dining room, once someone lights up, it doesn't go away."

Sometimes when people make reservations they explain they are allergic to any kind of smoke. Young designates an area with only a few tables as nonsmoking, and seats only nonsmokers in that area. "I wish," he said, "more people would ask for no-smoking. Then we would designate an area," permanently.

The question of nonsmokers' rights has become significant enough for the National Restaurant Association to issue a guide for restaurateurs on no-smoking sections. In a survey conducted by the association, between one-quarter and one-third of the eight hundred households responding considered a no-smoking section "important" or "very important." Ten percent considered it "somewhat important."

While there are no statistics on the increase in militancy among nonsmokers, I have certainly observed a change in attitude, not only among the nonsmokers but among smokers as well. Many smokers are less aggressive about their "right" to smoke than they used to be.

Every taxi driver I have asked to stop smoking has done so without a fuss. Would that that were true for every restaurant patron I have ever sat next to who blew smoke in my face. I have never asked them to stop smoking, just to blow the smoke the other way. The responses range from sheepishness to intense hostility. Smokers at private dinner parties have always been accommodating.

The hostile ones do not seem to be among the smokers questioned in a recent Gallup poll. According to that survey 55 percent of the smokers believe that they should refrain from smoking in the presence of nonsmokers. It is a feeling shared by 82 percent of the nonsmokers.

Whether or not one objects for health reasons to inhaling someone else's smoke, the question of aesthetics still remains. Smelling the fumes from a cigarette, or worse still, from a pipe or cigar, interferes with my enjoyment of the meal because it overwhelms the aromas of food. It is especially offensive in a small restaurant with poor ventilation.

A Change in Attitude

Julia Child, a former smoker, has become militant on the subject. Asked in an interview in *Cook's* magazine how she feels about smoking at the dinner table, she said: "I used to smoke, and I now don't smoke. I don't like it anymore. It gets in your hair and on your clothes. In fact, I'm rather rude about it now."

A recent survey of eighty-one restaurants and chains in New York City that was conducted by the New York Heart Association turned up only ten that provided no-smoking areas. Of those none were in the expensive category, four were in the moderate-priced category, and the rest were inexpensive restaurants, including two fast-food chains.

Rachou said he had thought of dividing his dining room into smoking and nonsmoking sections but couldn't decide what to do with a party of six in which there were three smokers and three nonsmokers. So, he says, he suffers.

"Once I asked a person not to smoke a cigar," Rachou said.

"He asked me where the sign was that said he couldn't. Since there wasn't one, what could I say?" Rather than confront any other smokers, Rachou moves the complaining party to another table.

But at the three restaurants owned by the Lattanzi family, Trastevere, Trastevere II and Erminia, all of them small and with tables close together, the management is harder on the rette smokers have been asked to stop.

"Once in a while we get a complaint," Maurizio Lattanzi said, "so I ask the person to put out the cigarette. If they won't I ask them to leave."

Richard Lavin is convinced that if smokers could see the condition of the filters on his air-cleaning machines after three days' use, they would stop smoking. "They are so blackened," her said. "we have to give them an acid bath twice a week."

Dining and Smoking: A Quandary
June 29, 1985

"If the lawmakers want no smoking in the restaurants, O.K.," said André Soltner, chef-owner of Lutèce in New York City. "They should say no smoking at all, and we would have no problem. But not just *part* no smoking. It makes it impossible."

Impossible, difficult, not practical. That is the reaction of many restaurateurs to Mayor Koch's request last week for voluntary no-smoking sections. Restaurants are being asked to set aside at least one-quarter of their seats for nonsmokers. Some restaurants are willing to try to work out a way to comply with the request; a few have already begun the process.

Diverse Assortment

As divergent an assortment of places as Il Nido, 251 East 53rd Street, La Côte Basque, 5 East 55th Street, Positano, 250 Park Avenue South, and Huberts, 102 East 22nd Street, have expressed interest in creating a no-smoking section.

"Eventually we'll probably have to set aside one part of the dining room in both places," said Il Nido's owner, Adi Giovannetti, alluding to his other restaurant, Il Monello, at 1460 Second Avenue, near 76th Street. "Probably we'll do it in the fall because there are a lot of people who complain about the smoke. We have air cleaners, but they don't seem to work."

Management at Positano, a large new restaurant that attracts a younger crowd than Il Nido, is even more enthusiastic. "I think it's a very good idea," said the general manager, Willy Moulin. "Health is threatened by other people's smoke, and when you are eating you want to taste your food, not the smoke. People do complain, particularly about pipes and cigars. Some people already ask if we have a no-smoking section, but once they find out we have one, even more of them will ask for it." Moulin said he hopes to make the changes in a week or two.

La Côte Basque may give it a try too, using one of its two dining rooms. "The way our restaurant is laid out, we would be in a perfect situation to put aside a section for nonsmokers," said Joseph Reyers, the maître d'hôtel. "We are perfectly willing to try it out. But eventually, I think, it will become law."

No Plans

Some restaurants, like Huberts, Jams and Vanessa, already ask people not to smoke pipes or cigars. But Vanessa has no plans to set up a no-smoking section. Skip Sharon, who is general manager at Vanessa in Greenwich Village as well as Hoexter's Market and Uzie's on the Upper East Side, says that Uzie's is the only place a section for nonsmokers would work. "It has a back room, and I think you need a whole separate room," he said, "but we haven't given it a tremendous amount of thought."

He acknowledged, however, that even though he smokes cigars, sometimes smoking in restaurants bothers him. "A guy lit up a cigar at Uzie's the other night," Sharon said, "and it was annoying me. I thought about all the people around him. I'm very, very conscious of my own cigar. I can't smoke it in my own home."

Even those who say it would be very difficult to set aside non-smoking sections in their restaurants like the thought. "I think it's a terrific idea," said Karen Hubert, co-owner and chef of Hu-

berts. "But I can't figure out logistically how to do it in my restaurant because it is so small. I wrote to the Health Department,
and I suggested a meeting of some small restaurants to discuss
this. Maybe someone smarter than I can figure out how to do it.
No one would like to be red-eye free more than myself."

Peter Stephan, manager of Cafe Luxembourg, at 200 West
70th Street, would be in favor of no smoking at all. "It's better
for the quality of the air," he said, "but this is a democracy. If you
do that, you are asking people to curtail their vices in public."
The restaurant's solution is to ask people to extinguish their
pipes and cigars if others around them complain and to move
those bothered by cigarette smoke to another area.

At Indochine, 430 Lafayette Street (near Astor Place), if they
see someone lighting up a pipe or cigar, they ask him not to. "We
try to stave off the complaints," said the manager, Michael Calla-
han, "and we have some people who complain. But it's kind of
hard here. Reservations are a nightmare as it is with the no-
shows."

How to manage the traffic seems to be the biggest worry. "It's
very difficult to do because you have to juggle the tables
around," said Melvin Master, co-owner of Jams on East 79th
Street. But Soltner doesn't see how he could juggle his tables
around at Lutèce, at 249 East 50th Street. "I fill my twenty-nine
tables at six," he said, "and then someone comes for an eight
o'clock reservation and they want a no-smoking table, but the
first table free is in the smoking section. What should I do? For
me there are only two solutions. Either you smoke in a restaurant
or you don't."

Smoking in Restaurants

The first column about smoking in restaurants was written in
1984; the second in 1985. In 1986 the Mayor and City Council of
the city of New York contemplated mandatory no-smoking sections in restaurants because the voluntary plan had absolutely no
effect on the city's restaurants at all. And from the comments

made by restaurateurs in the second column, it is easy to see why.

The first column brought a fair amount of applause, but the usual amount of criticism.

"Pipes and cigars have been mankind's boon companion for over two thousand years. The cigarette is a recent arrival. The most dangerous part of smoking is inhaling. Cigarette smokers inhale tobacco fumes and chemical fumes designed to keep the cigarette burning plus paper fumes. Fine cigar and pipe tobaccos have none of the above."

The Brooklyn critic continues: "If I am in a small restaurant and they do not allow smoking, this is agreeable. If they discriminate against the forms of smoking, which are really for enjoyment as opposed to sheer habit, I will walk out. If a restaurant has ashtrays and no signs, I will smoke after dinner if I wish. If a restaurant has a sign NO PIPES OR CIGARS, I will walk out and never eat there.

"If a waiter tries to stop me without a sign, I will not eat there again and I will let all my friends know the place is to be avoided."

Well, sir, I certainly am lucky not to be married to you. And I'm glad I don't work for you either.

A Manhattanite who claims to be a nonsmoker who enjoys an occasional cigar wants to know who determines "that the noxious fumes of cigarette smoke are more pleasant or less disruptive to a meal than cigar and pipe smoke, which at least have a fragrant aroma and are generally confined to the end of the meal."

One man's aroma is another man's stink. And the end of your meal may be the beginning of mine.

But the gentleman raises an important question. His solution: a ban on all smoking.

A New Jersey woman who likes cigars commented that "anyone who becomes so possessive as to claim airspace apparently thinks the world owes him something. Besides that, shouting and screaming are just a matter of poor upbringing, and cigar smoking can be considered akin to good breeding."

Several readers wrote in to remark on the restaurants, mostly abroad, where brandy and cigars, or whatever, are taken in a room separate from the dining room.

The owner of Gravetye Manor, a charming country-house hotel not far from London, which incidentally has a wonderful chef, wrote to comment on an article I had written about his place. He added that he had just completely banned smoking in the restaurant. "I will admit to considerable apprehension at the time," wrote Peter Herbert, "but in the event we have had but one complaint and a mass of compliments on our new policy. I know that a great number of my colleagues have been awaiting the results of our bold move, and I suspect from my conversations that there will now be quite a few of them following our lead. When one considers that we have been civilized enough to ban smoking from theaters and even tube trains, it *is* crazy that we allow the habit to continue in restaurants."

In the spring of 1986 on a trip to the Napa Valley in California we visited two restaurants where smoking is completely banned in the dining room: Mustard's Grill and Rose et LeFavour Cafe Oriental. Bruce LeFavour says he has had almost no complaints.

How Dining Bills Add Up
June 16, 1984

Few people study menus with the same care the I.R.S. uses to scrutinize tax returns. Often it doesn't make any difference because there are no hidden messages. But more and more restaurants are using the bottoms of their menus to list special charges, sometimes in print so small the charges are easily overlooked. This is, however, an improvement over the custom twenty years ago of surprising patrons with *le couvert,* the cover charge that "took care of the bread and butter" and often appeared on the bill, without warning, as "B & B."

While there are still a few places that retain a cover charge, New York City restaurants are more likely to have minimum charges and charges for splitting portions. Occasionally they will also have a 15 percent service charge in the fashion of European restaurants, and once in a while there is a corkage charge for patrons who bring their own wine.

A corkage charge is understandable at a restaurant that serves wine, especially one that prides itself on its wine list, such as Oenophilia, where the fee for bringing your own bottle is $5. But a corkage charge at a restaurant that does not yet have its wine and liquor license struck one reader as peculiar. "It's not my fault Evelyne's doesn't have their license yet," she wrote. "I think it's outrageous."

Helping Waiters

Maryann Mowrey, manager at Evelyne's, says the $1.50 goes to the waiters as part of their tip. "It's just a traditional charge," she said. "Most Americans tip on the food and wine, and this makes up for lost revenue for the waiters until we get our license." The charge does not apply to hard liquor or beer.

Almost as unusual as the corkage charge is the inclusion of a predetermined gratuity. At El Rio Grande adding a 15 percent service charge is discretionary. Joyce Steins, one of the owners, says she suggests such a gratuity "on occasion when there is a large party and they are having a wonderful time and they are drunk."

She adds, "I always remind them that the tip is usually 15 percent, and nobody fights back." Steins says she learned to do this when she worked at Tavern on the Green, which suggests a 20 percent gratuity for parties of twenty-five or more.

By far the most common restaurant charge is a minimum, which can be as low as $5 during dining hours at Chandra Gardens, an Upper East Side vegetarian restaurant, and as high as $35 at La Caravelle, an elegant French restaurant in midtown.

"The $35 actually is not even useful," André Jammet, one of the owners, said at first. "A normal person, even if he takes a normal entrée, will spend that." But there are no entrées that cost as much as $35 at La Caravelle. Then Jammet explained that "if someone comes and says I just want a cup of soup or a salad, we can use this."

Woods has three restaurants. Two have minimum charges, while the third and newest, in Gramercy Park, does not. Ronald Sharkey, manager of Woods on Madison, said the minimum charge of $15 for dinner is "to avoid people coming in for soup at eight o'clock." The $11 minimum at lunch is to keep out people who want "tea, and apple and cheese at one." Sharkey said the minimum is often waived if two in a party of three order a full meal while the third just wants soup or a drink. The new Woods has no minimums, Sharkey said, because it is much bigger and "is geared to serving people at the bar who want just a cappuccino."

A number of restaurants charge for splitting portions because, they say, it is more work for the kitchen. The charge at Oenophilia is $1, but Steven Goetz, a waiter at the restaurant, says it isn't necessarily enforced.

If it isn't enforced, why is it on the menu? "To discourage people from doing it," Goetz explained.

The impression left by talking to restaurateurs is that some of these rules are made to be broken. So if a careful perusal of a menu turns up an additional or unexpected fee, a patron might want to ask for specifics before deciding not to incur the charge.

Practical Prices for Practice Food
September 27, 1986

If Broadway shows charge preview prices while the cast is in dress rehearsal, why should restaurants charge full price when their dining room and kitchen staffs are still practicing? Every time I visit a restaurant in its shakedown phase and find the service and food less than professional, I wonder why I have allowed myself to be practiced on for full price.

There are those who want to be the first on their block to visit the newest restaurant, and for them, perhaps, the price for that thrill is not too high to pay. But restaurants could create a considerable amount of goodwill for themselves by taking a leaf from the theater notebook. The idea of preview restaurant prices came to mind recently because two newly opened places have instituted the policy.

Different Prices

At Chez Josephine at 42nd Street and Ninth Avenue in Manhattan the menu, in effect until Oct. 2, is called a preview menu. The prices are, according to Jean Claude Baker, the owner, about 15 percent less than they will be when the restaurant officially opens. And at Ménage à Trois at 48th Street and Lexington Avenue prices will rise 30 percent at the end of this month, when the restaurant will have been open four weeks. Antony Worrall-Thompson, co-owner of the New York City branch, said the five-restaurant chain has followed the same policy in Bombay and Melbourne, Australia, and at its two branches in London.

"I don't like going into new restaurants and getting all these excuses thrown at me," said Worrall-Thompson, "and then getting a full bill at the end of the meal. I don't think you should charge full prices for a dress rehearsal. Whenever you open a restaurant, you can't be as good as you are going to be in a month's time. There are always minor hiccups along the line.

"But," he added, "most restaurants don't have a large enough cash flow to do this. Luckily, we do."

Baker instituted a preview menu when he opened Chez Josephine earlier this month so he and his staff might practice. "I do it because I think it would be a rip-off if I don't do it," Baker said. "I am learning a trade that is new to me, and why should customers pay for mistakes that I make? If a restaurant is very professional and the chef is very professional, and they feel they can open without a preview, wonderful.

"But you know that even many famous places don't always run well, and there are always little adjustments," he added.

In the Minority

Chez Josephine and Ménage à Trois are in the minority. Restaurant Lafayette at 56th Street and Park Avenue, where dinner for two without wine is about $140, opened six weeks ago without preview prices. Tony Fortuna, the manager, is ambivalent. "Why should the first guests suffer?" he said.

On the other hand, Fortuna said he is uncertain that preview prices would have been appropriate. "It might be a little tacky for a restaurant in our category," he said. Before the restaurant opened to the public, employees from the other restaurant tried it out. But he added, "You can't really tell until the guests are actually there."

He did not foresee, for example, that in the small dining room guests might object to cigar smoke. Some did, causing quite a ruckus with the man smoking one. As a gesture of apology, the restaurant offered a sampling from the dessert cart to the table of guests who complained. The new menu will include a line prohibiting pipes and cigars.

Charles Bernstein, editor in chief of *Nation's Restaurant News*, a weekly newspaper about the food-service industry, said restaurants should have a preview period of two to four weeks during which they can iron out the kinks. During that time critics would be honor-bound not to review the restaurants. And most restaurant critics would be willing to abide by such ground rules if prices were also reduced. "Preview menus and prices would keep the critics at bay," said one reviewer.

Bernstein also acknowledged that preview prices make sense. "Clearly, if you aren't going to open officially for a month or two, then clearly you should not charge full price," he said.

Perhaps Ménage à Trois and Chez Josephine are on the cutting edge of a new and welcome trend.

Coping with Difficult Waiters
May 26, 1984

Service can make or break a meal. Even the most professional of waiters can spoil a dinner by acting unprofessionally. I don't mean in the sense that they pour scalding coffee down your back or stack plates on the table. These waiters may do everything properly in a technical sense, but by their demeanor they mar an otherwise pleasant experience.

The classic roadside restaurant scene in the movie *Five Easy Pieces* pits a customer against a hardened waitress who has heard it all before. The waitress tells Jack Nicholson that he cannot have what he wants because there are no substitutions. So Nicholson tries again, asking for an omelet, coffee and a side order of wheat toast.

The exchange between the waitress and Nicholson goes like this: "I'm sorry, but we don't have any side orders of toast. I can give you an English muffin or a coffee roll."

"You don't make side orders of toast?" he says. "You make sandwiches, don't you?"

Nicholson tries again, hoping that if he orders a chicken sandwich on toast and tells the waitress to hold the chicken he can get the toast. But the waitress says: "Do you see that sign, sir? Yes? You all have to leave. I'm not taking any more of your smartness and sarcasm." Nicholson then sweeps the dishes onto the floor and stalks out of the restaurant.

There are two satisfying responses to rude waiters or waitresses. One is the Nicholson variety, a tactic that makes you feel wonderful, but of which your mother wouldn't approve. Then there is the kind that many find equally effective: total disregard for the waiter's ill-mannered behavior, a plan guaranteed to confuse him.

Recently, when I ordered *rognons de veau* at one of New York City's most expensive, old-line French restaurants, the captain said in his most superior tone: "Those are kidneys, you know."

"That is why I ordered them," I replied.

He tried once more. "How do you want them done?"

"Pink," was the answer.

Trying to recover, he explained that many people order *rognons de veau* without knowing what they are.

That seems hard to believe.

Then there is the impatient waiter. The fact that he can remember all the specials doesn't help the diners much. A good waiter will gladly explain the specials again and go into all the detail needed. In more considerate restaurants the waiter includes the price with the list of specials. In the most considerate places the specials are written and clipped to the menu. One couple suggested this approach: "We refuse," they said, "on principle, to order anything offered orally."

Then there are the nonprofessional waiters who treat their jobs as a continuation of their social lives. Usually they regard their work as something to do until they can get a job in their chosen profession, often acting. Just the same, in a well-run establishment, waiters and waitresses who are out-of-work actors can be very pleasant because they know how to perform. When no one is minding the store, however, untrained waiters, instead of paying attention to their customers, often stand off to the side and chat. Sometimes they smoke.

Patrons are usually made to feel that they are intruding if they interrupt the conversation to ask for service. On occasion, chatting is not enough, and waiters and waitresses have engaged in horseplay in full view of the dining room. One reader wrote, "Even while our waiter was standing at our table taking our order, he was blowing kisses across the room."

But my favorite restaurant complaint involves a customer who said that there was something wrong with the food. To which the waitress replied. "There is? Here let me taste it." She lifted up the plate, pulled out a fork and sampled the diner's food.

Dinner "Special" Game:
Too Much to Remember
December 24, 1983

Ask someone to assume the role of restaurant captain and play this little game by reciting the dinner specials: "For this evening we have for a first course *vongole alla Capri*, spiedini, *cappelletti in brodo* or *taglierini* with truffles. The *taglierini* is also available for a main course. Or you may have *crostacei marinara, cotoletta Milanese, bocconcini di vitello, zuppa de pesce, fegato di vitello Veneziana, cervella dorata*. And the chef has prepared a special fritto misto this evening. If I can answer any questions..."

The second part of this game is for you to recall as many of the dishes as possible.

The question I always want to ask the captain is if he is planning to quiz us on the list. As five-year-olds in kindergarten we played a game that was designed to improve our memories. The teacher would place six or eight objects on a table and then ask us in turn to look at them carefully. She then instructed each child to close her eyes and recite as many of the things as she could remember. The one who remembered the most got a treat.

Sometimes when a captain drones on with the list of specials my mind wanders back to my kindergarten days. Will the restaurant offer a treat to the patron with the best memory? Will it be a free dinner, or a drink?

When the number of specials goes beyond two or three main dishes and one appetizer, it's time for a list. Even a mimeographed sheet will do. They are not fancy and sometimes the handwriting is illegible, but even illegible handwriting is preferable to no list at all.

George Lang, owner of the Cafe des Artistes, has an old mimeograph machine at his restaurant, and on it he prints each day's specials, which make up a third of the menu. He finds recitation of the specials "pointless and counterproductive to hospitality." He adds: "To have the restaurant test the memory of the guest is to humiliate them. They do it because they think it is stylish, they think it is merchandising. But I think it's gimmicky."

Of the twenty restaurants I have visited in the past three months that offer specials, four printed them and attached them to the menus. A restaurant like Da Silvano, which has about fourteen specials each day, doesn't think a printed list is "very classy." Christina Chastan, the restaurant's manager, says, "People are used to the specials when they come here."

Some of Da Silvano's new clientele may be in for a surprise if they can remember what is available. The restaurant does not always include the price of the specials, and some of them are considerably more than the regular items on the menu, the most expensive of which is $17.50. Venison and Dover sole, $22 and $23 respectively, are among the more expensive specials. "We would announce the price for something with truffles," Chastan said, "like the *taglierini*, which is $32. But very few people ask the price because it's a very sophisticated clientele."

Perhaps intimidated is a better word. Many hesitate to ask a price because they don't want others to think the cost is important.

Cafe Luxembourg doesn't print its specials, which number about five or six each evening, because "we would have to run back and forth to the mimeo shop," said Don Palladino, the maître d'hôtel. "All the waiters are required to give the price of specials," he said, but not all of them do. And the specials are sometimes $3 to $7 more than regular menu items.

But change may be in the wind. Le Cirque is coming around to the George Lang school of thought. Sirio Maccioni has decided that customers are entitled to read the seven or eight specials. "I feel many people would prefer to have it printed," Maccioni said. He has ordered a copying machine and after the first of the year will add specials to his menus.

Maccioni has decided that for people who do not often go to his restaurant a recitation of specials is confusing. "They will remain better in their heads," he said, "if we print them."

Let us hope Maccioni is a trendsetter.

Pet Peeves
September 6, 1986

"Every restaurant reviewer has his or her pet peeve," says *The Gallup Monthly Report on Eating Out.* "It might be iceberg lettuce, overcooked vegetables, tables too close together or any one of a hundred other annoyances. But the one peeve many reviewers have in common is the practice some restaurants have adopted of having daily specials recited by the servers, often without benefit of price."

When I was reviewing restaurants for *The New York Times,* I felt, as I still do, that a long list of specials recited without prices was designed to intimidate patrons rather than assist them in making selections. People out for an evening of relaxation are not interested in games that tax the memory.

Inconvenient Method

The report states there is no reason for presenting specials verbally "since it is inconvenient for the diner who is unlikely to remember more than one or two of the dishes mentioned."

The polling organization wondered what diners actually

thought of the practice, since no surveys focused on this. The pollsters asked 1,010 adults in a nationwide sampling how they preferred to be advised of the specials. Gallup gave five options: a list on a blackboard on the wall; a portable blackboard; a card attached to the menu; recitation by waiter with prices; recitation by waiter without prices. The organization also asked 504 restaurant owners how they informed customers about daily specials.

The vast majority—70 percent—of those queried said a list attached to the menu was best. Yet only 23 percent of the restaurateurs use that method. According to the survey, only 3 percent of the restaurants polled offer specials without giving prices. And a good thing too: Only 2 percent of the diners find this a satisfactory method.

Customers are not especially fond of the portable-blackboard method either. Only 3 percent find it satisfactory. And only 10 percent like to read the specials from a blackboard on the wall. That's easy to understand: The blackboard always seems to be at the other end of the room, much of the writing is smudged, and the handwriting is often illegible. But that doesn't stop restaurateurs, since 48 percent of them use a blackboard on the wall.

As for the recitation of specials with prices, even more patrons prefer that method to the blackboard attached to the wall, a surprising 11 percent. It is used by 20 percent of the restaurateurs who were surveyed.

But restaurants are in business to please their customers, and if 70 percent want to see the specials on a piece of paper with the regular menu, why won't restaurateurs provide that simple service? The excuses and explanations vary. To my mind, none justify the practice.

Time for a List

When there are more than three specials, it's time for a list. Even a mimeographed sheet of paper will do. No matter if the handwriting is illegible. Illegible handwriting is preferable to no list at all—especially when the specials cost more than the regular dishes on the menu. The arrival of the check may often hold a rather unpleasant surprise.

But some restaurateurs with whom I spoke don't think mimeographed sheets are classy enough. Others view the recitation of specials as a merchandising gimmick; still others say it is too much trouble to run back and forth to the printer each day.

Perhaps the computer age can lend a hand. Computers have become so inexpensive that many restaurants use them for keeping their books and their inventory. They ought to purchase the equipment to allow them to print a menu of daily specials painlessly.

Too Special

The specials problem appears to annoy diners more than snobby waiters, sloppy ones or rude ones.

These letters are typical of what most people had to say.

"Bravo! It's amazing the amount of pretension we are asked to endure in restaurants under the guise of sophistication."

And "Thank you! Thanks for dealing with the ubiquitous dinner 'special.' Granted your emphasis was on the quiz aspect rather than the comparative costs, but they were at least mentioned.

"Let's keep it up, even if some entrepreneurs don't think a printed list is very classy. Less class, less deception is my motto."

"For the record," wrote an Atlanta reader, "the scene with Jack Nicholson and the gruff waitress originally took place about thirty years before in *Rebel Without a Cause*. James Dean, dressed in a white T-shirt, jeans and hobnailed boots, orders toast for lunch at the local diner. 'We don't serve toast after breakfast hours,' replies the disdainful waitress. 'Then I'll have a chicken sandwich on white toast with lettuce and mayonnaise. Hold the chicken, hold the lettuce, hold the mayonnaise.'

"Incidentally, I think he got the toast."

Two years later, when the subject of specials was addressed again, not much had changed.

Sheryl and Mel London, cookbook authors, wrote to say that they always ask the price, no matter how long the list, "usually getting a response such as, 'You mean you want me to tell you the prices of all of them?' Following that, we generally send the establishment a copy of this *New York Times* editorial—and usually get no response."

Today's Special

Anyone who's been out to lunch in Manhattan lately knows there's a contagious nuisance stalking the restaurants. You've just sat down to lunch, gotten your drinks (Perrier for her, Goldstein for him) and started the conversation in earnest when a smiling man ("Hello, I'm LeRoy and I'll be your waiter") arrives to make a speech, a virtuoso performance honed and honeyed by repetition.

"I'd like to tell you," he says, "about today's specials." His face turns serious. "The pasta of the day is *pappardelle alla pizzaiola*. That's flat noodles cut at a slant and sauced with veal, tomatoes and garlic. For the main course, the special is *filet de turbot au brocoli* with mousseline sauce. That's fresh fish with a rich buttery hollandaise sauce lightened with whipped cream. The salad special today is..." He goes on, reciting soups and desserts. This is one performer who knows his lines.

Yet the performances are annoying. Some diners even despise them because of the interruption. Others resent the fact that, for all the buttery detail, there's rarely any statement of the price. People hesitant to look cheap are left wondering if they've just spent $19 for a special when something not quite so special could be had for $12.

Others object to the practice because so many items are cited. Invariably, somebody at the table has to ask, "What was the *pappardelle* again?" The fear that one sounds like an idiot is promptly confirmed by the waiter's patronizing smile.

These objections make such sense that we wonder why restaurants are so insistent on the today's special routine, especially when there's such an easy alternative. It's cheap. It can be easily supplemented every day. It requires no feats of memory. It endangers no one's self-respect. It is called a menu.

One smart restaurateur figured out a way to capitalize on the column. A few weeks after it appeared the following ad ran in the *Times:* "For diners who are tired of hearing waiters recite a litany of specials, here's a yearlong schedule of pasta specials, week by week, from Lello. Starting with Columbus Day 1986 through Columbus Day 1987. Happy Pasta Year."

What followed was a week by week listing of a different pasta dish—fifty-two in all.

Several restaurateurs wrote to describe what they do about

specials, and there was this interesting point of view from Roberta Churchill, owner of Roberta's, a restaurant in Princeton, New Jersey. Churchill says she despises specials, but she has

> learned that the customers expect specials and are most unhappy when none are offered. I, therefore, offer specials and make an effort to limit them to a maximum of two appetizers and two entrées. Even so, the waiters must also announce the daily soups and the recitation is of six items. I don't like to print these items both for lack of time and lack of space for a clip-on on my very small menu. It would look tacky and obscure the printed menu.
>
> I insist my waiters announce prices of specials. However, many customers stop them when they are doing this and express displeasure with this practice, as if it were too crass, or perhaps they do not want their guest to be made aware of costs. As a result, I constantly have to fight my waiters and to correct them when they do not give prices.

Churchill invited me to work in her kitchen for a week or two "and observe the daily problems and frustrations. Perhaps you would then be able to suggest a more satisfactory way of handling these problems."

The letter I found most fascinating, however, came from an old professional acquaintance of mine, Dr. Frederick Stare, professor of nutrition emeritus from the Harvard School of Public Health. In twenty years Stare has never liked a single thing I have written about nutrition. Stare is the professor who testified on behalf of the Cereal Institute before Congress in the late '60s, sticking up for the sugar-coated cereals.

"While we have different views on some aspects of nutrition," he wrote, "I do want to write that I am in complete agreement with your comment in today's *Times* that people out for an evening of relaxation are not interested in games that tax the memory."

Usually letters from Stare are to the editor of the newspaper where I am working at the time, complaining about something I have written.

Restaurant Noise: Does It Spoil a Good Meal?

October 29, 1983

Whatever happened to acoustic tile?

Time was when it automatically figured in the cost of opening a new restaurant, along with knives and forks. Not that I am suggesting acoustic tile as the most attractive way to control the noise level, but it beats tin ceilings, tiled walls and marble pillars.

By design a majority of the trend-setting restaurants opening these days do not consider the noise factor. A restaurant in which the decibel level is such that you must shout at your dinner companions is not my idea of a place where food is to be savored. It's a place where the food is secondary. And it's a place where I get an Excedrin headache.

So You Won't Notice the Fare

Frequently a restaurant in which the noise level is disturbingly high is one in which the restaurateur does not want you to notice what you are eating. But sometimes an unbearably noisy place has a chef who is serious about the food, and that's a pity.

Many of the newest New York restaurants have been designed for people who have spent most of their social lives in discos and want to dine in surroundings that feel familiar. It seems to me that people who consciously choose restaurants with ear-shattering noise levels don't care much about the quality of what they eat and don't really want to converse with their companions. They go to see and be seen, to count the number of feather boas and black leather pants.

Ernie's, an instantly popular watering hole on the Upper West Side in Manhattan, is an archetype of this sort of restaurant. It was designed to give patrons an opportunity to size up the new arrivals. Conversation is virtually impossible, but the restaurant is jammed. Even if Ernie's did not intend its food as an after-thought, and it did, it cannot be taken seriously.

At some restaurants in which food is the primary considera-tion, the noise, though several decibels lower than at Ernie's, still makes many people uncomfortable. Both the long-established Oyster Bar in Grand Central Terminal and the brand new Cafe Luxembourg have become as known for their noise as for their food.

It seems appropriate that the Oyster Bar, in the bowels of a train station, be noisy. Designed for quick meals, the Oyster Bar is not the place to linger over an expensive bottle of wine. It isn't just the tile surroundings that contribute to the din; tables are close together and waiters make no attempt to control the clatter of dishes. But a funny thing happens to the place when it has few patrons: It takes on a tomblike quality that makes you uncom-fortable because you feel conspicuous.

The Look and Sound of a Big Crowd

The Cafe Luxembourg could have been designed to be quieter if that was what the owners were seeking; they were not. They deliberately set out to create a space with a high energy level that would look and sound crowded and, therefore, successful, that would attract the young, affluent crowd. It's difficult to book a table because those who want to be part of the scene love the energy level. The tiled walls, terrazzo floor and zinc bar make the sound reverberate as the place pulsates. Any slack in conversa-tion is taken up by greatly amplified Muzak.

The owners repeated the successful formula they used at their other restaurant, Odeon. But the Cafe Luxembourg, like Odeon, is serious about its food. Unfortunately, if you have difficulty enjoying a good meal when you are overwhelmed by the noise, as I am, you will be most comfortable in places like these before or after the height of the dinner hour. Conversation, laughter, the clink of glasses and the clatter of plates are at a warm and friendly level. You can hear yourself think and can converse nor-mally with your companions. There was a time when that was called civilized dining.

More Diners Object to Restaurant Noise

April 16, 1985

If designers wonder about the impact their settings have on restaurant diners, they need only look at a new Gallup poll. The deliberate addition of loud music in restaurants—along with surfaces that reflect rather than absorb noise—has drawn much attention, not all of it positive.

According to the poll, only poor service is more likely than loud music to keep people from returning to a restaurant where they were satisfied with the food and the price.

One thousand people over the age of eighteen were questioned by phone nationally from January 7–20, and the results appear in the March issue of the *Gallup Monthly Report on Eating Out,* which tracks changes in the restaurant business. The report, with a margin of sampling error of plus or minus four percentage points, shows that there has been a significant rise in the percentage of people who find loud music offensive. In 1982, 50 percent of them said they would not patronize a restaurant again if the music was too loud. By 1985 the figure had jumped to 64 percent.

This is not because people have become more sensitive to noise but because there is more of it. On purpose. Restaurants where noise is more important than the food and service have increased dramatically in the past two years.

Such restaurants cater to a young crowd. But how young is young? According to the survey, loud music annoyed only 40 percent of those in the eighteen-to-twenty-four age group but 52 percent of those between the ages of twenty-five and thirty-four and 66 percent of those between thirty-five and forty-nine. The fifty-to-sixty-four-year-old category liked it least of all (88 percent).

Loud music also beat out slow service as an important complaint in this year's survey.

So far there has been no abatement in the number of new restaurants where noise comes first and food second. But perhaps after studying the results of the poll, restaurateurs will take a second look at their plans.

Restaurant Noise

A man from Miami offered a bravo for the column and wrote: "It is time that someone took these people to task who feel noise means action, i.e., business. I do not believe they really intend to insult their more affluent customers who are becoming quite aware of the new war cry of the savages—'If it's too loud, you're too old.'"

A Manhattan resident said he would be happy to refer the owners of Cafe Luxembourg, Odeon, Ernie's, etc., with the name of a good carpet man!

Another reminded me that all loud restaurants are neither necessarily just for the young nor are they new, adding The Palm and Le Cirque to the list of those that are extremely noisy.

In 1985 the city of New York surveyed the noise levels in a number of eating establishments. No one was terribly surprised to learn that eating in certain restaurants is like eating in the middle of a noisy street. They include America, McDonald's, the Hard Rock Cafe, Tavern on the Green, the Carnegie Deli, Canastel's, Gulf Coast, The Palm, Positano and Hatsuhana. Some are new-style restaurants; some have been around a long time.

The trend continues, but fortunately for us old fogies, serenely grown-up restaurants like Le Bernardin and Brive continue to open.

Now, if they could just figure out how to do an *inexpensive* grown-up restaurant.

Restaurant Tipping: How Your Money Is Shared

January 19, 1986

A friend of mine says she has solved the problem of how much to tip the captain and how much to tip the waiter on those credit-card receipts that have space for both. (She refuses to deal with the question of whether and how much to tip the maître d'hôtel.) My friend puts the combined tip for the captain and the waiter right through the middle of the two lines. "Let them fight it out," is her theory.

And that, indeed, is what occasionally happens. While waiters in the majority of New York City restaurants pool their tips, they do not pool them with the captains. And restaurant owners have had to lay down a few guidelines so that the captain does not get left out.

These days, the standard tip at restaurants is 15 to 20 percent of the total of the check, with one-quarter to one-third going to the captain—if there is a captain—the remainder to the waiter. (Of course, the quality of service can alter these proportions.)

In years gone by, especially in Europe, there was a system known as the *tronc*, from the word for a wooden alms box found at the entrance to churches. Under this system, all the tips are pooled and apportioned to the entire staff, including those in the kitchen, and a point system based on seniority is used.

In a limited survey of more than a dozen restaurants, ranging from the elegant and very expensive Quilted Giraffe to the extremely casual and moderately priced Italian steak house called Frank's, on West 14th Street, I found only one place where a modified *tronc* system is in operation, the Quilted Giraffe. And I found only one restaurant, the American Festival Cafe at Rockefeller Center, where each team of two waiters keeps its own tips, instead of pooling them with other waiters, and gives a percentage to the team's busboy.

At the Quilted Giraffe, at Second Avenue, and 51st Street, all tips are pooled, no matter what the diner leaves to whom on the credit-card slip. The tips are then apportioned according to the employee's experience. The owner, Barry Wine, said: "In our restaurant the captain is our most experienced waiter. In a typical restaurant this is not so. The second most experienced waiter is called the back waiter. He brings the dishes from the kitchen. Then comes the station waiter, who pours the water and serves the cheese. And finally the bread and coffee come from the least experienced waiter."

Equal Distribution

"Sometimes," Wine said, "the waiters give part of the tips to the cooks. If there has been a lot of money in tips, then they share some." But Wine said that because all the staff has about the same experience, the tips are divided "just about equally."

But for most restaurants, equal distribution of the waiters' pool and of the captains' pool is the rule. (This, of course, largely negates the impact of leaving a small tip because of poor service.) From the waiters' pool a certain percentage—it differs from place to place—is taken for the people who bus the tables and sometimes for the bar service people. And for the most part, according to André Soltner at Lutèce, Jean-Jacques Rachou at La Côte Basque and Sirio Maccioni at Le Cirque, it works fairly well.

"From time to time there is a little problem," Soltner said. "I require that even if the customer puts on a tip only for the waiter, the waiter gives one-quarter to the captain. I have no full power over it," said Soltner with a laugh, "and sometimes I have to act like a little judge."

At La Côte Basque, Rachou expects the waiter to give something to the captain, but he said, "It's very difficult. If they don't split it, sometimes the captain follows the customer to the door. It happened here once, but I put a stop to it."

It is not clear exactly what happens at Le Cirque. According to Maccioni, "If people leave without specifying whom the tip is for, it is at the discretion of the waiter." But Maccioni added, "It is funny that you should call because next week I am scheduling a meeting with the staff to talk about this. If the waiter gets too much, he should give some to the captain, and if the captain gets too much, he should give some to the waiter."

As for the maître d'hôtel's tips, one of the owners, who requested anonymity, said: "Oh please, madame. I have no comment. He works for himself. You really don't want to know what's going on. There is still plenty of selling of tables. If you give a good tip, you get a better table."

Whatever You Do, Please Do Not Tip

July 12, 1986

"Do Not Tip," says the guest check at the Casual Quilted Giraffe, the sleek, stainless steel and black Art Deco restaurant opened in the AT&T building by the owners of the more expensive Quilted Giraffe. And in case a customer misses the admonition, the tip line on the credit-card form is crossed out.

In place of the tip the owners, Barry and Susan Wine, have added an 18 percent service charge to the meals at the restaurant at East 55th Street and Madison Avenue. This will go to the house, not to the waiters, and will be used to defray the cost of paying the dining room staff higher salaries.

"I'm taking a leadership role," Wine said, "trying to convert being a waiter into something more professional. We are guaranteeing the waiters a salary close to $25,000 a year, and now their living is not dependent on how many people come for dinner, what shift they are on or what tables they get." Waiters at comparable restaurants earn anywhere from $350 to $600 a week, with their tips, depending on business.

Rarely Done

Wine did not think up this idea. European restaurants, and private clubs and inns in the United States, have added a service charge for years, but it is a rarity here. Restaurant Raphael on West 54th Street tried it and gave it up. But Michael's in Santa

Monica, California, has stuck with the concept for 5½ years. Michael McCarty, the owner, said, "I wanted to develop the people in the front of the house instead of having them as free agents."

But the plan was not met with universal approval when it began. Many of the waiters quit. Today's staff comes up through the ranks in the front of the house, beginning as busboys, just as they do in the kitchen.

Melvyn Master, who owns the Manhattan restaurants Jams, Bud's and Hulot's with Jonathan Waxman, approves of the idea but points out the risks. Not only is the payroll increased, there are additional payroll taxes. "It could be bad for the house," he said, "because it still must pay the salaries even when business is slow. It's a security for the waiters, and it makes them more legitimate because one of the biggest problems is getting waiters to declare all their tips. But they certainly could end up with less because they would have to pay taxes on all of it."

Having fully salaried waiters also eliminates certain unsavory practices that restaurateurs do not like to talk about—waiters who tip the maître d' to get better tables, better shifts and bigger tippers. And, added McCarty, it eliminates the bickering. "I couldn't stand the fighting when the waiters divided up their tips at night," he said. "And the busboy was complaining he only got $1 when he knew the waiter had made $200. All that is gone now. The result is a better, more sophisticated, more stable employee."

Wine also sees it as a way to "eliminate the indignities connected with being a waiter, with always seeming to have your hand out."

Gilbert Le Coze, the chef-owner of Le Bernardin in New York City and in Paris, approves of the idea. At his Paris restaurant, a 15 percent service is added to the bill. "It makes the waiters better, and they are more interested," he said.

Le Coze has no plans to institute the service charge at his New York restaurant, however, because he doesn't see any reason "to change a system that works."

An Unsuccessful Try

Raphael Edery tried it at Restaurant Raphael, but ended it three years ago. "The staff," he said, "honestly prefers it without the service charge. The restaurant critics did not like it. Some customers did because they didn't like to do the accounting in front of their guests, but in my opinion some people thought it was an imposition." Especially, he said, when it was added to an expensive bottle of wine or Champagne.

And what about the customer who wants the option to tip according to the quality of the service? Wine said that anyone who does not wish to leave 18 percent does not have to. And anyone who insists on leaving more is free to do so, the extra going to the waiter.

Joe Baum, who owns Aurora on East 49th Street, feels Americans prefer the option of tipping. "They think they have an opportunity to reward poor service accordingly, even if it is more in the mind than in practice," he said. All the restaurateurs said that few people leave less than 15 percent.

"And if you are a great waiter," McCarty said, "you will make an additional $5,000 or $6,000 a year from the people who leave an extra tip."

No Tipping

It is always foolhardy to say anything is a first. Because as certain as God made little green apples, it isn't.

"The famed Longchamps restaurant chain observed a 'no tipping' policy from the mid-1920s until just about the end of World War II," wrote a former office boy in the executive offices of the chain. "Fifteen percent was added to the check to cover waiters, busboys and captains. Table tents on each table warned the customers that an employee would be dismissed if he or she accepted a gratuity."

Our correspondent says the no-tipping policy was abandoned in 1945 "due to pressure from the restaurant union when the

Longchamps group finally unionized around that time."

And, in fact, restaurateurs have told me many times that the unions are strongly opposed to the type of plan Barry and Susan Wine have instituted. Despite that attitude the Wines have now instituted the same policy at the Quilted Giraffe.

Restaurant Attitudes Toward Women Without Men
March 3, 1984

Do restaurants still discriminate against women?

A reader from Washington, D.C., thinks so and finds it shocking. But I don't think the situation is as bad as it was fifteen years ago, when another woman and I had dinner at Paul Bocuse's restaurant in France. We were shown to the least desirable table although there were many empty ones in better locations. They remained empty throughout our meal. The waiter was imperious and rude. We had to ask for the wine list twice and were told we would not enjoy what we had chosen for dinner. The only thing we did not enjoy was our treatment.

The Washington reader, who wrote on behalf of his wife and grown daughter, had suggested a restaurant to them as one he liked, but was chagrined to find that when they dined there without him "they were treated rudely and served badly." "The irony," he said, "is that they reported that they enjoyed the food, which is, of course, what a restaurant should be judged on." He wondered if a restaurant should not be judged on its treatment of customers as well.

"It has often occurred to me," he added, "that we men, as we go about our business, do not notice wrongs or slights that don't affect us. Those of us who are blessed with wives and daughters of spirit, however, do learn and should act. I took for granted that in this enlightened world, particularly in Washington, people who run restaurants are alert."

People who run restaurants are certainly more alert and aware than they were when my friend and I were stuck in a corner at Paul Bocuse. Fewer restaurants are guilty of such discrimination, which restaurateurs admit was, and still is, based on their belief that women do not tip as well as men.

Perhaps that was true when there were fewer women in the business world. But it hardly applies today. And it hardly explains why some maître d'hôtels and waiters still think they can treat women rudely and get away with it. Perhaps it is because some men still do not think of women as important and often powerful members of society, and perhaps it is because some men were raised to think women ought to be in the company of men when they dine out.

On a visit to Le St. Jean des Prés, a Belgian cafe in TriBeCa, last summer I was in a group of eight women. The menu was in French, but that was no problem since everyone spoke French. There was no difficulty in deciding what we would have, though there was some discussion about who would have what.

During our discussion the maître d'hôtel walked over and said, "Do you understand French well enough to read the menu?"

"Yes," replied one of our group, "but we don't understand Belgian." Afterward she said, "I only wish I had told him that in French."

Would a maître d'hôtel have phrased his question in such a fashion if there had been a man in our group? I think not. More likely he would have said, "Can I explain anything on the menu for you?"

Last winter at the Gibbon on Manhattan's Upper East Side, as a female friend and I sat talking over our coffee, the maître d'hôtel asked us to leave because, he said, he needed the table for another couple. He invited us to have a drink on the house at the bar. We had been at the restaurant less than 2½ hours, but that was not the point. The occupants of several other tables for two had come in before us and had finished eating but were not asked to leave. The only noticeable difference was that at those tables one of the diners was male.

Not quite as annoying as these examples of discrimination is the ludicrous throwback to another era, the custom of giving women menus without prices. Perhaps the few restaurants that still do so would stop if everyone reacted as a recent guest of mine did.

At lunch my male companion was handed the menu with prices. Though he had quite conspicuously exchanged menus with me, when the check came it was presented to him. He said to the waiter: "You've made a mistake. The check, like the menu with the prices, should have been given to my hostess."

The waiter, a man older than forty, mumbled something that sounded like "Liberation!" and fled.

Who Says a Woman Can't Pay?
October 6, 1984

Restaurants are among the last bastions of male supremacy. Ask any waiter or captain. No matter how clear it is that a woman in the party is paying the check, at least 99 percent of the time it is presented to one of the men. I speak from experience.

But there is hope, for even Emily Post is coming around. In the 1975 edition of her book *The New Emily Post's Etiquette,* written by her daughter-in-law, Elizabeth L. Post, women were advised that, to ease men's "embarrassment," they should either carry a credit card or have a charge account in a restaurant.

Post commented: "This situation can be so awkward that many women without charge privileges prefer to give their guest a sum of cash large enough to cover the bill before they enter the restaurant, thus relieving the man of any embarrassment before the waiter. Incidentally, this solution also serves for the husband who has left his wallet behind or has insufficient money with him."

I acknowledge that twenty years ago I too passed my husband money under the table. But this is 1984. And ever since I started to contribute to the family's support, my husband has been delighted to let me pay. He calls it the best part of the meal.

In the 1984 edition, *Emily Post's Etiquette,* subtitled *A Guide to Modern Manners,* this arbiter of taste has shifted emphasis—ever so slightly. When a woman invites a man to a restaurant, Post says, it is not usually a problem "among people who are accustomed to this relationship between men and women, but it is a matter of concern to men who were brought up to feel that paying a woman's expenses was not only an obligation but a pleasure and a privilege."

Are there really men who feel it is their obligation to pay, even when a woman has made it clear that she is extending the invitation? On business occasions it has not been my experience that men are any more likely to offer to pay than other women. But the book says there are still men who feel uncomfortable when a woman does so.

However, in what can surely be construed as an acknowledgment that women have as much right to pay a check as men without embarrassment, Post comments: "Waiters are the worst offenders. They still automatically hand the check to the man, even when a woman has acted as hostess by ordering the meal."

In such circumstances, she suggests, the woman should firmly take the check from the man and say something such as "Don't be silly. You're my guest." She adds, "Perhaps in time waiters will learn and men will begin to like it!"

I hold out little hope for the waiters. And age has nothing to do with it. On the occasions when I have been paying the bill, either in a group or with a man, only one waiter, at a restaurant in Cambridge, Massachusetts, has ever returned the change or credit card to me. Perhaps he was a Harvard student and more observant than most.

Even though I often request the wine list and sometimes ask more questions of the waiter than anyone else at the table, and even though the waiter sees me take the check, I never get it back. It is rather astounding. Especially since the first name on my credit card is apparently a woman's.

I gather they never look at the name. But that's another story.

Women in Restaurants

Do not, for one minute, think that everyone agreed with the column about how women are treated in some restaurants.

One woman in New York asked what was so ludicrous about a restaurant's giving women menus without prices. "I earn about twice as much as my husband, and I like receiving the ladies' menu. I also like having the door opened for me and being sent flowers."

O.K.

Next came a letter from a restaurant in Allentown, Pennsylvania.

"Happily, we at Judith's do not discriminate against women diners. But, they *do deserve* the bad press they get, at least in the hinterlands.

"They are often late, talk endlessly so that the waiter has a hard time finding an appropriate moment to approach the table, always obviously divide the bill at great length and leave very poor tips.

"As a woman, I have tried to give them every advantage, but many times I am embarrassed."

The owner at Judith's should pay heed to this customer from Cambridge, Massachusetts. "The double standard of service is hard to change, for if a man leaves a small tip, the waiter probably gets a message about the service, but if a woman leaves a small tip, the system blames the victim, not the server. The question that does not seem to occur to waiters and maîtres d'hôtel is why should a woman tip as well as a man when she does not receive as good service as a man? The alternative of explaining one's dissatisfaction with poor service is hardly effective because it encounters stereotypes about women complaining and making a scene."

The writer's sentiments were echoed by several others, but as one suggested, the situation is worse in the older restaurants than in the ones in which young owners, young chef and young staff have grown up with the idea that, at least on the surface, women are the equal of men.

Saying It in English vs. . . .

January 21, 1984

On a recent evening in a fine French restaurant one of my dinner companions threw up his hands in disgust after peering at the menu for about five minutes. "I don't see why they can't print it in English or at least give it subtitles," he said. "I don't understand a word."

The idea of having the captain, waiter or one of us translate everything on the menu did not mollify him. He said that was even more confusing. A discussion at the table ensued: Should restaurants in the United States expect their patrons to understand menus in foreign languages?

Most of us thought that only the French and Italians would be unlikely to provide translations. But some small authentic ethnic restaurants, usually those that expect to cater only to their own ethnic group, provide no subtitles. As they become more Americanized, the subtitles appear.

André Soltner, chef-proprietor of Lutèce, said his menu is entirely in French, "because my predecessor started it that way twenty-three years ago and I have never changed it." Soltner said that was "not a good excuse."

"But," he added, "I've never had problems. Once or twice I have thought to underline in English, but my captains explain everything."

On the other hand, Soltner said, if he were opening a restaurant now, he would use English subtitles. "Absolutely."

Some restaurants cannot decide whether they should assist patrons with menu translations for all the items or for just some of them. This results in a menu in which, for example, *fegato Veneziano* is translated into bite-size calf's liver with onions, wine and vinegar, while *bistecca ai ferri* is carried without translation. Is this an indication that the restaurant management is more eager to sell the liver than the broiled steak or that it thinks non-Italian-speaking patrons would prefer the liver to the steak?

The menus at Il Nido and Il Monello have English subtitles because, Adi Giovannetti, the owner, says: "I don't think it's fair to guests when you have to do a lot of explaining. When the full menu is in a foreign language, whether it's Italian, Chinese or French, after they ask you about two or three dishes, they stop. And even if they've had something good, when they leave your place, they wonder if they got what they really wanted.

"We are imposing our will on them if we do that," he said. "I think some people do it to be a little snobby."

Some Menu Listings Are for Reading, Not Eating

July 14, 1984

Sometimes nothing makes lighter reading than restaurant menus with their misspellings and garbled translations. The hand-lettered daily specials tacked up outside restaurants to entice passersby can also be amusing window shopping. Often, usually inadvertently, the advertised specials turn off potential customers.

Take, for example, one Greek-owned coffee shop that posted a sign saying that all its entrées were served "with a cup of sour coffee." Did the writer confuse sweet and sour? This passerby never found out.

The Chinese restaurant that said it was featuring "sliced prawns vs. pork Hunan style" must have given pause to many who wondered if they might be watching a wrestling match while eating dinner. And diners who considered ordering "General Tseng's historic chicken" were bound to wonder just how old the chicken was.

I wonder how much sliced pork Sichuan style was sold after patrons read this description: "Sliced pork, broccoli, baby corns (better than big ones, any day) and bamboo shoot (specially selected)." And what, I wonder, was the general reaction to a meal said to be made up of "bean treads"?

Was a Middle Eastern eating place in Greenwich Village appealing only to anthropologists when it offered lunch of "Hommos and hommos delux"? And who could help but be intrigued by a chalkboard outside an Italian restaurant in midtown featuring "chicken caccatore"?

The proper translation of *le carré d'agneau au thin frais et petits légumes* has never been forthcoming. Rack of lamb and little vegetables to be sure. And fresh something. But thin continues to be a puzzler.

Medallion de lotte aux fruites de mer is clear to anyone who understands French but its translation into English, I think—"burbot with seafruit"—is bizarre.

Sometimes it takes just a few readings to get the drift. In one restaurant each item was listed in French with an English translation below it. So I can be forgiven, I hope, if it took a while to realize that "mixed tableside" was not a translation for a specific dish, "steak tartare," but a description of where the dish was prepared.

Misspellings like "corn beef" always conjure up images that restaurateurs surely don't have in mind. That one makes me think of some exotic breed of cattle. In all likelihood "straw berries" are simply an honest evaluation of their taste.

Candidates for Franglais include "fish of the day en papillote," "swordfish escalopes," "pears en croûte," "bay scallops de la région aux lames des amandes" and, my favorite, "roast beef au jus sauce."

Over the years perhaps no menu spelling has confounded more editors of food sections and writers of restaurant columns than that for the liver of a calf. It emerges as calves', calves, calfs or calf's liver. Restaurants seem to be equally divided over the proper spelling. Since the usual serving is from a single calf, calf's liver would seem the most appropriate.

Menu Translations, Continued

January 26, 1985

The French government, in a never-ending effort to keep the language pure, has outlawed the use of 127 foreign words, including le hot dog. I wonder what the French would think of some of the menu entries that have come across my desk since I wrote about odd translations last summer.

A number of the correspondents were happy to help decipher *carré d'agneau au thin frais*. One suggested that perhaps the restaurant had meant *thon* instead of *thin*. *Thon* is tuna in French. The writer said he had never heard of lamb with tuna sauce, but then, he added, "I've only been interested in serious cooking since 1953." Another suggested that if, indeed, *thin* should have been *thon*, "perhaps Provençal cooking had gone the way of surf and turf."

Others wrote in to suggest that *thin* should have been *thym* and that the lamb was cooked with thyme. This makes perfect sense, but an even newer menu from the same restaurant continues to spell thyme *thin*.

Another observant menu reader offered several charming goofs from his own collection to add to mine. Among them were *asperges avec sauce hollandaise* translated as asparagus with Dutch gravy, and the notation on the New Haven Lawn Club menu that said: "All entrées served with starch du jour."

"Every Wednesday," wrote a former soldier stationed in Baghdad, "in a garden overlooking the Tigris, the menu featured 'glassy sheep bones.'" But he said that he was then nineteen years old and did not have the nerve to try it. To this day, he does not know what it was.

The writer who observed the following sign in the window of a restaurant in Texas, HO-MADE PIE, suggested it might have been the work of a Vietnamese baker.

For sheer volume of amusing mistranslations, the menu from a Greek restaurant in Athens was the winner. In addition to "ricepuddink" and four kinds of "homelettes," with ham, potatoes, cheese or sausages, there was "chicken smashed pot," "utmost of chicken as Hungarian" and "bowel of origan." And everywhere there were "macaronis": with sauce, with cream, with ma, though I'm not sure what ma is.

My favorite from the menu, however, was an item listed under vegetables. It was called "blight."

Menu Mistranslations

Mistranslations of other people's cuisines is, of course, universal. The original column of menu miscues brought forth so many new entries from readers that a follow-up column was necessary. The second column prompted another bag of mail, including copies of other newspaper articles on the same subject and a book devoted to them. There was this letter too.

Those who cast stones are often caught between a rock and a hard place. Your article in this morning's paper was a fair example. Your typesetter seems to have gone awry with the quotation marks, applying them askew and atilt. They are amusing, as amusing as your comments were not.

I find racial prejudice impossible to take at any time. I think your article smacks of it. You seem to think that an Athenian restaurateur would be able to handle the vagaries of the English language with aplomb. I feel strongly that you cannot handle Greek that well. It is one thing to point out the snobbishness of a Manhattan eatery and quite another to hit someone who is only trying to help their customers. They may not do it well, but they try.

I am sure that it is foolish of me to expect good taste from a woman who has admitted in print that she has taken up every food fad in the last twenty years (or longer) including thinking that gelatin salads were edible, but I would think that a sensitivity to your readers would give you some sense.

Then, warming to the subject, my critic, who is obviously a careful reader of everything I write, not just my column, went on:

I hope in the future you will take others into consideration. You might even give some thought to the fact that not everyone eats too much fat, too little carbohydrate, not enough fiber, too much protein and not enough polyunsaturated food. Some of us are healthy, have low blood pressure, below normal cholesterol levels and though perhaps could lose a few pounds are not on death's door or even headed toward it within the next forty years. Perhaps your previous excesses in regard to food have put you into trouble, but don't blame all of us for a lack of intelligent eating habits. Because you have spent a fair amount of your time and money on frozen, canned and apparently out-of-season foods does not mean the rest of the world has gone along with your innate laziness.

I look forward to more interesting articles from you.

Other readers, I am thankful, have not misinterpreted a column I hoped would be taken in good humor. Heaven knows I admire anyone who attempts to cope with English as a second language. I certainly can't speak a word of Greek.

One of the additional entries from a reader was a list from a tourist restaurant in Verona, Italy, complete with English translations: Sausage of pure swine, Turkey—cook's breasts, Gilded brains, Season mixed edges, Blackened salmon.

Gilded brains and season mixed edges have me completely stumped, but blackened salmon does not seem strange at all since Paul Prudhomme made blackened redfish so popular.

A writer from Ohio had these to add from a menu in Yugoslavia: Hemendeks (say it fast), Wisky Skots.

And from a Parisian menu: Rawsberries, no doubt done by someone who learned English in England.

From Madrid came these two: Rignones con Tio Pepe—Uncle Pete's Kidneys; Rape a l'Amoricaine—Rape American Style.

Not all menu mistakes are made abroad. Take this one from a Russian restaurant in the Brighton Beach section of Brooklyn: Meat Patties Zodiac (chooped chicken meat stuffed with utter and dell); Chooped Chicken with Salary and Dell; Beef Choop with Shredded Bits.

A reader in California had spotted these in Kentucky: Chateaubriand with catfish sauce. (According to our correspondent it turned out to be a cut of beef, not as advertised, with some kind of tartar sauce.) And a sign that said HERE MADE PIES, probably a variation on homemade.

A friend showed me one she had discovered in a carryout shop specializing in salads: Marinated herrie covert. Stumped? Try reading the last word with a French pronunciation, with the accent on the last syllable and a silent "t."

Translated into its original tongue, it would be spelled *haricots verts,* the tiny green beans.

My favorite, however, was found by a Queens, New York, reader:

"While on a recent visit to Bangor, Maine, I saw a large illuminated sign which read FRESH ITALIANS. On closer examination things became much clearer; the sign on the window advertised ITALIANS MADE FRESH DAILY. No doubt a local variation of the submarine, hoagie, hero, grinder or, possibly, a shop specializing in delicacies for cannibals."

A recent added starter was sent from Niantic, Connecticut, and it came on a menu for a hospital benefit dinner dance. For dessert they were serving "Ice Cream a la Mode" and the contributor had penned a question at the bottom: "With a scoop of apple pie?"

Another just arrived from a Stamford, Connecticut, reader traveling in Mexico: "The copywriter for a hotel dining room went quite astray with the overworked U.S. grandiosity of 'From the Sea,' 'From the Garden,' etc. His/her caption for the listing of beef entrées was more riveting than planned. In both English and Spanish it read 'From the Stable.'

"Fearing the worst (and its possible truth) and briefly pondering the approaching Kentucky Derby, we ordered from the seafood list."

Snubbed: Decaffeinated Coffee
October 1, 1983

Manhattan's better restaurants, where dinner for two can easily cost $150, spare no expense to serve the finest food on the best china in the most opulent surroundings. The silver is imported from France; the china is by Villeroy & Boch; fresh flowers are arranged every other day.

The chef orders only plume de veau and aged prime beef and

has the Dover sole flown in fresh twice a week. The unsalted butter is molded into little flowers. Crisp French rolls are either warmed and served in a damask-napkin-lined silver bread-basket or carefully placed on the butter plate with a pair of silver tongs. The coffee is Columbian, the espresso fresh dark French- or Italian-roasted beans.

Almost an Afterthought

But serving decaffeinated coffee is almost an afterthought. The waiter plunks down the cup of hot water—occasionally it is actually a pot—with a shiny little packet of instant coffee in front of the hapless diner, who proceeds to make the best of a rather dreary and tasteless end to an otherwise splendid meal. It's the kind of do-it-yourself service one expects in fast-food carryouts and tourist class on the airlines.

When diners who are about to spend $150 ask for decaffeinated coffee, as more and more of them are doing these days, their chances of getting a freshly brewed pot are no better than fifty-fifty. Only half of the eighteen fashionable Manhattan restaurants I called this week serve a brewed decaffeinated blend; the other half offer instant powder inelegantly presented in individual packets. These same restaurants would never dream of putting a carton of cream on the table.

Such restaurants have a blind spot about decaffeinated coffee. While they treat those who order espresso or regular American coffee to a steaming hot silver or copper pot accompanied by a silver sugar bowl and creamer or carefully sliced slivers of lemon peel, they serve those who order the decaffeinated version with the same disdain they accord people who order Cokes with their poached red snapper in beurre blanc.

It would be a slight improvement if they offered a pot of instant decaffeinated coffee. Not that a pot of instant coffee actually tastes as if it had been brewed, but it does taste a bit better than the do-it-yourself version made in a cup of tepid water. Sometimes the water has spilled over the side of the cup and has soaked the packet so that when it is opened, some of the contents lump together and all the stirring in the world won't dissolve them.

Hardly a Rarity

It isn't as if decaffeinated coffee beans are a rarity. Every supermarket carries them and every coffee wholesaler can supply them. But some restaurants say they do not have enough call for the ground beans. Robert Meyzen, co-owner of La Caravelle, says only four or five people order it at lunch or dinner. "We could do it in a small coffeepot," he said. But they don't.

Meyzen feels that people who drink decaffeinated coffee don't care what it tastes like. "There is not much pleasure in drinking it," he said. "People only do it because they have to." Perhaps he has never had a cup that has been brewed. Restaurants that serve it and people who drink it know that, if properly made, it can be almost as good as a cup of regular, full-strength coffee.

Despite the many restaurateurs who have yet to come around, the situation has vastly improved in the past ten years. A decade ago there was no option, just instant powder. Today some restaurants think brewed decaffeinated coffee is worth printing on the menu. And they don't even charge extra.

Decaf in Restaurants

The value of this column on decaffeinated coffee, written in 1983, is historical. The situation has changed significantly in the past three years.

There are still plenty of holdouts, especially among the old-style French restaurants, the spaghetti-and-meatball Italian restaurants and some ethnic establishments, but on the whole, brewed decaf's time has come.

At the time I wrote the original column, I received a very enlightening letter from the owner of one of New York's oldest coffee merchants, Gillies 1840.

"The cost of preparing a superb fresh-brewed decaffeinated is less than commercial instant varieties," wrote Donald Schoenhold, one of the company's owners.

Schoenhold acknowledged that a restaurant would have to buy

separate equipment and allow additional space, not to mention effort, in order to provide decaf along with regular coffee, but once the original expense for the equipment had been amortized, the restaurant would save money on the coffee itself.

Almost everyone who wrote was in full agreement, and several readers pointed out that New York City was behind the times.

"Nearly every decent restaurant in the Midwest and in California served brewed decaf. I think I even encountered it in Philadelphia," wrote one woman from Long Island.

"If they can spend so much money on flowers and other needs for their restaurants, I'm sure they can spend $50 for a pot to brew decaf," wrote another.

Some people really get exercised over instant decaf. "I have vowed that the next restaurant that attempts to ruin my dinner will have the Sanka and hot water poured all over the tablecloth. It is an insult to a good dinner," said a Denver reader.

Anytime you write about coffee, you always hear from at least one tea drinker who thinks it is a "disgrace how prevalent Lipton tea bags are in our best restaurants. I recently questioned the maître d'hôtel at Le Cygne about this," wrote one tea fancier, "and he seemed amazed that I might expect something so radical as a tea infusion ball and a pot of hot water."

And then the lone dissenting voice from Milton, Massachusetts:

"Could it be that true restaurateurs cannot bring themselves— despite their instinct for elegance otherwise—to serve decaffeinated coffee except offhandedly. If they have anything of their patron saint Brillat-Savarin about them, they must shudder at the idea of a coffee from which the primal element has been removed—that element being caffeine, the only bodily reason for growing and brewing and drinking coffee in the first place. Imagine the reaction of the late Henri Soulé, for instance, if, at the close of a Pavillon dinner, anyone asked for a Cognac without alcohol. So with decaffeinated coffee, like a rose made of red tissue paper."

Recycling Butter Makes It Anything but Sweeter
April 7, 1984

For several months I have eaten more old, reused, stale or rancid butter in restaurants than anyone should be required to sample in a lifetime. It is a sure sign of sloppy restaurant housekeeping. Even worse than that, reusing butter is prohibited by a New York City regulation. Butter that has been served and then left in a dish must be discarded, according to the New York City Health Department, but the regulation is difficult to enforce and seldom does anyone try.

There is no other food that so readily picks up the flavors and odors of just about anything with which it comes in contact— and not just strong-smelling foods like onions and garlic but even household cleaners and tobacco smoke that may be in the vicinity.

Directions for storing butter always recommend that it be placed in the coldest part of the refrigerator in airtight packaging. Yet it is common to see unwrapped butter sitting out at service stations, and even on the tables in restaurants, awaiting the arrival of the patrons.

The custom of serving butter in crocks compounds the problem. Seldom do the diners consume all the butter in one of those little pots at one meal. And despite the city regulation against it, restaurants return the partially filled crock to the kitchen, where, instead of being thrown out, it is refilled and served to the next customer. Butter pats served from a communal dish placed on the table are also recycled.

Chances of getting fresh, sweet-tasting butter improve when a busboy serves individual pats, curls or balls from an iced dish. Yet many restaurants prefer the communal plate because it requires less service, and because they may feel that putting an unlimited amount of butter on the table seems generous. Less generosity and higher standards would be appreciated.

Butter's natural ability to absorb other odors so readily is related to its composition, which is 80 percent fat and 20 percent water and milk solids. The fat soaks up odors like a sponge. Warm butter soaks them up even more quickly.

The best butter, graded AA, is made from sweet cream with very, very few off-flavors. Off-flavors that are acceptable to a butter grader include only a slight taste of the feed that the cows ate or a slightly cooked taste from especially high heat used during pasteurization. As the grade of butter decreases, more soured cream is used, and there are more off-flavors.

The off-flavors are most apparent in unsalted butter, which has a more delicate flavor than salted butter. The use of salt in butter improves its keeping qualities and also disguises odors. So on every score, the best-tasting butter in the grocery store is likely to be unsalted. Because of its fragility, unsalted butter is likely to be handled more expeditiously and carefully between the farm and the store.

Sometimes butter becomes stale. This is a function of age. It is possible for butter to be free of off-odors and still be stale. Rancidity, which is caused by a chemical change and marked by offensive odors, has nothing to do with staleness or the absorption of off-flavors. While rancidity becomes more apparent with age, the enzyme that causes it is present in the butter when it leaves the farm. As it grows older, the chances of the rancidity's developing increase. The custom of recycling butter in restaurants certainly increases the customers' chances of being served rancid butter.

Perhaps the reason I have had so much terrible butter in restaurants lately is because more of them have switched to unsalted butter or what is sometimes called sweet butter. This is a move in the right direction. But it also means that restaurants have to handle their butter with even greater care. According to the American Butter Institute, unsalted butter accounted for only 5 percent of total butter consumption in 1980 and now accounts for 15 percent.

The United States Department of Agriculture contends that the characteristic flavor of the best butter is indescribable. To me the finest butter is sweet and creamy with a slight nutlike flavor.

Butter

"Just a note to express our appreciation for your 'fresh' view of restaurant dining. In particular, your remarks on the state of table butter and the aromas of waiters and their uniforms won great commiseration from us (page 299). I would add that, since the butter is usually stinky, the occasional dank waiter can combine for a TKO." This New York writer says that the problem lies with ill-informed Americans who don't know "the uncomplicated smell of sweet butter."

Since I wrote the column in 1984, I think the situation has improved, and it is probably because there are fewer and fewer of us who are uninformed. As restaurant patrons we have become more and more sophisticated and more and more demanding every year, and restaurants are responding.

Only fresh, sweet butter will do in this Greek speciality, melt-in-your-mouth *kourambiedes*.

KOURAMBIEDES

½ *pound unsalted butter*
2 *tablespoons confectioners' sugar*
½ *egg yolk*
3 *cups flour*
6 *tablespoons finely chopped blanched almonds*
  Additional confectioners' sugar

1. Melt the butter, bring to a boil and stir occasionally. Remove and turn slowly into a mixing bowl.
2. Add the 2 tablespoons sugar and egg yolk and beat for 2 minutes.
3. Add the flour gradually, mixing constantly. Knead vigorously for about 30 minutes. At this point the dough is crumbly but smooth.
4. Add the nuts and knead thoroughly for about 10 minutes. Pinch off small amounts of dough and form into ¾-inch balls.

5. Place on baking sheets ¾ inch apart. Bake at 375 degrees about 30 to 40 minutes. Cool.

6. Sift some confectioners' sugar into a large bowl and roll the cookies in it. The cookies will keep for two weeks in a tightly covered container.

YIELD: 2 dozen

CONSUMERISM

This is the section in which I have an opportunity to sound off about practices in the food business that rip off consumers. After ten years of consumer reporting on television in Washington, D.C., some of this stuff seems tame and it certainly does not produce the volume of mail that other columns do.

But it made me feel better to get some of the complaints off my chest and if that seems self-indulgent, then you can skip this section. It's short anyway.

Soon You'll Know
What's In a Burger
May 17, 1986

After July 1 patrons of McDonald's restaurants in New York State will be able to find out exactly what goes into Big Macs, french fries, Chicken McNuggets and just about everything else sold in the chain. The attorney general's office describes the decision as an "unprecedented action," but Burger King has beaten McDonald's and the attorney general to the punch.

Burger King has voluntarily decided to make ingredient information available in its outlets all over the United States. And if Senator John H. Chafee, Republican of Rhode Island, has his way, all fast-food chains will eventually be required to provide this information. Earlier this week he introduced federal legislation to make ingredient labeling and nutrition information mandatory in fast-food restaurants.

Request for Information

At the same time, Attorney General Robert Abrams has written to five fast-food chains requesting that they provide this information voluntarily to New York residents. The idea of providing ingredients in fast food has been promoted by the Center for Science in the Public Interest (C.S.P.I.) for many years, and now everything seems to be coming together.

The catalysts for the McDonald's agreement were two petitions filed by the Washington, D.C.–based center, a consumer organization. In the summer of 1985, the center asked New York to prohibit what it described as McDonald's false advertising for Chicken McNuggets. The ad said the product was "made only from tender juicy chunks of breast and thigh meat," when in fact

355

it also contained chicken skin and was fried in beef tallow. The consumer group also asked the state to enforce current laws requiring ingredient labeling of fast foods.

Possible Remedies

The attorney general began a formal inquiry into the charge of false advertising and invited McDonald's to discuss possible remedies. The case was handled by Stephen E. Mindell, assistant attorney general in the bureau of consumer frauds and protection. He said he told the fast-food chain that the office would like "to open a dialogue which would encompass concerns of the attorney general as well as the C.S.P.I. in getting nutrition information and ingredient information generally available to the public."

According to Mindell, McDonald's was told that the attorney general's office was also "seriously concerned about the impact of the current advertising campaign" because it was likely that consumers viewed Chicken McNuggets as healthful.

After seven months of negotiations, on April 23 McDonald's agreed to provide not only nutrition information, which had been available, but also ingredient information similar in form to what is provided on all packaged goods, that is, in descending order of importance. And it agreed to include the cooking medium used.

In a statement released jointly by the office of the attorney general and the chain, the president of McDonald's U.S.A., Edward H. Rensi, said, "McDonald's has made this type of information available for over a decade through our corporate office."

In fact, when consumers requested ingredient information from the corporation, this is the type of reply they received as recently as June 1985: "I hope you can understand, in a business such as ours, why we cannot release complete ingredient lists."

After the agreement with New York, McDonald's also announced that it would stop using beef tallow or beef fat to fry Chicken McNuggets and Filet-O-Fish sandwiches and to cook those items in vegetable oil instead. Nutritionists consider vegetable oil preferable to beef tallow because it is a less saturated fat. But McDonald's will continue to use beef tallow to cook its french fries because, the company says, people prefer them that way. "If we could find a vegetable shortening for cooking the french fries that gives the taste, consistency and quality our customers have come to expect, we certainly would use it," said Robert Keyser, a spokesman for McDonald's.

McDonald's says it will provide the materials in all its New York restaurants for one year and then assess the level of interest among consumers. If the company should decide to discontinue the program, it is required to consult with the attorney general's office in advance.

Should the attorney general's office disagree with the decision, the office says it might use "whatever remedies" it has to try to make such information available. That also applies to other fast-food chains. On May 6, the attorney general wrote and asked five of them, including Burger King, to provide the same information voluntarily.

Roy Rogers, a division of the Marriott Corporation, says it "considers ingredient information proprietary." Wendy's and Arby's say they will provide ingredient information if customers ask; Kentucky Fried Chicken said ingredient information will be available at its outlets in August, and Arby's said it will meet with the attorney general later this month.

McDonald's Ingredient Labeling

Shortly after the column on ingredient labeling for fast foods appeared, McDonald's new brochure made its debut. It will take at least twenty minutes to plow through all the material the pamphlet contains that has nothing to do with ingredient labeling.

McDonald's is using the brochure as another source of promotional literature, for which, by the way, the franchisee must pay after the initial shipment of free brochures has been exhausted.

In New York State the franchisee has no choice but to buy these brochures because, by law, they must be available to patrons.

Senator John H. Chafee, Republican of Rhode Island, has offered national legislation to require ingredient information at fast-food restaurants, an idea to which the McDonald's corporation is opposed.

Senator Chafee responded to McDonald's in a letter to the editor of the *Times:*

> McDonald's suggests that my bill creates a new and costly requirement. However, federal law already requires fast-food ingredient labeling. Unfortunately, the agencies responsible for enforcing those laws—the Food and Drug Administration and the Department of Agriculture—have failed to act. My bill simply compels those agencies to enforce what the law already requires.
>
> I'm also concerned about what McDonald's has offered as a substitute for labeling: its new ingredient brochure. That pamphlet—which the company calls "useful and easy to understand"—contains several questionable claims about the nutritional value of McDonald's products. For example, the brochure suggests that fat in the diet is necessary to absorb certain vitamins. But diets that are high in fat increase one's risk of heart disease and certain types of cancer.
>
> I do applaud McDonald's for beginning to disclose its ingredients. However, I question the company's claim that it has made ingredient information available upon request "for more than a decade." A letter dated October 10, 1984, from McDonald's to the Center for Science in the Public Interest stated, "McDonald's does not give out complete ingredient lists for their food products."
>
> The new McDonald's brochure, and other brochures that may soon be available at other fast-food chains, are certainly a step in the right direction. But they are by no means the whole solution. To be truly useful to the consumer, fast-food information should be universally available and conform to agreed-upon standards. Otherwise, it is just more advertising—and possibly misleading advertising at that.

Advertising indeed. If McDonald's were truly performing a consumer service, the ingredient information found in its 37-page brochure could have been condensed into four easy-to-read pages that would have cost the franchisees a whole lot less money.

New Salmon: Less Bone, Fat, Calories and Taste

March 8, 1986

Chicken of the Sea has come up with a canned salmon that could pass for canned white-meat tuna packed in water or for any other nonfishy-tasting fish.

This was not an accident but a deliberate response to consumer demand, according to a spokesman for the canner, the Van Camp Seafood Company.

The packer has taken the mildest variety of salmon—pink—removed the skin and bones and packed what is left in spring water.

"It has been designed to be very appealing to salmon lovers," said Ron Penoyer, manager of financial communications for Van Camp.

It is more likely that it has been designed to appeal to people who basically don't like fish, especially fish with a distinctive taste. And since most Americans prefer the mild flavor of whitefish to stronger-tasting fish such as red salmon, this new version should have many fans.

Flying in the Face of a Fad

But in the process of turning a mild-tasting fish into a bland one, Van Camp has flown in the face of the current fad for calcium. Without the bones, Chicken of the Sea canned salmon no longer has any calcium. Regular canned salmon has always been considered an excellent source of calcium because of the bones, which dissolve when mashed with a fork. A 3½-ounce serving contains 20 percent of the U.S. Recommended Daily Allowance for calcium.

But according to Penoyer, most Americans were not eating those bones anyway. "Over 85 percent of the consumers Van Camp surveyed remove the bones from the salmon before eating it. Calcium," he said, "is not an issue."

The company decided to pack the salmon in water to reduce the calorie and fat content. "Consumers, overall, are less in favor of oil pack for tuna and prefer water pack," he said, adding that it applied to salmon also.

Figuring Out the Fat

And, indeed, there is a significant difference in both calories and fat content between regular pink salmon and water-packed pink salmon, although the industry certainly makes it difficult to figure out.

Of all the canned salmon bought in New York City, only Chicken of the Sea, Bumble Bee and S&W Fine Foods list nutrition information, but all use a different-size serving: Bumble Bee uses 3.5 ounces, S&W 3.75 ounces and Van Camp 2 ounces. Based on the realistic 3.5-ounce serving, Chicken of the Sea pink salmon has 105 calories and 3.5 grams of fat, while Bumble Bee's contains 160 calories, 8 grams of fat and 20 percent of the RDA for calcium. Bumble Bee blackback, a premium grade of red salmon, has the same nutrition profile, while Bumble Bee Alaska Sockeye, another red salmon, has 180 calories, 10 grams of fat and 15 percent of the RDA for calcium.

But since most people eat because food tastes good, not because it's good for them, I decided to taste a variety of salmons from two local supermarkets. For those who really like salmon, even in a can, nothing beats the blueback, a red salmon named for the color of its skin. Bumble Bee's was the best, but Icy Point and Rubinstein's were good too. S&W Fine Foods also packs a delicious blueback, although it is too salty.

Second choice in canned salmon would be the sockeye from Bumble Bee. The sockeye from Icy Point had an off, overly fishy taste.

Pink salmon from Bumble Bee, Icy Point and house brand from A.&P. were much milder in flavor and a can of pink salmon from Gill Netters Best was too salty.

Mildest of all, of course, is the skinless, boneless Chicken of the Sea packed in water.

Which variety you choose depends on what you want to do with it. For this recipe, loosely based on a superb creation of Jeremiah Tower at Stars, his new restaurant in San Francisco, either kind of salmon can be used. The intensity of the spices compensates for a mild-tasting variety. At the same time, the spices are a perfect counterpoint for a richer, more full-bodied can of blueback.

SALMON HASH WITH SALSA

1 15½-ounce can salmon
1 small red onion, chopped
2 tablespoons bread crumbs, approximately
½ serrano chile, minced
½ teaspoon cinnamon
¼ teaspoon cloves
1 teaspoon cumin
2 tablespoons corn oil
4 warm (10-inch) flour tortillas
4 tablespoons thick plain yogurt
   Cilantro for garnish
   Salsa (see recipe)

1. Drain and rinse the salmon. Process with the onion in a food processor; add the bread crumbs, chile, cinnamon, cloves and cumin and process to form a paste. (If necessary, add more bread crumbs so the mixture will hold its shape.)
2. Shape the mixture into 4 patties and sauté in hot oil until lightly browned on both sides.
3. Meanwhile, warm the tortillas by wrapping them in aluminum foil and placing in a hot oven or toaster oven for 8 minutes.
4. Top the patties with yogurt and cilantro and serve with warm tortillas and salsa.

YIELD: 4 patties

SALSA

¾ pound plum tomatoes or tomatillos, finely chopped
½ serrano chile, minced
⅓ cup chopped red onion
1 teaspoon lime juice
2 tablespoons fresh cilantro leaves

Combine all ingredients and serve with salmon hash.

Salmon

You shoulda stood in bed aptly describes how I felt after the mail began to pour in following the appearance of the boneless salmon column.

This Summit, New Jersey, resident put it succinctly:

"Your De Gustibus column featuring the salmon hash recipe was largely unfathomable. Not only did you omit the recipe (as indicated 'see recipe') for salsa, but more importantly, you neglected to inform us what to do with the main ingredient—the salmon.

"Does one add it to the food processor with the onion mixture? Or if that would render it too mushy, perhaps it is coarsely chopped or mashed by hand and folded in.

"Really. This sloppiness is unbecoming a food editor of the *New York Times*."

Right on!

I am totally responsible for omitting directions for the use of the salmon (corrected in this copy), but I had a big argument, which I lost, with my editor about including the salsa recipe. When it was cut out, the copy desk forgot to remove the "see recipe."

Fortunately some people read the column for its information and not the recipe and were confused for other reasons. "I guess it is *non est disputandum*," wrote a San Mateo, California, fan. "Why would a company package or the public demand an expensive can of salmon made to taste like a less costly, indeed cheap by comparison, can of tuna? I'm sure people will buy it— they'll also rush out and buy calcium supplements made from the bones removed from the salmon cans because of their lack of aesthetic appeal. In our house there was always a rush of volunteers to open the salmon can—the opener got the bones!"

Tuna: A Multiplicity of Choices
November 23, 1985

The makers of the first no-salt-added canned tuna previewed their product at a lunch several years ago. Most of the guests were certain afterward that someone had sabotaged their efforts. The tuna that was prepared and presented was fishy, dry and singularly unappealing.

But dedicated cooks soon learned that, with ingenuity, salt-free tuna could be turned into a respectable salad or sandwich. And despite those first discouraging efforts, canned tuna without salt or with less salt is becoming increasingly common.

On a recent stop at the tuna section of a supermarket, the number of low-sodium and no-salt-added tuna products was astounding. In the past five years there have been changes that affect the can itself, the nutrition labeling, serving sizes and varieties from which to choose.

In a slightly-larger-than-normal Manhattan supermarket, there were nine different canners represented by 3¼-ounce cans, 12½-ounce cans and 6½- or 7-ounce cans. (Not so long ago the 7-ounce size was standard, but little by little canners have been switching to 6½ ounces with no commensurate drop in price.)

Within the past five years most of the canners, including the three largest, Bumble Bee, Chicken of the Sea and Star-Kist, have been switching from three-piece cans (top, bottom and sides) with lead-soldered seams to two-piece seamless cans (the bottom and sides are made of one piece). It has been more than ten years since health professionals sought the change because the lead-soldered seams leak lead into the tuna. Of the nine brands, four are still being sold in three-piece cans: Season, Geisha, Progresso and S&W. Progresso said its newer cans are made without the lead-soldered seam.

A spokesman for one of the companies explained why the

lead-soldered cans are still being used: "It costs many, many thousands of dollars to retool. I personally don't know when the plant that cans our tuna will change over."

The Different Types

Aside from the type and size of can, there are many other decisions to be made. Tuna comes in solid white in oil, chunk white in oil, chunk light in oil, solid light in oil, chunk light in water, chunk white in water, solid white in water, chunk light with 50 percent less salt, chunk white "very low sodium," chunk white with 60 percent less salt and diet chunk white.

The designation of "solid," which is the same as "fancy," means that there are large pieces; "chunk" means smaller pieces; flaked or grated means small bits. But sometimes there appears to be no difference between solid and chunk.

White-meat tuna must always be albacore. It is considered the choicest of the tunas because it is the least fishy tasting. It is the most expensive because it is the scarcest. The so-called light tuna —beige-brown with a deep pink cast—is usually either yellowfin or skipjack, both with a more pronounced fish taste.

Despite inroads made by water-packed tuna, the oil-packed variety remains the best seller. The ingredients are some combination of oil and salt and more often than not hydrolyzed protein and/or pyrophosphate. Hydrolyzed protein is a flavor enhancer. Pyrophosphate is used to prevent the formation of struvite, which can occur in white-meat tuna. Struvite is a harmless crystalline substance, but consumers occasionally confuse it with pieces of bone or shards of glass.

The oil most frequently used is soybean. On occasion it is cottonseed. And in the case of Progresso, an Italian-style tuna, olive oil. The amount of salt can also vary, and the S&W tuna was by far the saltiest.

Oil-packed tuna can contain anywhere from two to 2½ times more calories than tuna packed in water and as much as ten times more fat. But it is not always easy to make comparisons. While most cans suggest two ounces as a serving size, a 6½-ounce can of Chicken of the Sea chunk white meat was designated as a single portion. A spokesman for the company said it was in the process of changing its labels so that two ounces would be the suggested serving size.

In addition, several companies—Geisha, S&W, Season, Bumble Bee and Progresso among them—provide no nutrition information. A Bumble Bee spokesman said with the exception of the smallest cans—3¼ ounces—all the tuna packed after August 1985 will have nutrition labeling. Irving Brodwin, senior marketing manager of Progresso Quality Foods, said, "Quite candidly, it never occurred to us to put nutrition labeling on. The tuna is packed in olive oil, and it appeals primarily to Italians for use in antipasto."

Progresso also appeals to those who care about the taste of tuna unadorned by the usual accompaniments: It tastes good all by itself.

People choose water-packed tunas because they are considerably lower in calories than oil-packed tunas. And they contain virtually no fat. They are usually seasoned with vegetable broth, salt and hydrolyzed protein and/or pyrophosphate. Those that are low in sodium contain just tuna and water.

With the exception of Bumble Bee, nutrition information was available on each can of water-packed tuna purchased. The number of calories is approximately the same in all the products.

Which tuna to choose for making a sandwich depends on whether fat, calorie and sodium consumption are a consideration. The next consideration is appearance: White-meat tuna is more attractive looking. But there are some light-meat tunas, especially those packed in water, that taste no different from white-meat tuna after they are combined with the requisite mayonnaise and choice of condiments. It isn't always necessary to buy the most expensive tuna to get the best results.

Searching for Truth in Ads and Labels

March 24, 1984

Coca-Cola has agreed under pressure from New York State to change its advertising and its labeling for Diet Coke and Diet Sprite. But it is not the only company making claims that are not quite precise.

In the Coca-Cola case, the state charged that advertising and can labels failed to make clear that even though the new sweetener aspartame is being used in the drinks, they still contain saccharin. Without admitting any wrongdoing, the company agreed to the changes.

While the attorney general's office negotiates with other soft-drink companies over their references to the sweetener, other companies are not so candid.

Del Monte asserts that its canned vegetables are "as nutritious as fresh-cooked, cause they're picked, cooked and canned the same day." But the study on which Del Monte bases its claim shows that most canned vegetables contain considerably less of the water-soluble vitamins (C, B1, B2, B6, niacin and folacin), minerals (iron, magnesium and copper) and potassium than fresh-cooked equivalents. Del Monte agrees that there are less of these nutrients, but says the difference is not enough to cause nutritional deficiencies.

Some advertising obfuscates. A campaign of the National Coffee Association asserted that coffee "picks you up" while it "lets you calm yourself down." Caffeine stimulates the central nervous system, so coffee does "pick you up." How then can it be calming? As advertisements for decaffeinated coffee suggest, coffee makes some people jittery.

The association has changed this advertising. The commercial now says, "Coffee is the calm moment that lets you think," meaning that the coffee break itself is what is relaxing.

Finally, there are the advertisements that emphasize a single characteristic of a product, implying that similar products don't have this attribute. For example, a vegetable oil might say it has "no cholesterol." No vegetable contains cholesterol.

While any consumer may complain about false advertising to the Federal Trade Commission or the Better Business Bureau, it is usually a consumer group or a rival advertiser that does the complaining. However, under the Reagan administration, the commission's budget for monitoring food advertising has been cut almost 90 percent. Commissioner Michael Pertschuk, who was chairman of the agency during the Carter administration, asserts that the commission "has largely abandoned any effort to deal systematically with food and nutrition advertising."

The Center for Science in the Public Interest did petition the commission to ban the Coca-Cola advertisements, but the agency has not acted.

NutraSweet, a brand name for the synthetic sweetener aspartame, is being used by Coca-Cola, Pepsi, 7-Up and Diet-Rite in combination with saccharin. Advertisements for these products play up the addition of NutraSweet, all but ignoring the continued presence of saccharin, a carcinogen in animals. The label on the Diet Coke can, for example, says, "Now with NutraSweet."

The implication on the cans and in the advertising is that NutraSweet has replaced saccharin, but it has done so only partially, and Attorney General Robert Abrams of New York says such advertising is misleading.

In its agreement with New York State, Coca-Cola says that substantially all the containers that the attorney general objects to will be gone from the state within four months. On new cans sold in the state, labels that highlight NutraSweet will say "NutraSweet blend" with a large asterisk. The asterisk will refer to the list of ingredients on the can, showing the presence of saccharin.

The company has also stopped radio, print and television advertising that similarly emphasizes NutraSweet. Coca-Cola has agreed to pay $30,000 in costs to the attorney general's office. The attorney general is still negotiating with Pepsi, 7-Up and Royal Crown Cola, the manufacturer of Diet-Rite.

"The Coca-Cola company did not agree with contentions that it had engaged in conduct that violated New York State law," Rob Martin, a spokesman for the company, said in Atlanta. He added, according to the Associated Press, "We would really like to note that the agreement with the state is in keeping with our long-standing cooperation with legislative and regulatory bodies.

It is unlikely that a company will change its advertising and can labels in just one state; it is much easier to make the changes nationwide, which is, according to Martin, what Coca-Cola has done for Diet Coke.

If other states pursue the the same course as New York, companies might find it necessary to produce different labels and advertising for each of those states. These companies might wish that the Federal Trade Commission would increase its monitoring of advertising.

Labels on Soups: Read with Care
February 22, 1986

The soup aisle will never look the same. There are so many new varieties of soup that it is almost impossible to make intelligent choices. It isn't just the varieties of soup today—most of them still by Campbell's or Lipton—that confuse shoppers. It is also the labels, many of which have one or more of the following: No preservatives. No artificial ingredients. No artificial flavors. No artificial colors. No additives. All natural.

Either directly or by implication, these phrases are used to indicate that the product is better than soups that contain ingredients with unpronounceable chemical names. But whether the words on the front of the package bear any relationship to the list of ingredients depends on interpretation.

Campbell's new line of dry soup mixes comes in the standard varieties the company has made in cans for years. The front of four of five packages says "No preservatives. No artificial ingredients." Beneath that line on the front of the noodle soup package are the words "other than vitamin and iron enrichment."

One of the noodle soup ingredients is hydrolyzed vegetable

protein. It is described this way in *The Complete Eater's Digest and Nutrition Scoreboard* by Michael Jacobson, director of the Center for Science in the Public Interest: "H.V.P. consists of vegetable (usually soybean) protein that has been degraded by chemicals or enzymes to the amino acids of which it is composed."

Caramel Powder

The onion soup and onion mushroom soup contain caramel powder as a coloring agent, to make the soup look darker and richer, and as a flavoring agent.

A sixth variety of soup, Cheddar cheese, says "No preservatives. No artificial flavors," instead of no artificial ingredients. Presumably it is the enzyme-modified blue cheese listed as an ingredient that prevents this soup from making the same claim as the others.

Andy Whitelaw, vice president for technical administration at Campbell's, says: "There is nothing artificial in these products. According to government regulations these are not artificial ingredients."

Lipton dry soup mixes have also been repackaged. Five varieties say "No preservatives. No artificial ingredients." So it came as something of a surprise to find monosodium glutamate listed as an ingredient of four of the soups. In parentheses it is described as "a natural flavor enhancer."

Asked how monosodium glutamate could be considered a natural ingredient, Enio Feliciotti, senior vice president of science and technology for Thomas J. Lipton Inc., said: "It is a natural ingredient. In fact, all of our soups have been reformulated in keeping with consumers' desire for less chemicals." Other natural ingredients in these products include caramel color and hydrolyzed vegetable protein.

International Classics

Lipton has another new line, International Soup Classics. Above the list of ingredients, each package says, "There are no artificial flavors, colors or preservatives, only select ingredients to give these fine soups a delightfully fresh cooked taste." Among

these select ingredients, are xanthan gum, an emulsifier and sta-
bilizer.

Jacobson says these companies are "walking that thin line,"
that what they are doing is "somewhat deceptive because these
claims imply to people that the foods are made from basic ingredients found in one's kitchen. Even if the words are truthful, it is
deceptive labeling."

But whether or not consumers care if these ingredients are
artificial, they may care about taste. And despite the fact that
some of these soups have premium prices, they don't taste any
better than the cheaper versions that do not claim to be natural.

And like the old-fashioned packaged soups, they are loaded
with sodium, even those that claim a reduction. Lipton Golden
Onion, for example, has "25 percent less salt." That still leaves a
single serving with 730 milligrams of sodium.

Soup Labels

"Maybe you can write a column about the deceit of soup companies," suggested a reader from West Orange, New Jersey.

"I remember when Campbell had two portions in a can of
soup. Then they raised it to 2½ portions in the same 10½-ounce
can. Now they have 2¾ portions in the same 10½-ounce can.
They have the same amount of salt but claim they have less salt
per portion.

"In the 10½-ounce can there are 2,000 milligrams of sodium.
For two portions there are 1,000 milligrams of sodium per serving. For 2½ servings there are 800 milligrams per serving. For
2¾ servings there are 727 milligrams per serving."

If that reader is angered by the sodium content, what kind of
reaction would this information bring?

According to the Center for Science in the Public Interest, a
Washington, D.C.–based consumer group, a Campbell Soup
Company executive has finally admitted what we have all known
all along: "To partly compensate for real and perceived loss in
flavor with low- and reduced-sodium products," said Dr. George

Dunaif, "there is a necessity to add more ingredients, i.e., meat, vegetables, spices and herbs. This adds substantially to the cost of these products."

Chicken, garlic, carrots—no telling what they might add next.

The Delayed Approach to Sodium Labeling
May 24, 1986

More than five years ago Dr. Arthur Hull Hayes, then the Commissioner of the Food and Drug Administration, told a congressional hearing that if companies did not voluntarily label packaged products soon with their sodium content he favored forcing them to do so. Asked later what he meant by "soon," Hayes said "within six months."

Hayes is long gone from the F.D.A.; he resigned three years ago to become dean of New York Medical College. The chairman of the subcommittee that heard the testimony, Albert Gore, Jr., Democrat of Tennessee, has moved from the House of Representatives to the Senate. And there is still no law that says all packaged food must contain information about sodium content.

F.D.A. Proposing a Regulation

Two years ago the F.D.A. published a proposed regulation to make sodium labeling mandatory under certain circumstances. If there are no delays, the regulation is scheduled to take effect July 1. Almost a dozen companies have asked for extensions in order to comply. One of them, Coca-Cola, says it may be reformulating its Tab soda and would like to relabel when it reformulates. Other companies have other reasons.

The new labeling regulation falls far short of what Hayes wanted. It would require only that manufacturers who give nutrition labeling on their foods include the sodium content on the nutrition label.

About 55 percent of all prepared foods have nutrition labeling, so under the proposed regulation, nearly half the packaged foods sold in this country would not have sodium information unless the manufacturer provides it voluntarily. Manufacturers who want to offer only sodium information without the rest of the standard nutrition label would be free to do so.

Describing the Amount of Sodium

The proposed regulation defines the way a manufacturer may describe the amount of sodium in a product:

• To be called "sodium free," a food must have less than five milligrams a serving.

• "Very low sodium" products may contain no more than thirty-five milligrams a serving.

• "Low sodium" foods may have no more than 140 milligrams a serving.

• "Reduced sodium" would mean that the sodium in the food has been reduced by at least 25 percent.

Even if the proposal goes into effect, shoppers would still have to be alert for such phrases as "no salt," "no salt added" and "salt free." Such descriptions do not mean the product is sodium-free.

Such "salt free" foods may contain monosodium glutamate, sodium bicarbonate, sodium saccharin or other sodium-based ingredients that add sodium to the diet.

The only way consumers can protect themselves against ingestion of unwanted sodium is by carefully reading the ingredient statement, which is required by the F.D.A. While a manufacturer can use any sort of fanciful phrase or terminology on the label, it is much harder to hide the facts on the ingredient statement.

Calcium, Fat and Sodium: Caveats for Teenagers

February 14, 1987

The dairy industry has taken up the battle against osteoporosis with vigor. After years of being criticized for emphasizing nutritious but fattening products—whole milk, ice cream, etc.—the industry has seized upon the opportunity to campaign for increased consumption of calcium to prevent the crippling bone disease that afflicts older women.

But if teenage girls follow the industry's recommendations with any regularity, they'll be full of calcium all right, but they'll be fat.

At a recent meeting in Manhattan sponsored by the National Dairy Board, a research and promotional arm of the dairy industry, two calcium researchers discussed "The Calcium Crisis Among Teenagers." The crux of their reports: young women need to consume more calcium to prevent osteoporosis later in life.

Dr. John J. B. Anderson of the University of North Carolina at Chapel Hill made several recommendations to assure what he called "optimal bone values." And the first, quoted from the text of his speech: "Eat foods that contain many nutrients from the Basic Food Groups rather than energy-dense (nutrient poor) snack foods. Calcium-rich foods are especially needed."

To accompany the researchers' presentations, the dairy board offered a pamphlet with suggestions on how young girls can get enough calcium. Nowhere does the pamphlet suggest, even hint, that it might be a good idea to choose foods that are calcium-rich and low in fat. Asked about this, Anita Fial, a spokesperson for the National Dairy Board, said that perhaps the pamphlet should have discussed fat as well as calcium. "However, kids who know they should be watching their calories are going to watch their calories," she said. "They know what to look for. But it's mostly when they are at home that they can select them."

These are some of the "calcium-boosting hints" offered in the pamphlet:

• "When you're eating out order quiche, lasagna, tacos, cheeseburgers, nachos with cheese, chicken Parmesan and cheese-stuffed potatoes."

• "Walking around the mall, order milkshakes, double cheese-burgers, pizzas and salads topped with cheese."

• "Going to a picnic or sports event, take wedges of cheese or cheese kebabs; yogurt; tuna, potato and macaroni salads with shredded cheese, and yogurt fruit drinks or hot cocoa made with milk."

Unquestionably, these foods are full of calcium, but are they the best sources of calcium for teenagers—instead of such low-fat sources as sardines, spinach, kale and skim milk? Or are they, instead, the same energy-dense, nutrient-poor foods Dr. Anderson mentioned—and high in salt to boot? A check of several guides to calories, fat and sodium provided some interesting answers:

• A single serving of lasagna contains about 450 calories, 17 grams of fat and 1,500 milligrams of sodium.

• A cheeseburger contains 300 to 500 calories, 17 to 27 grams of fat and 800 to 1,400 milligrams of sodium.

• A cheese-stuffed potato contains about 500 calories, 22 grams of fat and 500 to 600 milligrams of sodium.

• Pizza contains 300 to 600 calories, 15 to 39 grams of fat and 500 to 1,700 milligrams of sodium.

• A milkshake contains 300 to 700 calories (1,000 calories for a large shake), 8 to 11 grams of fat and 200 to 300 milligrams of sodium.

All you have to do is consume an extra 175 calories a week beyond your needs to gain 2.6 pounds a year. At that rate, by the time these teenagers are thirty or forty years old, they may well have gained 30 or 40 pounds.

Or, if they follow the National Dairy Board's suggested regimen carefully, they could do it sooner.

True Fat

The National Dairy Board did not call. They did not write. In fact, no one did, except one of the editors on *The New York Times* editorial page. I like the editorial so much, I thought you might, too. Here is part of the editorial from February 22, 1987:

True Fat

Concern about osteoporosis, a crippling bone disorder that afflicts mainly elderly women, has spawned a cynical campaign by the dairy industry aimed at the teenage girls.

Studies show that calcium deficiency is not a factor in most cases of osteoporosis. But increasing calcium intake during adolescence, experts say, can help build a heavier and denser skeleton that is more resistant to the bone-wasting disease.

An eye-catching new pamphlet being distributed nationwide by supermarkets by the National Dairy Board endorses the worst in teenage eating habits. In a near parody of bad diet, the "Teen Guide" urges increased consumption of a high-fat, high-sodium diet.

Such an artery-clogging diet will indeed provide ample calcium. But, as our colleague Marian Burros warns, as regular fare it can also condemn adolescents to lifetime bouts with obesity and high blood pressure.

The dairy industry can't be blamed for seeking to boost sales. But it can be blamed for pushing badly erroneous health advice on vulnerable youngsters.

What's in Supermarkets
November 24, 1984

Most of us spend as little time in the supermarket as possible. We move quickly and knowledgeably down the aisles, plucking the items on the shopping list off the shelves, never looking to the left or right of them. Before we notice a new product or an old product in a new guise, we have usually heard of it through advertising or from a friend.

I haven't been paying much attention lately to what is on the shelves except for the things I need. But on a shopping visit last week I found that the contents of some cans of tomatoes had shrunk, that the amounts of sugar and salt were reduced in some dry cereals, that some so-called health foods had become sweeter, not healthier, that tofu seems to have found a larger audience, and that the produce in at least one market was a joy to behold.

I found out about the canned tomatoes when I stopped to compare prices. That's when I discovered a Del Monte can that appeared to contain sixteen ounces of tomatoes but did not. The label said it was filled with just 14½ ounces of tomato solids and liquid. Other cans of tomatoes on the shelves, such as Redpack and S&W, contained the full sixteen ounces.

"Competitive Pressure"

Del Monte says its 14½-ounce can was a result of "competitive pressure." Bob Paden, a products manager for the Del Monte Corporation, explained that "our major competitor was at 14.5 ounces and so we met them." The price, however, did not change. Del Monte's major competitor is Hunt-Wesson. Paden said that all manufacturers of canned tomatoes would soon be selling only 14½-ounce cans.

Usually manufacturers say they change their products in response to consumer demand. I wonder when consumers demanded fewer whole tomatoes in a can for the same price they used to pay for more?

Elsewhere in the store the demand for healthful foods was reflected in modifications of existing products and in some new products. In the cereal aisle, where I had gone to pick up a box of bite-size shredded wheat, response to consumer demands was obvious in two old standbys.

On the Cheerios box it says, "No artificial colors or flavors." Wheaties now reads, "Low in sugar." The amount of sodium in Wheaties has been reduced as well, from 370 milligrams per one-ounce serving to 275 milligrams, a 25 percent reduction.

In the frozen-food section tofu appears to have come of age. There must be a lot of people out there who want it if a large supermarket chain stocks a variety of tofu-based frozen dinners. At the Food Emporium in Manhattan considerable shelf space has been given over to Legume's TV dinners. They offer tofu lasagna, tofu tetrazzini, stuffed shells Provençal, vegetarian lasagna, tofu Bourguignonne, sesame ginger stir-fry, cannelloni Florentine. While I would argue with the company's claim that its products are all-natural when some contain hydrolyzed plant protein, it is accurate to state that they are free of cholesterol.

The health-food trend can also result in changes in existing products that do not make them more healthful. Granolas have never been particularly low in calories or fat, especially those made commercially. No sooner did granola become a popular new cereal in the early '70s than cereal manufacturers began experimenting with ways to turn granola into what they call healthful food. That set the stage for the arrival of the granola bars, the cereal mixture further sweetened, hardened and pressed into the shape of a bar cookie.

Now Quaker has added chocolate chips and coated the granola bar with milk chocolate. As a result the primary ingredient in the chocolate chip Granola Dipps is milk chocolate, in which the most important ingredient is sugar. The second ingredient in the granola bars is called crisp rice which also contains sugar. Rolled oats and semisweet chocolate chips are the third and fourth ingredients. They are followed by brown sugar, corn syrup, partly hydrogenated vegetable oil that, according to the label, may or may not be soybean, cottonseed or palm oil. Chocolate is 50 percent saturated fat; palm oil is 80 percent saturated fat.

Elsewhere in the ingredient statement there are corn syrup solids, something called "invert sugar" and honey. Dipps are artificially flavored and preserved with BHA. Although they look like candy bars, have approximately the same number of calories as candy bars and taste like exceptionally sweet candy bars, they are not sold with the candy bars; they are next to the cereal section.

While Quaker's original granola bars are no great shakes nutritionally either, at least their primary ingredient is rolled oats.

In Marvelous Variety

Not far behind is Pillsbury's entry into what it calls "the healthy snack food category." Each Milk Break Milk Bar, described as an alternative to candy bars, contains the equivalent of half a glass of nonfat milk. They do provide fair amounts of certain desirable nutrients: Each 1½-ounce bar contains 15 percent of the Recommended Daily Allowance (RDA) for calcium, 10 percent of the RDA for vitamin D, 10 percent of the riboflavin and 10 percent of the protein. But each bar also contains thirteen to fourteen grams of fat, much of it saturated.

Some of Manhattan's larger supermarkets now stock a marvelous variety of truly healthful foods—produce. Counters are laden with almost as many unusual fruits and vegetables as shoppers find at Oriental produce stands.

At the Food Emporium there were vibrant yellow peppers from the Netherlands, American red peppers, sweet melons from Israel, bright orange persimmons, kiwis, celery root, fennel, both red and white sunchokes (also known as Jerusalem artichokes), Kirby cucumbers, plum tomatoes, hydroponically grown tomatoes and even out-of-season asparagus. It is the kind of choice that propels the cook out of the store and into the kitchen.

Not-So-Natural Foods
January 24, 1987

Natural foods have gone big time. The movement into the mainstream may have begun when the first spoon of sugar was attached to the first cold cereal, but it was probably the first spoon of grape jelly put into a carton of plain yogurt that marked the beginning of the end of natural foods.

In the process of moving from counterculture to mainstream the packaging has been changed, or, in the words of the Lempert Report, a marketing service, the products "have shed the dull and wordy packaging often found in health-food stores for more colorful, simpler wraps." It is not the new gussied-up exteriors, however, that are troublesome: it is the new interiors, which have been undergoing drastic revisions.

When plain yogurt became fruit-flavored yogurt no one realized what the mainstreaming of natural foods would mean. They were soon to find out, as yogurt went on to bigger, though arguably not better, things. Some yogurts were frozen and turned into "healthy" alternatives to ice cream, but in fact many contain more calories than ice cream. Yogurt now has the distinction of having been the first junk health food.

The Tofu Alternative

Tofu is not far behind. That plain, bland, low-calorie, high-protein substitute for meat is valuable just because it has no flavor of its own and therefore can be combined with savory ingredients to simulate meat. But now most tofu is unrecognizable, especially in its frozen form. Tofu was supposed to be a nutritious alternative to ice cream, but some tofu-based desserts, like yogurt before them, have more calories than ice cream. What is more, despite tofu in the name, there are frozen tofu desserts with very little tofu.

Perhaps as a child you were allowed to eat fruit leather, fruit that had been dried into sheets in the sun (or the oven). General Mills has learned how to manufacture a version of fruit leather, Fruit Roll-Ups, that contain added sugar, partly hydrogenated soybean oil, guar gum, xanthan gum and artificial color.

Even herb teas have not escaped. In addition to the herbs you would expect to find in them, Lipton's also adds natural flavors and citric acid.

Of course C. W. Post and John W. Kellogg would have been struck dumb by the liberties that have been taken with the health foods they called cereals. Cereals that are 40 percent sugar are not uncommon. Nor are cereals shaped like chocolate chip cookies and graham crackers and cinnamon toast.

Once the manufacturers ran out of ideas for making cereal look like cookies, turning cereal into candy was the next step. Granola, a staple of the health-food store, soon became a granola bar filled with caramel and chocolate. But we have Ralston to thank for the latest permutation, a granola bar coated with "real blueberry pudding" or "real chocolate pudding." These granola bars stick to your teeth as effectively as any Snickers and perhaps better than a Hershey with almonds.

And while Quaker Oats oatmeal has long since been manufactured with a variety of seasonings, the latest version shows a fertile brain at work. Quaker Fruit and Cream Instant Oatmeal contains "artificial flavor peaches and cream," or, if you prefer, "artificial flavor blueberries and cream." There is no cream in the product and the one made with blueberries contains "dehydrated blueberries coated with partially hydrogenated vegetable oil."

There is, however, a bright side to the mainstreaming of natural foods: They are now more readily available. It's simply a matter of picking your way through the mine fields in search of those that have not been "improved."

Sparkling Waters' Latest Twist—Flavors

August 17, 1985

Never mind old Coke, new Coke, Cherry Coke and Diet Coke. Forget about Diet Pepsi with NutraSweet, with caffeine or without caffeine. There is another revolution going on in the beverage industry, and so far no one is paying much attention to it, perhaps because it has just begun.

The labels on bottles of Perrier—or more specifically, Perrier with a Twist—come in different colors, and the labels on bottles of Vintage seltzer have also changed. Sparkling waters are no longer just sparkling waters. There is a new category called flavored waters making its way eastward from California, and most often the flavors, like those for Perrier, are orange, lemon and lime.

According to Jesse Meyers, the publisher of *Beverage Digest,* a trade journal, the flavored waters are still just a blip on sales charts. "It's not a big speck on the beverage spectrum," Meyers said. But even so it is nothing to sneeze at. Meyers said that business for flavored sparkling waters had tripled in the past three years, and "it looks like it may triple again in the next three."

Perrier introduced its flavored waters last spring, and according to Barbara Long, director of marketing for the Perrier Group, there has been a "50 percent increase in sales in three months."

Flavored waters came to my attention several years ago when a friend asked me to sample a lemon-flavored sparkling water he raved about. It was not my cup of seltzer. The flavoring had a bitter quality reminiscent of the dried peel of the fruit. To me it was anything but refreshing. I didn't think much about flavored waters again until this year when someone served me flavored Perrier.

According to Meyers, Canada Dry had flavored club soda in

four or five markets, and Schweppes and Seagram's are marketing flavored club sodas. And some of the soft-drink companies, like Royal Crown and Pepsi, are entering the market.

Unlike soft drinks, however, flavored waters contain no sweetening agent, though they may seem to be sweeter than plain sparkling water. They contain no artificial colors and none of the other chemicals usually found in soft drinks. In other words they fit right in with the popular image of natural and healthful foods. And because their image may be more sophisticated than that of soft drinks, they can be an appropriate alternative to spirits. While Coke hardly seems to go with grilled tuna in beurre blanc, lemon-flavored seltzer doesn't sound so bad. The rise in popularity of the flavored waters also coincides with—or is a product of—increased concerns about alcohol consumption.

Barbara Long of Perrier said the flavored waters also provide a convenience: "According to our surveys 85 percent of those who drink Perrier have it with a wedge of lemon or lime. Now they don't have to carry the lime and knife around with them."

For those of us who like our sparkling water plain, I hope this doesn't mean a repeat of what happened to those of us who like our yogurt plain. There was one depressing sign already this summer. I asked my host for some seltzer or club soda at a barbecue, and all he had to serve was lemon-flavored Perrier.

Flavored Sparkling Waters

Jesse Meyers was prescient.

But several readers were not. "Let us pray," wrote one from Maryland, "that flavored Perrier and Vintage (and all the rest) come a cropper with the 'new' Coke."

You can hardly count the number of flavored sparkling waters on the market one year later.

"My tastes have fallen afoul of the mass market many times before," wrote one reader a year later. "But can it honestly be true that I am the only one, winter and summer, who keeps a supply of fresh lemons/limes to add to my seltzer, soda, Perrier?

Artificially flavored seltzer and soda are a far cry from the same liquids bubbling, cold and with fresh citrus."

"Can anything be done? The situation is desperate."

More desperate than you know.

In the summer of 1986 I went to a very elegant party where Champagne flowed like seltzer and anything you wanted to drink, from a Pimm's cup to a soft drink, was available. But I couldn't get a plain glass of seltzer. All they were serving was lime-flavored Perrier!

Extending Precious Coffee
January 23, 1986

Coffee prices are rising again, in a repeat performance of a situation American shoppers faced nine years ago. The reason appears to be the same: a frost in Brazil.

In 1977, suggestions for ways to extend each precious pound abounded. There was the method used regularly by New Orleans residents since the Civil War, when coffee was also scarce: mixing the coffee with chicory. The ratio of chicory to coffee depends on how much you like the bitter taste of chicory. Some people use half chicory and half coffee. But then some people drink just plain chicory.

Most of the other suggestions for extending a pound of coffee were pretty bizarre. Drying out coffee grounds overnight or in an oven that has been heated to 450 degrees and then turned off does not produce a very palatable cup of coffee the second time around. But perhaps with enough milk and sugar the coffee taste is unimportant.

Bad Ideas

Leaving coffee grounds in the filter paper and using them again produces approximately the same result. And reheating leftover coffee is worse yet: The coffee tastes bitter.

So much for bad ideas. There was one excellent suggestion, however, from Dr. David Kessler of Silver Spring, Maryland. I have made my coffee following his directions ever since.

The method has a very technical name, but it is really quite simple. It is called sequential extraction. Kessler explained that it is based on the chemical extraction methods used in laboratories.

Three-Stage Process

Because the solubility of coffee is quite low, you can get at least 25 percent more from coffee filtered through paper if you add the water in three stages.

It works like this: Spoon into the filter the amount of coffee you would use for six cups. Then pour in three cups of boiling water (some people say the water should have stopped boiling); wait until the water has gone through. Then pour in another three cups and wait until it has gone through. Then pour in two additional cups.

When coffee goes on sale, don't hesitate to stock up, as long as you can store the coffee in the freezer. Even if you don't buy more than a pound at a time, that's a good place to keep coffee fresh. The second best place is the refrigerator; the worst is the cupboard.

Coffee

The stack of mail that arrived after this piece staggered me. It included a variety of conflicting information, designed to prove that either (a) I was ignorant, (b) I was naive, (c) I was stupid. So read on and take your choice.

From Philadelphia: "It was with an amused smile that I read your reporting of the suggestions of Dr. David Kessler, who is either rather young or unobservant. I have been using the sequential-extraction method for fifty years, and my mother-in-law, who taught it to me, used it for many years prior to that. The sequential-extraction method has been used by Europeans for years."

From Newark, New Jersey: "Your recent article can do more harm than it can do good.

"Dr. David Kessler has an erroneous concept of the soluble contents of coffee and the physical action which takes place when brewing. There is an absolute maximum amount which should be removed beyond which only bitters and acrid extracts are removed."

The letter goes on in some detail about the proper length of time that the water should be in contact with the coffee, suggests an experiment to prove that the method is right and then continues:

"Note also that ground or bean coffee is destroyed by exposure to air, and even more so by exposure to moisture. The only place in your house that has higher humidity than your refrigerator is your freezer, therefore, your recommendation to store coffee in either must bear the admonition that it be stored 'only in an airtight container.' Even removing the lid from an airtight container before the product reaches room temperature will cause moisture to condense on the beans and rapidly cause deterioration." A point worth noting.

From New York and points north, west and south: "I cannot understand how you, a 'food person,' have never heard of the Chemex coffeepot. It was invented by a chemist and is similar to the method you describe."

Then came alternative suggestions. A New Yorker said the best way to save money on coffee is to roast your own. Green beans are ⅓ the price of roasted coffee, and they can be stored in the cupboard. "Roasting coffee," he wrote, "takes approximately ten minutes in a West Bend Corn Popper."

The Luzianne people were not especially happy with the reference to the bitterness of chicory, which they use in their premium-blend coffee, so their public relations office sent along two pounds of chicory to demonstrate "the mild and mellow flavor characteristics of chicory, not bitterness." The letter blamed the bitterness of coffee with chicory on "over-roasting, poor-quality coffee beans and improper brewing."

From Denver came a package called Coffee S-T-R-E-T-C-H,

natural- and artificial-flavor coffee extender. It contains coffee, caramel color, natural and artificial flavor (starches, dextrins, vegetable oil, chicory, acids, vanillin, alcohols, lactones).

But why would anyone want to put all that junk in their coffee?

Of all the mail the column produced, there was only one outraged letter about the cost. After so many years of inflation the high cost of products no longer infuriates many people. We have become inured.

A Florida reader expressed the righteous indignation we ought to feel but don't. "What a fraud! What a rip-off on the consumer! The warehouses are bursting at the seams with surplus coffee. The Coffee Trust (or the Coffee OPEC?) headed by the two major growers, Brazil and Colombia, deliberately set a quota to keep prices artificially high. All we have to do to bust the fraud wide open is to *boycott coffee!* In a short time you'll see the prices tumble."

Plastic Is a Bubble Killer
February 1, 1986

Glass soft-drink bottles may become as scarce as bottle openers and as obsolete as bottle stoppers if the present trend continues. So scarce, in fact, that in our family we have started a small collection of the quart (or thereabouts) size.

Not many. Just enough so that when we open a two-liter plastic bottle we can pour the remainder into a reusable glass bottle. It's the way we preserve the carbonation.

At first we discarded several dozen half-filled plastic bottles of seltzer, assuming that we had gotten an improperly sealed or processed batch. We returned half a case to the store, explained the problem and were promptly given a new half case. But the same thing kept happening.

The National Soft Drink Association acknowledges the problem. "Plastic bottles do have a shorter shelf life," said Julie McCahill, vice president of communications for the trade association. "Carbonation retention is supposed to be improving," she said, but if it is, we certainly haven't noticed it in our family."

Half the Shelf Life

In fact, according to Ralph Armstrong, general sales manager for Continental PET Technology, a division of the Continental Can Company in Stamford, Connecticut, the bottling industry has "basically agreed that plastic bottles have a sixteen-week shelf life; glass bottles have a six- to nine-month shelf life." Carbonation is lost because plastic is permeable.

We are no longer brand-loyal. Vintage comes in cans or two-liter bottles in the supermarkets where we shop. Instead of buying it, we buy whatever seltzer we can find in glass bottles. If glass isn't available, we buy Vintage and switch bottles after opening.

But Armstrong says the plastic of the bottles has nothing to do with the perception that the contents go flat more quickly than in glass bottles. He says the loss of carbonation has to do with the size of the bottle rather than its composition. He explained that when a two-liter bottle is half empty, there is more head room in which the gases are diffused than there is in a half-empty one-quart bottle.

Reasons for the Shift

Several factors are responsible for the shift to plastic, according to McCahill. Plastic bottles are much lighter so they are more convenient. In addition, McCahill said that in New York, where there is a returnable-bottle law, people who used to buy six-packs of cans or bottles have been switching to two-liter plastic bottles because of the deposit. The deposit on a six-pack is 30 cents, on a two-liter bottle it is 5 cents.

Armstrong said bottling companies were switching to plastic because they are easier for them to handle. Under the bottle law, the bottler is responsible for disposing of empty soft-drink containers. "It is much easier for the route man to sling a plastic bag filled with plastic bottles up onto a truck, than boxes filled with glass bottles," he said.

Some people have simply switched to cans. In 1984, 56 percent of the soft drinks sold came in cans, 37 percent in refillable and throwaway glass in 16-ounce and 28- to 32-ounce sizes, and only 6.5 percent in plastic of any size. When the 1985 figures are available, there are certain to be some changes. And by the end of 1986 they should be dramatic. If the supermarket in my neighborhood is typical, the only sparkling water sold in glass is likely to be such designer beverages as Perrier and San Pellegrino.

One unintended—or perhaps intended—effect of the switch to plastic must certainly be the increased sales of soft drinks. After all, what can you do with a bottle of unsparkling sparkling water, Coke or Pepsi?

Open another.

Plastic Bottles

The response to my complaints about plastic bottles reminded me of the response to the column on stretch coffee. There was a lot of mail about what was wrong with my science.

I will not bore you with the details, or the tests that were suggested to prove that I was wrong, despite the fact that even the soft-drink companies acknowledge that soda in plastic bottles has a shorter shelf life.

But a letter from a researcher in chemistry at Brown University, who was especially persistent, writing not once but twice, is worth repeating: "The important part is that solubility of gases in liquids tends to increase as the temperature goes down. Chill the bottle overnight before opening it, and after filling your glass, recap it immediately and put it back in the refrigerator."

One letter said the reason so much of the fizz left my bottles was because I opened them too much. But I don't open them any more often than I open glass bottles.

Another letter came from a woman whose husband's research group invented the plastic bottles at Du Pont. She suggested that if I can't buy a one-liter bottle I buy a two-liter bottle and "enjoy one fizzy liter and flush the other liter down the john."

On the other hand, there were several readers who were delighted to find their suspicions confirmed. "For years," wrote a woman from Pelham Manor, New York, "I have been complaining that even the brand of soda or seltzer did not seem to matter to the effervescence in most bottles once they were opened. The real crusher came last night when I opened a fresh, recently purchased plastic bottle to discover no bubbles at all.

"My question to you is this: Is there any secret (or open) code by which one can determine the freshness of a bottle on the grocer's shelf? Isn't there some way in which we consumers can protect ourselves from the worst of the duds?"

Every bottle is dated, but the code is secret.

A better suggestion is to save the dud and take it back to the store the next time you go shopping. I can't think of a store in the country that will not take the bottle back, especially since they can return it for credit to the bottler.

Another reader was thrilled to find out that carbonation was not lost because the cap had not been screwed on properly. "Probably saved a lot of arguments in the house. 'Johnny, I told you to put the cap back on tight after you drank the Coke,' etc."

"Plastic ruins the carbonation, which is what makes soda fun! If one is going to imbibe (!) unhealthy drinks, one should enjoy them," wrote a Brooklyn Heights reader.

Warming to the subject, he continued: "All plastic bottles cause taste-destroying qualities. I will not buy soda in plastic or twist-top bottles. Cans are a passable substitute for glass. However, glass with a tight top is the only medium for the best taste of any drinkable liquid. If you and all other food writers keep pointing this out, maybe the soda manufacturers will return to glass."

There is always one reader who has a suggestion. This one is reprinted in its entirety. "I have discovered that if you squeeze the bottle and force the air out when the cap is replaced, it holds the carbonation over a longer period of time. I am assuming that there is less surface for the carbonation to dissipate. In addition, you get a vacuum condition that holds the screw cap tighter to the bottle."

Now the good news. Recently I have noticed that the fizz is

lasting longer in the plastic bottles. The National Soft Drink Association said carbonation retention is supposed to be improving, and I think it is.

Natural, Fancy: Food Lines Blur
September 2, 1985

The people who sell so-called gourmet or fancy foods emphasize taste; those who sell natural foods emphasize health. They would seem to have nothing in common. But, in fact, many of the products at the Natural Food Expo '85, which took place in Washington, D.C., last weekend, would have been right at home at an earlier New York City show called Taste, where fancy foods starred.

A few, very few, of those who sell the fancy foods are aware that there is a market for their products among those who care about their health and nutrition and vice versa. Those who don't are losing a good bet.

Not, of course, that purveyors of ginseng-flavored soft drinks are likely to win any converts among people who prefer Chardonnay with their mesquite-grilled chicken. Or that putting miso into spaghetti sauce, chili or barbecue sauce makes these canned sauces taste any better.

But there were a host of products at the natural-food show that would fit right in at a shop like Balducci's in New York City or Sutton Place Gourmet in Washington, D.C., if the producers knew how to merchandise them and, in some instances, if they simply improved the containers.

One of the people who recognizes the potential is W. Park Kerr, owner of the El Paso Chile Company in Texas. "There is such a natural bridge between these two industries," said Kerr, who was selling his salsa at both shows. "For the past two years these natural-food stores have been buying my salsas, so I thought I would cross over." But Kerr's impression of the buyers at the natural-food show is that they are not very sophisticated.

"They don't know who Williams-Sonoma is and don't get the Neiman-Marcus catalogue," he said. "They keep coming up to my booth and saying 'God, this is gourmet.'

"But so is that apple butter over there," he said, pointing to a plain Jane wrapper on jars at the nearby booth. "Look at the packaging."

Underneath Packaging, Fine Food

Underneath some of that homely packaging is some very fine food.

Nouvelle Sorbet from San Rafael, California, for example. Even the name is likely to turn off some potential customers. One of its big selling points for the natural-food market is that it is made without refined sugar. The sorbet is sweetened with fruit juices. The result is a superior, intensely fruity product that comes in five flavors: strawberry, raspberry, apricot, lemon and passion fruit.

Nasoyanaise, in addition to its undistinguished label, has a name that is difficult to pronounce. It tastes as good as any traditional commercial mayonnaise, but only those who are deeply concerned about their health are likely to try it. Made with tofu by Nasoya Foods in Leominster, Massachusetts, it contains half the calories of regular commercial mayonnaise.

Some companies see that people interested in gourmet foods are also interested in natural foods and that they can appeal to both markets.

The cranberry sauce put out by R.W. Knudson of Chico, California, is better than any commercially packaged cranberry sauce I have tasted. Made with whole cranberries and sweetened with white grape juice, it is refreshingly tart. Knudson, a large health-food company, is quite sophisticated about merchandising, and its literature emphasizes that: "Festive cream, burgundy red, green and gold package design, an eye pleaser for gift packs and holiday baskets."

Somerset Farms, deliciously fruity preserves from England without sugar and only twelve calories per teaspoon, are also attractively packaged and displayed to suggest old-fashioned goodness. They are imported by Signature Foods, Hunt Valley, Maryland.

Old-fashioned hominess is a characteristic of the all-natural breads baked by Matthew's All Natural of Boston. The label on the English muffins says they are whole wheat, and that is what they are. Unlike other so-called whole wheat English muffins, which contain only a little less white flour than whole wheat flour, Matthew's are 100 percent whole wheat. They have body, texture and flavor. That they are made without sugar and without additives is a selling point that should appeal equally to the patron of a fancy-food shop and a natural-food store.

Good-looking bottles of fruit juice from the Winter Hill Natural Juice Company of Highland, New York, contain 100 percent fruit and some of the pulp from the fruit. The result is a cloudy drink, which the company has turned into a marketing tool. Their advertising says: "We'd like to make something clear: Winter Hill pure and natural fruit juices are not clear. Let's face it, they're cloudy." Some of the sediment of the unfiltered juices settles to the bottom of the bottles.

Separating the good products from the bad at the Natural Foods Expo '85, as at the fancy-food show, takes time and careful reading of labels, not to mention a lot of tasting. Much of it is not worth eating. But anyone looking for new products with which to stock a healthy, tasty larder or a store would find a surprising number of quality choices.

Recipe Index

General Index

About the Author

Marian Burros has been writing about culinary concerns for more than twenty years. Before taking the lead food writing position at *The New York Times*, she wrote for *The Washington Post* and reported on television about consumer affairs. She has written several successful cookbooks. Ms. Burros lives in New York City.

Marian Burros, author of
THE BEST OF DE GUSTIBUS
Published by Simon & Schuster
Photo credit: Jill Krementz